Architecture, Philosophy, and the Pedagogy of Cinema

Philosophers on the art of cinema mainly remain silent about architecture. Discussing cinema as 'mass art', they tend to forget that architecture, before cinema, was the only existing 'mass art'. In this work author Nadir Lahiji proposes that the philosophical understanding of the collective human sensorium in the apparatus of perception must once again find its true training ground in architecture.

Building art puts the collective mass in the position of an 'expert critic' who identifies themselves with the technical apparatus of architecture. Only then can architecture regain its status as 'mass art' and, as the book contends, only then can it resume its function as the only 'artform' that is designed for the political pedagogy of masses, which originally belonged to it in the period of modernity before the invention of cinema.

Nadir Lahiji is an architect. He holds a Ph.D. in architecture theory from the University of Pennsylvania. He is most recently the author of *Architecture or Revolution: Emancipatory Critique after Marx* (Routledge, 2020) and *An Architecture Manifesto: Critical Reason and Theories of a Failed Practice* (Routledge, 2019). His previous publications include, among others, *Adventures with the Theory of the Baroque and French Philosophy* (2016), and the co-authored *The Architecture of Phantasmagoria: Specters of the City* (Routledge, 2017).

'Articulated with rare philosophical intelligence and political incisiveness, Nadir Lahiji's new book proposes architecture as the preeminent art of the masses, one that is closer to cinema than to the other arts. A training ground for our wider confrontations with a technological capitalist modernity, architecture emerges once again as the best hope for a political pedagogy of the masses and for the formation of new political subjectivities. Brilliantly reading Walter Benjamin with Alain Badiou, psychoanalytic criticism with film theory, *Architecture, Philosophy, and the Pedagogy of Cinema* summons us to rethink the very project of architectural production today.'

—**David Cunningham**, *Institute for Modern and Contemporary Culture, University of Westminster*

'A seminal contribution to the political philosophy of architecture that extends, updates, and actualizes some of Benjamin's most far-reaching reflections on the crisis of perception towards a new perspective on architecture as a "mass art" in the time of digital capitalism, after the end of cinema. For sheer intellectual stimulation, few can match Lahiji's inquisitive probing of architecture's contemporary predicament.'

—**Libero Andreotti**, *Professor Emeritus of Architecture, Georgia Tech*

'*Architecture, Philosophy, and the Pedagogy of Cinema: From Benjamin to Badiou* puts forward the challenging case for architecture as the only living mass art with revolutionary political potential. Nadir Lahiji argues persuasively that the emergence of the masses as "*historical subject*" is aided by a radical restructuring of perception; as cinema in the modern period reshaped the social imaginary, so architecture can perform this role today.'

—**Christopher Kul-Want**, *Course Leader, MRes Art Theory & Philosophy, Central Saint Martins, University of the Arts London*

Architecture, Philosophy, and the Pedagogy of Cinema

From Benjamin to Badiou

NADIR LAHIJI
FOREWORD BY TODD MCGOWAN

LONDON AND NEW YORK

First published 2021
by Routledge
2 Park Square, Milton Park, Abingdon, Oxon OX14 4RN

and by Routledge
605 Third Avenue, New York, NY 10158

Routledge is an imprint of the Taylor & Francis Group, an informa business

© 2021 Nadir Lahiji

The right of Nadir Lahiji to be identified as author of this work has been asserted by him in accordance with sections 77 and 78 of the Copyright, Designs and Patents Act 1988.

All rights reserved. No part of this book may be reprinted or reproduced or utilised in any form or by any electronic, mechanical, or other means, now known or hereafter invented, including photocopying and recording, or in any information storage or retrieval system, without permission in writing from the publishers.

Trademark notice: Product or corporate names may be trademarks or registered trademarks, and are used only for identification and explanation without intent to infringe.

British Library Cataloguing-in-Publication Data
A catalogue record for this book is available from the British Library

Library of Congress Cataloging-in-Publication Data
Names: Lahiji, Nadir, 1948– author.
Title: Architecture, philosophy, and the pedagogy of cinema:
from Benjamin to Badiou / Nadir Lahiji.
Description: Abingdon, Oxon; New York: Routledge, 2021. |
Includes bibliographical references and index.
Identifiers: LCCN 2020051450 (print) | LCCN 2020051451 (ebook) |
ISBN 9780367762810 (hardback) | ISBN 9780367762827 (paperback) |
ISBN 9781003166252 (ebook)
Subjects: LCSH: Architecture–Philosophy. |
Architecture–Political aspects.
Classification: LCC NA2500 .L346 2021 (print) |
LCC NA2500 (ebook) | DDC 720.–dc23
LC record available at https://lccn.loc.gov/2020051450
LC ebook record available at https://lccn.loc.gov/2020051451

ISBN: 978-0-367-76281-0 (hbk)
ISBN: 978-0-367-76282-7 (pbk)
ISBN: 978-1-003-16625-2 (ebk)

Typeset in Univers
by Newgen Publishing UK

Film begins with D. W. Griffith and ends with Abbas Kiarostami.
—**Jean-Luc Godard**

But the human need for shelter is permanent.
—**Walter Benjamin**

Contents

Foreword
TODD McGOWAN ix
Preface: Architecture after cinema xiii
Acknowledgments xxii

Introduction: Architecture at the 'end' of cinema 1

1 **Returning to the philosophy of masses: Benjamin and Badiou** 10

2 **From the photographic moment of critical philosophy to the optical unconscious** 25

3 **Mass art and impurity: Reading Benjamin with Badiou** 39

4 **In and out of Plato's cave** 55

5 **Theory of distraction: Tactile and optical** 71

6 **Poverty of experience** 85

7 **Dialectics and mass art** 94

8 The proletarian *mise-en-scène*   120

Epilogue: The art of the masses in the age of pornography   141

References   157
Index   165

Foreword

Todd McGowan

The title of mass art or art for the masses has historically belonged to architecture, even if this title remained largely unclaimed. Since building provides a basic requirement for living, architecture has always had a definitive claim for being the art most closely associated with the masses and their requirements. This changes in the twentieth century. After the development of cinema, architecture cedes its position as the art of the masses to the cinema, which dominates the imagination of the twentieth century. The availability of cinema for the masses and its attempts to speak to their desires give it a position that supersedes that of architecture. But cinema's hour has reached its conclusion, or so asserts Nadir Lahiji (following Jean-Luc Godard and Alain Badiou) in his book *Architecture, Philosophy, and the Pedagogy of Cinema: From Benjamin to Badiou*. After cinema no longer functions as the primary mass art, we can calculate its lessons and rethink architecture in light of them. This is the wager of Lahiji's book.

But we must start from the acknowledgment that theorists of architecture have largely failed to seize on its role as art of the masses. The central contention of *Architecture, Philosophy, and the Pedagogy of Cinema* is that it is only after the reign of cinema as mass art has come to an end that we can properly think architecture itself as a mass art. As cinema moves aside, architecture's place as a mass art can become apparent in a way that it never was before. Architecture can also learn valuable lessons from cinema's successes and—even more so—its failures as an art for the masses. Cinema has in it a radical potential that remains primarily unrealized, and it is this potential that theories of architecture can avail themselves of.

Cinema has historically vacillated between exposing contradictions and obfuscating them. Although early theorists of cinema emphasized its radical political potential, later theorists have acknowledged that the basic political tendency of cinema actually points in the other direction—toward the dissemination of ideological fantasies. Early on, the verdict seems more positive. The great works in the history of cinema, such as Sergei Eisenstein's *Battleship Potemkin* (1925) and Orson Welles's *Citizen Kane* (1941), take pains to reveal the contradictions that divide modern society from itself. Eisenstein shows how the power of authority can be cut up through a cinematic editing process, while Welles exposes the emptiness of the fantasies that capitalist society promulgates. These two instances speak to the radical potential of cinema to topple the capitalist regime.

But as it develops as an art for the masses, cinema takes up the side of those in power and abandons its connection to the masses. It works to sell the fantasies that keep the capitalist regime afloat. In *Star Wars* (George Lucas, 1977) and *Forrest Gump* (Robert Zemeckis, 1994), to choose two celebrated examples, all contradictions collapse in the face of the force of fantasy. *Star Wars* shows that teen existential isolation houses a heroic destiny conquering the power of evil. In the imagination of this film underwritten by capitalist ideology, there is nothing that one cannot accomplish. *Forrest Gump*, for its part, takes a similar tack, proffering the fantasy that anyone can succeed, no matter their intellectual deficit, so long as they keep a positive attitude. There is not much ideological difference between *Forrest Gump* and the lotto. In both of these films (and countless others), the social contradictions of capitalist society miraculously fall away. By depicting fantasies of this ilk, cinema functions as a mass art only in the worse sense: it serves to manipulate the masses into accepting their fate within capitalist society.

If we take the temperature of cinematic politics in the twentieth century, the results are execrable. For every *Battleship Potemkin* or *Citizen Kane*, we have a hundred films like *Star Wars* and *Forrest Gump*. Cinema has betrayed its role as an art for the masses by obscuring social contradictions rather than highlighting them, by immersing the masses in a flow of images that provide fantasmatic deliverance from the suffering unleashed by capitalist society. The investment in the healing power of the image leaves the masses out in the cold.

For Lahiji, Alain Badiou represents one of his touchstones in *Architecture, Philosophy, and the Pedagogy of Cinema*. The other is Walter Benjamin. Both of these thinkers position themselves between cinema's radicality and its ideological functioning. Both Badiou and Benjamin see the political potential of cinema—something Benjamin even finds in figures such as Mickey Mouse—but they also recognize how cinema has betrayed this political potential. Although neither Badiou nor Benjamin connects the plight of cinema as a mass art to that of architecture, in *Architecture, Philosophy, and the Pedagogy of Cinema* Nadir Lahiji does it for them. Here, we view how the sad political fate of cinema offers lessons that can provide the foundation for constituting architecture as a genuine art for the masses.

As it reaches its end point as a dominant art, cinema plays a major role in the development of what Badiou labels our *pornographic age*. Cinematic revelations of formerly unseen domains—not to speak of actual pornographic films—create a sense that there is nothing that cannot be seen. This tendency toward total exposure bears directly on the project of architecture and its attempt to create a public space. This pornographic age is what architecture must confront and dethrone. This means that architecture must create public spaces that reveal rather than conceal the social contradictions of our time.

Architecture does not inherently challenge the spirit of pornography. To do so, it must work against the cinematic tendency to create an image that allows spectators to disavow the underlying contradictions. This is the vision that Lahiji has of architecture as a newly claimed art of the masses. In the final line of the book, Lahiji insists, 'Building in our time must "disimage" in order to overcome the obscenity of our Pornographic Age'. Where cinema has failed to stress what resists the image, architecture has to highlight these points of resistance, points that reveal the contradictions of capitalist society. Where cinema has succumbed to the image, architecture can break its spell.

The great triumph of *Architecture, Philosophy, and the Pedagogy of Cinema* is that it calls us to rethink the contribution that cinema has made to the theory of art. Rather than confining speculation about the cinema to the realm of cinema itself, Lahiji does something much more valuable. He recognizes that the lessons of cinema are universal lessons. Cinema's ultimate failure to constitute a successful art for the masses and its capitulation to the forces of capital on which it depended do not preclude another art taking up cinema's lessons in a more politically fecund way. This is precisely what Nadir Lahiji envisions for architecture.

Preface

Architecture after cinema

Cinema for Alain Badiou is 'democratic' because, on the philosophical ground, it is an 'art of contradiction'. It is 'a democratic dialectic' and therefore an 'exceptional' art. As a Platonist, Badiou puts forward a persuasive argument which goes as follows: While Plato, with his famous 'allegory of the cave', was saying that we have to escape 'the potency of the image', today, we must say, on the contrary, that in a certain sense, 'we must go to the cinema'. 'So we must go into the cave', Badiou says: 'in the modern cave where the spectacle of images is more elaborate'.[1] He further declares:

> If we say something concerning the relationship between cinema and philosophy we must say that cinema is for philosophy today the new allegory of the cave which is 'go to the cave, go to the cave'. It's only by going to the cave that we can find the new means to go outside, because precisely the cinema is the immanent conflict between what is the bad presentation of images, the troubled fascination of images on one side, but on the other side the possibility of clear vision by images themselves of the possibility of an orientation in the real.[2]

By going into the cave, which for Badiou is 'our cinema today', we also 'participate in the democratic dialectics. And so it's part of our modern education'.[3] This is the crux of the matter: After Plato's *Republic* there must be a *new* pedagogy: The pedagogy of the masses.

Badiou never brought up architecture in his complex philosophical thoughts on cinema. But Walter Benjamin did. I claim that it is architecture, well *before* cinema, that must be given pride of place to be the 'art of contradiction'—on the same philosophical ground. But this claim comes with a caveat. Architecture needs to learn the philosophical lessons offered by our radical philosopher on cinema. Thus it is most instructive to take Badiou's thought-provoking point on 'contradiction' seriously in this respect.

By suggesting the title 'Architecture after cinema', I mean to pose a defensible dilemma. Underlying it is a central thesis which goes as follows: Before the advent of cinema, architecture was the *only* 'art of contradiction' and it remains so after the invention of cinema. I will present the argument in support of this thesis after undertaking a major exploration. I first attempt to re-read Walter Benjamin's 'The Work of Art in the Age of Its Technological Reproducibility' in the light of Badiou's philosophical thoughts on cinema. I then use the result of this reading to advance the thesis that architecture has to recover its original function that, according to Benjamin, was taken over by cinema in the early twentieth century. Once again, as I argue, it must assume its task as the *training ground*—Benjamin's term—for the *perceptual apparatus of the human sensorium* grounded in the political subjectivity aimed at a pedagogy of the masses in the modern mass-mediated society. The nature and character of this 'mass-mediated society' in the twenty-first century is a problematic one that will require examination. The central claim here is that re-reading Benjamin with Badiou's philosophy of cinema will yield categories and concepts necessary for the renewal of critical analysis of architecture. I base my contention on the claim that architecture, today, is incapable of resisting, let alone confronting, the dominant political subjectivity arising from an ideology imbedded in contemporary capitalism that Badiou has termed 'democratic fascism'. The meaning of the latter term, as I will try to demonstrate, is in the political lineage of the seemingly 'perplexing' thesis that Benjamin put forward in the Epilogue of his Artwork essay almost seven decades ago.

My attempt to read Benjamin with Badiou holds a twofold objective. On the one hand, I situate Benjamin's Artwork essay and his theory of 'experience' on a *philosophical* ground going back to critical philosophy in Kant and Hegel. On the other, against the ambivalence of some, I consider Benjamin a quintessentially Marxist thinker, notwithstanding his '*weak* messianism', who had a certain idea of communism and a clear idea about the notion of the 'proletariat'. This is a specific figure of

'Benjamin' that I want to associate with a specific figure of 'Marx' associated with the 'post-1989' political conjuncture. Let me explain this. I follow Boris Buden's perceptive argument about Marx and the nature of 'Marxism' related to the 'translation' enterprise of *Capital* in the post-1989 era, with 'the restoration of capitalism' against the ideology of the so-called 'democracy'. This is the time when Marx was *liberated* from the previous official Marxism associated with the totalitarian communist police states of the Eastern Bloc. Suffice it to remember here the genuine idea of 'communism' originally belonging to Marx in the specific conjuncture in 1844 when an intense intellectual struggle was going on around him, leading to his eventual argument in *The German Ideology*. As Buden, invoking Kant's idea of 'public use of reason', observes:

> the post-1989 liberation of Marx's writings might be understood as a sort of reappropriation by public reason. It has liberated Marx as author, who is now finally free—to address, as a scholar (*Gelehrte*), 'the intellectuals of the world', or, in Kant's parlance, the society of the world citizens.[4]

Buden, following Marshall Berman, further writes that 'Karl Marx went through a double liberation: a life freed from Marx has recovered *Marx freed for the intellectuals of the world*'[5] (emphasis mine). It is in this sense that we might consider Benjamin as *freed* in the aftermath of 1989 in terms of his idea of communism for the 'intellectual of the world'. In this sense he is *a thinker of the Proletariat*. This notion of the proletariat in Benjamin had already been liberated from both abuses, from fascism and the later Eastern Bloc 'communism'. As I will argue in this work, it is in this context that we must consider his seemingly puzzling, and much misunderstood, statement at the end of his Artwork essay. I therefore envision a secure place for Benjamin among the contemporary radical thinkers on the Left who have unabashedly returned to the Idea of Communism, notably Alain Badiou and Slavoj Žižek.

Theses on pedagogy of the masses

> Just as Philosophy finds its material weapons in the proletariat, so the proletariat finds its spiritual weapons in philosophy; and once the lightning of thought has struck deeply into this naïve soil of the people

the Emancipation of the Germans into men will be accomplished. [...] Philosophy cannot be actualized without the abolition [*Aufhebung*] of the proletariat; the proletariat cannot be abolished without the actualization of philosophy.

Karl Marx, 'A Contribution to Hegel's
Philosophy of Right: Introduction'[6]

In this book I advance a central thesis, the premise of which goes as follows: The *collective human sensorium* in the apparatus of *perception* that, to put it strictly in Benjaminian terms, will perform a new task of *apperception*, must once again find its true *training ground* in architecture. This art of building is here understood in 'photographic' parallax as a 'thing-in-itself' in Kantian terms.[7] Building art puts the collective mass in the position of an 'expert critic' who identifies themselves with the technical apparatus behind the building. Only then can architecture *regain* its status as 'mass art', as I will contend, and resume its function as the *only* 'artform' that is destined for the political *pedagogy of the masses*, which originally had always belonged to it before the invention of cinema.

By examining the constitutive elements of this pedagogy, and by delving into the politically vague notion of 'masses', I will take up a *philosophical* investigation into the foundational *contradiction* inherent in the dialectic of *building experience.* The work of Benjamin and Badiou's philosophy on cinema are the main sources for constructing my theses. At the same time, I deploy a broader philosophical-political concept that underpins their works. At times, I incorporate an integrated Marxian-psychoanalytical theory with references to the tradition of critical philosophy from Kant to Hegel and critical theory in Marx.

At this point a brief explanation about the heading 'Architecture *after* cinema' is in order. The word 'after' is to be understood in its semantic variations: 'later in time', 'in the manner of', 'in agreement with', or 'in search of'. Granting that architecture must now come *after* cinema, it must be thought, paradoxically, as coming *before* cinema. The preposition '*before*' is taken not in a trite sense that there was building before the advent of film in the history of humankind, but rather to imply that building is *eternal*, we cannot take leave from it, it will never disappear, it will never die. Alain Badiou would retort that cinema *also* cannot disappear, or cinema is as old as Plato's cave. Granted. But, however we want to view it, we must consider that one provocative point has been brought to our attention just recently: That long after the invention of cinema, we have reached the point where cinema is said to be possible only *after* its death. I am referring to Jean-Luc Godard's declaration that film ended with the cinema of Abbas Kiarostami, the Iranian filmmaker.[8] It is after Godard that Badiou posed his own question in this regard: 'Why not the possibility of cinema which is the cinema of the death of cinema? Or the cinema of non-cinema; of the impossibility of cinema …'[9] It is hard to say these things about building art. We *cannot* talk about the *impossibility* of building. Why not? In the course of the investigation in this book I will address this question.

In thematic chapters before the Epilogue, I variously examine Benjamin's theses on architecture in connection to cinema and Badiou's philosophical thoughts on cinema *absent* architecture. This absence in the work of our prodigious philosopher is the cause for serious concern. To recall, the principal premise for Benjamin in his Artwork essay was the concern that, to the extent that it has become possible for art to perform the 'new tasks of apperception', and insofar as 'individuals are tempted to evade such tasks', 'art will tackle the most difficult and most important task' when it is able to mobilize the masses, and it is currently film (in Benjamin's time) that in the form of '*reception in distraction*' is able to do this. In this task, cinema, as a technological apparatus, aspired to architecture as an artform to affect the *collective human sensorium*. We must not, therefore, forget that it was cinema as a 'mass art' that *retroactively* enabled architecture to be conceived as a 'mass art', in the conflictual meaning inherent in the term. In our own twenty-first century, as I claim, the task is different. In a short outline, the task now is the *restoration* of architecture in order to enable it, once again, to regain its original function as 'mass art' after the supposed 'death' of cinema. Paradoxically, as will be argued, architecture cannot regain this function if it does not *revert* to the *dialectic of modernity*, to the status it enjoyed in the early decades of the twentieth century that, to put it in Benjamin's term, we can name as 'new, positive barbarism'. I have devoted a chapter to shedding light on this 'barbarism'.

At the center of the proposed pedagogy of the masses, I insist, is the question of *philosophy*. In Badiou's term, it is presented as a reciprocity: 'cinema *as* philosophy', or 'philosophy *as* cinema'. This is indeed an 'exceptional' relationship in the mind of our great philosopher, because he believes that cinema is the fundamental *symptom* of 'our history', if not of our modernity. But Plato told us to escape the 'potency of images', to get out of the cave, or what is known as the 'allegory of the cave', Badiou reminds us. Yet, Badiou urges us that 'we must go into the cave', in a certain sense. He says: 'we must go to the cinema', 'in the modern cave where the spectacle of images is more elaborate'. But he qualifies this act of going into the cave: 'If we say something concerning the relationship between cinema and philosophy we must say that the cinema is for philosophy today the new allegory of the cave that we can find the new means to go outside …'[10] What I will do in this work is rather *shameless*: I will *expropriate* the powerful philosophical concepts and categories that Badiou has attributed to cinema only to reclaim them for architecture. This, in effect, amounts to saying that, with due respect to our great philosopher, these concepts and categories inherently belong to building art prior to their conspicuous manifestations in the art of cinema, or 'cinema *as* philosophy'. Let me mention here the most important ones Badiou has brought up: impure art, *non-art* of the art, cinema as contradiction, cinema as democratic and dialectic, hence cinema as 'democratic dialectic'. In this book, I will avoid taking up the question of 'architecture *as* philosophy' or 'philosophy *as* architecture', in analogy to Badiou's terms. That would be a major undertaking and would require an entire book by itself.[11] I will therefore confine myself to contending that Badiou's powerful philosophical lessons on cinema can refreshingly bring about a new *actuality* of Benjamin and his theses on cinema in which the 'masses' play a central role. It will be my task to foreground the ideas of both our prominent thinkers, with two different philosophical groundings, to critique architecture, which in our contemporary setting has been emptied of its main function as the 'art of masses' by the forces of technological capitalism, which is responsible for the *anesthetization* of the apparatus of the *human sensorium*.

I hasten to point out here that, recalling Marx's paragraph cited above, in terms of the *philosophical project of the masses*, the notion of the 'proletariat' requires constant 'actualization of philosophy' until the 'abolition [*Aufhebung*] of the proletariat'. Concluding this preface, it is noteworthy that the notion of the 'proletariat' began its circulation in 1844 in Germany at the time when Marx embraced the idea of 'communism' and wrote his 'A Contribution to Hegel's *Philosophy of Right*: Introduction'. Gareth Stedman Jones depicts the intellectual circumstances in which the relationship between 'philosophy' and 'proletariat' was presented:

> The proletariat represented the '*passive* element, a *material* basis' in the process of revolutionary change. In Feuerbach's vision, it represented 'the *heart*—the feminine principle, the *sense* of the finite and the seat of materialism'. The spark must come from elsewhere, from philosophy, 'the *head*—the masculine principle and the seat of idealism'. Germany's revolutionary past was theoretical—the Reformation. Just as present-day Germany was trapped in the clutches of an outdated *ancien régime*, so 'official' Germany on the eve of the Reformation had been 'the most unconditional *slave* of Rome'. But 'as the revolution then began in the brain of the *monk*, so now it begins in the brain of the *philosopher*.[12]

As Marx himself put the matter:

> *The emancipation of the German* is *the emancipation of the human being*. The *head* of this emancipation is *philosophy*; its *heart* is the *proletariat* … Once the lightning of thought has squarely struck this ingenious soil of the people, the emancipation of the *Germans* into *human beings* will take place.[13]

Notes

1. See Alain Badiou, 'Cinema and Philosophy', in *Badiou and His Interlocutors: Lectures, Interviews and Responses*, eds A. J. Bartlett and Justin Clemens (London: Bloomsbury, 2018), 27.
2. Alain Badiou, 'Cinema and Philosophy', 27.
3. Alain Badiou, 'Cinema and Philosophy', 27.
4. Boris Buden, 'It Is Getting Darker around the Central Sun of Freedom: *Capital* Translation and the Re-feudalization of Capitalism', in *Capitalism: Concept, Idea, Image, Aspects of Marx's Capital Today*, eds Peter Osborne, Éric Alliez, and Eric-John Russell (London: CRMEP Books, 2019), 138.
5. Boris Buden, 'It Is Getting Darker around the Central Sun of Freedom: *Capital* Translation and the Re-feudalization of Capitalism', 151. Buden asks: 'What actually happened in 1989?' He explains that

it seems that there is today almost no disagreement about it: a democratic revolution that, following the ideals of the greatest emancipatory events of world history, liberated East European masses from the yoke of communist totalitarianism. In short, it was all about freedom. After 1989 people who had been previously subjected to various forms of repression, above all by an alienated one-party state and its ideology, were finally free—to speak out in the public sphere, to form political parties and choose their representatives in free elections, to exercise their religious beliefs, to pursue their economic interests or to move wherever they want to. If we are to believe [Marshall] Berman, after 1989 even Karl Marx went through a double liberation: a life freed from Marx has recovered Marx freed for the intellectuals of the world.

Buden here is referring to Marshall Berman's essay entitled 'Tearing Away the Veil: The Communist Manifesto' that originally appeared as the introduction to the Penguin Classics Deluxe Edition of *The Communist Manifesto,* published in 1989, also see www.dissentmagazine.org/online_articles/tearing-away-the-veils-the-communist-manifesto. Further, Buden states that

while the whole world was still celebrating the final victory of freedom, the new political elite turned the state into political instrument and immediately used it to change property and production relations. This was the third and final stage of the historical turn of 1989—the restoration of capitalism.

6 Karl Marx, 'A Contribution to the Critique of Hegel's *Philosophy of Right*: Introduction', in *Critique of Hegel's 'Philosophy of Right'*, trans. Annette Jolin and Joseph O'Malley, ed., intro., and notes Joseph O'Malley (Cambridge: Cambridge University Press, 1970), 142.
7 In this I will be following Kojin Karatani's extraordinary exposition of 'Parallax' in his *Transcritique: On Kant and Marx* (Cambridge: The MIT Press, 2003).
8 As Negar Mottahedeh reports,

Responding to the New York Film Critic Circle's proposal for a tribute to him on the occasion of the centenary of cinema, Jean-Luc Godard wrote a highly publicized open letter listing his own worst mistakes. One of the mistakes he regretted was his failure to convince the Academy Award selection committee to award the Oscar for best foreign language film to Kiarostami rather than Krzysztof Kieślowski. This, he said, was one of the greatest sins for which he would have to atone: 'Film begins with D. W. Griffith and ends with Abbas Kiarostami'.

Negar Mottahedeh, *Displaced Allegories: Post-Revolutionary Iranian Cinema* (Durham and London: Duke University Press, 2008), 90

9 See Alain Badiou, 'Cinema and Philosophy', 25.

10   Alain Badiou, 'Cinema and Philosophy', 27. Badiou goes on to say,

> because precisely the cinema is the immanent conflict between what is the bad presentation of images, the troubled fascination of images on one side, but on the other side the possibility of clear vision by images themselves of the possibility of an orientation in the real. So to go to the cave, which is today the cinema, is also to participate in the democratic dialectic. And so it's part of our modern education.

11   Architecture's relation to philosophy is a vast and difficult subject that goes beyond the main concern I have in this book. It is a subject matter that I will take up in my forthcoming work, tentatively entitled 'Philosophy and the Will to Architecture'.

12   See Gareth Stedman Jones, *Karl Marx: Greatness and Illusion* (Cambridge: The Belknap Press of Harvard University Press, 2016), 154. Also see Karl Marx, 'A Contribution to the Critique of Hegel's *Philosophy of Right*: Introduction', 137–138. Stedman Jones usefully provides a context for the passage I quoted. He writes:

> For in Germany there was no class capable of acting like the French 'Third Estate' in 1789. Every class was struggling against classes both above and beneath it. That meant that in Germany it was not 'radical revolution' or 'general human emancipation', but 'political emancipation', 'the partial, the merely political revolution', which was the utopian dream. In Germany 'universal emancipation' was 'the sine qua non of partial emancipation'. What was now required was a 'human' transformation carried through by a class outside and beneath existing society, a class with only 'a human title', 'a class with radical chains', a 'sphere' that 'cannot emancipate itself without emancipating ... all other spheres of society'. In Germany, such a class was already coming into being. This was the proletariat, a class arising from '*industrial* development' and from the '*drastic dissolution* of society'. It was 'the completion of Man' and 'the dissolution of the hitherto existing world order'. For radical revolution to occur in Germany it would not be enough for 'thought to strive for realization ... reality must itself strive towards thought'. This requirement was now being met, for 'by demanding the negation of private property ... the proletariat merely rises to the rank of a principle that society has made the principle of the proletariat'.

13   Quoted in Gareth Stedman Jones, *Karl Marx*, 154.

Acknowledgments

I would like first to express my gratitude to my publisher at Routledge, Francesca Ford, for her persistent support of my work and for making the publication of this book possible.

I am indebted to Trudy Varcianna, the Senior Editorial Assistant at Routledge, for her great assistance throughout the process. I especially thank her for her helpful advice and prompt communications.

I would like to thank Kristina Wischenkamper for her excellent editorial work on the final draft of the manuscript.

My special thanks go to Steven Holt for his excellent copyediting work on the manuscript. The final text benefited tremendously from his thorough and meticulous intervention.

Introduction

Architecture at the 'end' of cinema

> Film begins with D. W. Griffith and ends with Abbas Kiarostami.
> —Jean-Luc Godard, in *The Cinema of Abbas Kiarostami*[1]

> There's no film. Cinema is dead. There can't be film anymore. If you want, let's have a discussion.
> —Guy Debord, *IndieWire*[2]

> The alignment of reality with the masses and of the masses with reality is a process of immeasurable importance for both thinking and perception.
> —Walter Benjamin, 'The Work of Art in the Age of Its Technological Reproducibility'[3]

The study of architecture in the academy remains insulated from philosophical thoughts on cinema. The implication of this fact, at the very least, is that the political theory of 'masses' is absent in the theory and pedagogy of architecture. This absence is an indication, among other things, that teaching Walter Benjamin has never entered in any serious fashion into the pedagogy of architecture in the academy. In the early twentieth century, Benjamin was the only thinker who coupled *building* with *film* as two fundamental *technologically* conditioned 'mass arts' as the *training ground* for the *perceptual apparatus* of the *human sensorium*. In the third version of 'The Work of Art in the Age of Its Technological Reproducibility'—henceforth the Artwork essay—Benjamin wrote: 'The masses are a matrix from which all customary behavior towards works of art is today emerging newborn'.[4]

The mediated reception of architecture and cinema must be measured by the same matrix. At the same time, Benjamin emphatically asserted that before the invention of cinema, architecture had always been a 'prototype' of an artwork received by the collective. And the reason being that 'Buildings have accompanied human existence since primeval time'.[5] In modern mass-mediated society, by definition, 'masses' are *encoded* in architecture. Benjamin has reminded us that many forms of arts 'have come into being and passed away', but architecture has persisted, primarily because: '*the human need for shelter is permanent*', adding that 'Architecture has never had fallow periods. Its history is longer than that of any other art, and its effect ought to be recognized in any attempt to account for the relationship of the masses to the work of art'[6] (emphasis mine). That is, *until* the advent of cinema. As a technological apparatus, cinema *took over* the function of architecture. It radically changed the modality of *reception* of the work of art. He wrote: '*Reception in distraction—the sort of reception which is increasingly noticeable in all areas of art and is a symptom of profound changes in apperception—finds in film its true training ground*'.[7] This had far-reaching consequences. Technological reproduction put an end to the '*authenticity*' of the work of art. It radically changed the modality of 'mass art'. For the first time, *reproducibility* allowed *politics* to enter its practice. Benjamin took an enormous *political* step: '*But as soon as the criterion of authenticity ceases to be applied to artistic production, the whole social function of art is revolutionized. Instead of being founded on ritual, it is based on a different practice: politics*'.[8]

Nearly 80 years after Benjamin's Artwork essay, cinema is pronounced *dead*. Jean-Luc Godard famously said: 'Film begins with D. W. Griffith and ends with Abbas Kiarostami'.[9] Alain Badiou, a sympathetic interlocutor, who appeared in two of Godard's films, turned the filmmaker's dramatic statement into an absolute affirmation and astonishingly said: 'It will not be a disaster if cinema disappears. Godard, for example, says that cinema is dead, cinema is finished, except maybe the cinema of Godard because it's a cinema of the death of the cinema'.[10] Cinema keeps on living after its 'death'. But *building can never die*. It will never disappear. Because, as Benjamin said, and I repeat, 'the human need for shelter is permanent'. Building will continue to live on the ground of human existence—indefinitely.

Interestingly enough, before Badiou's pronouncement, it was Gilles Deleuze who in *Cinema 2: The Time-Image*, published in 1985, wrote about the death of cinema as the 'art of masses' in a particular political conjuncture in the twentieth century. He wrote the following:

> How strangely the great declarations, of Eisenstein, of Gance, ring today; we put them to one side like declarations worthy of a museum, all the hopes put into cinema, art of masses and new thought. We can always say the cinema has drowned in the nullity of its production [...] Cinema is dying, then, from its quantitative mediocrity. But there is a still more important reason: the mass-art, the treatment of masses, which should not have been separable from an accession of the masses to the status of true subject, has degenerated into state propaganda and manipulation, into a kind of fascism which brought together Hitler and Hollywood, Hollywood and Hitler. The spiritual automaton became fascist man.[11]

And further:

> As Serge Daney says, what has brought the whole cinema of the movement-image into question are 'great political *mise-en-scène*, state propaganda turned *tableaux vivants*, the first handling of masses of humans', and their backdrop, the camps. This was the death-knell for the ambitions of the 'old cinema': not, or not only, the mediocrity and vulgarity of current production but rather Leni Riefenstahl, who was not mediocre [...] There has been no diversion or alienation in art of the masses initially founded by the movement-image; on the contrary the movement-image was from the beginning linked to the organization of war, state propaganda, ordinary fascism, historically and essentially. These two joint reasons, mediocrity of products and fascism of production, can explain a great many things.[12]

As Christopher Kul-Want observes, 'Deleuze recognized that the hopes and aspirations for a truly mass art realizable through cinema were over in the sense that Benjamin, as well as the great filmmakers of the early modern period, had hoped for'.[13] Benjamin of course in his Artwork essay had already laid out his concern about the technological art of cinema with the 'instrumentalization of technology', as

Kul-Want puts it, by the 'combined forces of capitalism and fascism'. Now, Deleuze's judgment about 'mediocrity of products' is reinforced by Badiou who understands cinema as '*first and foremost* an industry'. In his 'Cinema as Philosophical Experimentation' he writes: 'In any film, there are whole bits of it that are banal, images that are pointless, lines that could disappear, over-done colors, bad actors, rampant pornography, and so on'.[14]

An elementary thesis would go as follows: Cinema as a genuine 'mass art', exemplified by the great cinema of Hitchcock and Godard, is *dead*—literally and metaphorically. It has lost its function. But its *ends* persist. Architecture, on the other hand, as the oldest art of the 'masses' in the history of mankind, outlives cinema—because, to reiterate, 'the human need for shelter is permanent'. This permanent 'mass art' is exploited in the era of capitalist modernity by the unchanging material property relation and cultural mythology of fascism. Given the *denial* of the primordial function of architecture under this exploitation, it is imperative that its *ontology* be *rethought*. To this end, it is the contention of this work that architecture must re-learn the lessons of the early-twentieth-century cinema as 'mass art' in order to regain its function as the genuine art of masses. This means that its *practice* must be brought back again to *politics*. Subtracted from its *Schein*, or semblance, architecture must recover its function as the *training ground* for the *perceptual apparatus* of the *human sensorium*, to deepen the *apperception* of the individual, as Benjamin put it in the case of cinema. This task can be fulfilled only when architecture's mode of existence comes under the twofold modalities Benjamin specified, and when the *philosophical theory of masses* is allowed to enter its discourse.

More than 80 years ago an ontological question was posed about cinema by André Bazin. He famously asked: 'What is cinema?' I want to pose the same ontological question addressed to architecture: 'what is architecture?' Central to any possible answer is the call for a *re-opening* of Benjamin's 'The Work of Art in the Age of Its Technical Reproducibility'. In the past 50 years many intelligent readings of Benjamin's Artwork essay have been offered by its scholars and commentators. The most comprehensive one is offered by Miriam Bratu Hansen in her indispensable *Cinema and Experience*.[15] Learning from her work, I attempt a different reading. Here it is useful to cite

Hansen's succinct 'rough sketch' highlighting the main argument in the Artwork essay. She writes:

> The technological reproducibility of traditional works of art, what is more, the constitutive role of technology in the media of film and photography have affected the status of art in its core. Evolving from the large-scale reorganization of human sense perception in capitalist-industrial society, this crisis is defined, on the one hand, by the decline of what Benjamin refers to as aura, the unique modality of being that has accrued to the traditional work of art, and, on the other, by the emergence of the urban masses, whose mode of existence correlates with the new regime of perception advanced by the media of technological reproduction. The structural erosion of the aura through the technological media converges with the assault on the institution of art from within by avant-garde movements such as dada and surrealism.[16]

And further:

> In terms of the political crisis that is the essay's framing condition, two developments have entered into a fatal constellation: first, the cult of decaying aura qua belated aestheticism (from *l'art pour l'art* to Stefan George) and on the part of avant-gardists such as futurist F. T. Marinetti who supply an ideological link to fascism; second, fascism's wedding of aestheticist principles to the monumental, particularly in the spectacular formations of the masses that give them an illusory sense of expression and culminate in the glorification of war. In this situation of extreme emergency, Benjamin concludes, the only remaining strategy for intellectuals on the left is to respond to the fascists' aestheticization of politics with the 'politicization of art' as advanced by communism.[17]

Hansen quite instructively makes it clear that the Artwork essay is

> neither 'about' film as an empirical phenomenon nor, for that matter, about any other reconstituted, given object. Rather, it is concerned with the structural role Benjamin ascribes to film as a hinge between the fate of art under the conditions of industrial capitalism and the contemporary political crisis, which pivots on the organization of the masses.[18]

We have not overcome this political crisis—quite the contrary. Hansen further reminds us that Benjamin 'forges his text into an area of crisis', and that '[t]he essay does not *describe* a given crisis; it rather *stages* a crisis through the particular construction of the essay'.[19] Hansen interestingly looks at the preface and epilogue along with the 15 sections that together form the structure of the Artwork essay as 'alternating camera setups', or, using Benjamin's own words, 'sequences of positional views', and suggests that we might think of them as 'master shots taken from the larger perspectives of, respectively, the institution of art and the aesthetic, including film; reproduction technology and changes in human sense perception; and the political formation of the masses'.[20]

In this work I have the same sense of 'extreme emergency' and the 'remaining task' for the intellectuals on the Left for architecture, in response to the same 'fascists' aestheticization of politics with the "politicization of art" as advanced by communism', as much as this latter statement has puzzled various commentators, to which I will attend. In my reading, I attempt to put the Artwork essay on a higher philosophical plateau in the intersection with the philosophical thoughts of Alain Badiou on cinema. This intersection is warranted by a twofold notion central to the thoughts of both, that is, the political notion of 'masses' and thoughts on 'Communism'. In the center of this thought, pronounced more explicitly in Benjamin than in Badiou, resides the notion of the *proletariat*. I examine the concept through a Marxist lens.

Badiou refers to Benjamin's Artwork essay once in his magisterial *The Century,* although only in passing, and to the best of my knowledge, he never discussed any work of Benjamin in his philosophical work on arts and in his vast writings on cinema.[21] Had he taken up Benjamin, in line with his affirmative response to André Bazin and Gilles Deleuze, Badiou might have found a sympathetic interlocutor not only in relation to the ideas about cinema as a 'mass art', but more specifically on the notion of 'masses' as quintessentially a *political* entity. In his 'On Cinema as a Democratic Emblem', which I will discuss in this work, Badiou poses a seemingly simple question to which he offers an illuminating answer. He writes 'the point is this: "mass art" defines a paradoxical relationship. Why? Because "mass" is a political category. Or more precisely a category of activist democracy, of communism'.[22]

He further notes that 'The Russian revolutionaries were able to define their action as being that of the era when "the masses mounted the stage of History"'.[23] He further points out that 'Nowadays we oppose "mass democracy" to representative and constitutional democracy. "Mass" is a fundamental political category'.[24]

This work explores the way Benjamin places the notion of the 'proletariat' within the political category of 'masses' that would bring him into proximity with Badiou's 'Idea of communism'. I explore its implications for the fundamental ontological question I pose: 'What is architecture?' Forcing the theory and philosophy of architecture to learn from the theory and philosophy of cinema, I deploy psychoanalytical-Marxian theories of film, particularly following the work of Slavoj Žižek, Todd McGowan, and Joan Copjec.

Notes

1. See Negar Mottahedeh, *Displaced Allegories: Post-Revolutionary Iranian Cinema* (Durham and London: Duke University Press, 2008), 90. Also see the front cover of Alberto Elena's book, *The Cinema of Abbas Kiarostami* (London: Saqi, 2005). Kiarostami was the world-known Iranian filmmaker who passed away in 2016. Badiou has prominently said that cinema is about knowing the Other, and in this case, knowing Iran through cinema one needs to study Kiarostami's films. For further discussion on Kiarostami see Mehrnaz Saeed-Vafa and Jonathan Rosenbaum, *Abbas Kiarostami*, Expanded Second Edition (Urbana: University of Illinois Press, 2003, 2018).
2. www.indiewire.com/2012/10/sound-the-death-knell-again-a-brief-history-of-the-death-of-cinema-105354/.
3. Walter Benjamin, 'The Work of Art in the Age of Its Technological Reproducibility', Third Version, in *Walter Benjamin, Selected Writings, Volume 4, 1938–1940*, general ed. Michael W. Jennings (Cambridge: The Belknap Press of Harvard University Press, 2003), 256.
4. Walter Benjamin, 'The Work of Art in the Age of Its Technological Reproducibility', Third Version, 267.
5. Walter Benjamin, 'The Work of Art in the Age of Its Technological Reproducibility', Third Version, 268.
6. Walter Benjamin, 'The Work of Art in the Age of Its Technological Reproducibility', Third Version, 268.
7. Walter Benjamin, 'The Work of Art in the Age of Its Technological Reproducibility', Third Version, 269.
8. Walter Benjamin, 'The Work of Art in the Age of Its Technological Reproducibility', Third Version, 256–257.
9. For the cinema of Kiarostami see especially Alberto Elena, *The Cinema of Abbas Kiarostami* (London: Saqi, 2005) and Mehrnaz Saeed-Vafa and Jonathan

Rosenbaum, *Abbas Kiarostami*, Expanded Second Edition (Urbana: University of Illinois Press, 2003, 2018). As Petra Kettle and Robert Pfaller note, 'Cinema's death was proclaimed more than once. It seems that every time a new technological mutation—the talking film, television, video tapes and recorders, DVD-players, streaming services, etc.—came out, somebody called for cinema's last rites'; see Petra Kettle and Robert Pfaller, 'The End of Cinema as We Know It: Or How a Medium Turned from a Promising Graduate into an Old Folk', in *Crisis and Critique* 2, vol. 7 (June 2020).

10 Alain Badiou, 'Cinema and Philosophy', in *Badiou and His Interlocutors: Lectures, Interviews and Responses*, eds A. J. Bartlett and Justin Clemens (London: Bloomsbury, 2018), 25. Badiou makes his comments specifically in response to Alex Ling's presentation entitled 'An Inessential Art?: Positioning Cinema in Alain Badiou's Philosophy', also published in the same collection.

11 See Gilles Deleuze, *Cinema 2: The Time-Image*, trans. Hugh Tomlinson and Robert Galeta (Minneapolis: University of Minnesota Press, 1989), 164.

12 Gilles Deleuze, *Cinema 2*, 164–165. In the footnote Deleuze cites Paul Virilio affirmatively and brings up the logic of perception:

> the system of war mobilizes perception as much as arms and actions: thus photo and cinema pass through war and are coupled together with arms (for example, the machine gun). There will increasingly be a *mise-en-scène* of the battlefield, to which the enemy replies, not now by camouflage, but by counter *mise-en-scène* (simulation, trickery, or giant illuminations of the air defense). But it is the whole of civil life which passes into the mode of the *mise-en-scène*, in the fascist system: 'real power is henceforth shared between the logistics of arms and that of images and sounds'; and, to the very end, Goebbels dreamt of going beyond Hollywood, which was the modern cinema-city in contrast to the ancient theatre-city. Cinema in turn goes beyond itself towards the electronic image, civil as well as military in a military-industrial complex.
>
> 309–310

See also Paul Virilio, *The Logics of Perception*, trans. Patrick Camiller (London and New York: Verso, 2009).

13 See Christopher Kul-Want, 'Introduction', in *Philosophers on Film from Bergson to Badiou: A Critical Reader*, ed. Christopher Kul-Want (New York: Columbia University Press, 2019), 9. Kul-Want adds that 'Deleuze brings to bear a similar argument to that of Adorno and Horkheimer in their essay "The Culture Industry: Enlightenment as Mass Deception" to explain why Benjamin's revolutionary hopes for the relationship of cinema and the Masses failed', 9. This link, as Kul-Want notes, connecting masses to cinema and mass art was severed by fascist and capitalist ideology.

14 See Alain Badiou, 'Cinema as Philosophical Experimentation', in *Cinema*, texts selected and introduced by Antoine de Baecque (Cambridge: Polity, 2013), 230.

15 See Miriam Bratu Hansen, *Cinema and Experience: Siegfried Kracauer, Walter Benjamin, and Theodor W. Adorno* (Berkeley: University of California Press, 2012).

16 Miriam Bratu Hansen, *Cinema and Experience*, 85.
17 Miriam Bratu Hansen, *Cinema and Experience*, 85. Hansen here adds that

> As has been noted, this conclusion raises more questions than it answers. What did communist art politics mean in 1936 (or for that matter, in 1939)? What did Benjamin mean by politics? What was his concept of revolution? Which 'masses' did he have in mind—a utopian collective, the proletariat, the moviegoing public, or the psychopathological mass mobilized by racist-nationalist politics? How does the dichotomous conclusion tally with the argument about the revolutionary role of film in relation to art, sense perception, and urban industrial technology?

18 Miriam Bratu Hansen, *Cinema and Experience*, 85.
19 Miriam Bratu Hansen, *Cinema and Experience*, 88.
20 Miriam Bratu Hansen, *Cinema and Experience*, 88–89.
21 See Alain Badiou, *The Century* (Cambridge: Polity, 2007).
22 Alain Badiou, 'On Cinema as a Democratic Emblem', in Alain Badiou, *Cinema*, texts selected and introduced by Antoine de Baecque (Cambridge: Polity, 2013), 234.
23 Alain Badiou, 'On Cinema as a Democratic Emblem', 234–235.
24 Alain Badiou, 'On Cinema as a Democratic Emblem', 235.

Chapter 1

Returning to the philosophy of masses
Benjamin and Badiou

> The increasing proletarianization of modern man and the increasing formation of masses are two sides of the same process.
> —Walter Benjamin, 'The Work of Art in the Age of Its Technological Reproducibility'[1]

> 'Mass' is a political category, or more precisely a category of activist democracy, of communism.
> —Alain Badiou, *Cinema*[2]

> Mass reproduction is especially favored by the reproduction of the masses.
> —Walter Benjamin, 'The Work of Art in the Age of Its Technological Reproducibility'[3]

There has never been a philosophical *theory of masses* in the theory and critique of architecture. The current categories and concepts, institutional practice and pedagogy, not only leave architecture exposed to the exploitation of ruling technological-industrial capitalism, but worse, make it *useful* for it. Against this state, I first invoke Walter Benjamin's methodological introduction to his Artwork essay. Benjamin begins the introduction by invoking Marx's 'Preface' to *A Contribution to the Critique of Political Economy* and ends by stating that he will offer *concepts* that are '*completely useless for the purpose of fascism*'. It goes as follows:

> When Marx undertook this analysis of the capitalist mode of production, this mode was in its infancy. Marx adopted an approach which

gave his investigation prognostic value. Going back to the basic conditions of capitalist production, he presented them in a way which showed what could be expected of capitalism in the future. What could be expected, it emerged, was not only an increasingly harsh exploitation of the proletariat but, ultimately, the creation of conditions which would make it possible for capitalism to abolish itself.

Since the transformation of the superstructure proceeds far more slowly than that of the base, it has taken more than half of a century for the change in the conditions of production to be manifested in all areas of culture. How this process has affected culture can only now be assessed, and these assessments must meet certain prognostic requirements. They do not, however, call for theses on the art of the proletariat after the seizure of power, and still less for any on the art of classless society. They call for theses defining the tendencies of the development of art under the present conditions of production. The dialectic of these conditions of production is evident in the superstructure, no less than in the economy. Theses defining the developmental tendencies of art can therefore contribute to the political struggle in ways that it would be a mistake to underestimate. They neutralize a number of traditional concepts—such as creativity and genius, eternal value and mystery—which, used in an uncontrolled way (and controlling them is difficult today), allow factual material to be manipulated in the interests of fascism. *In what follows, the concepts which are introduced into the theory of art differ from those now current in that they are completely useless for the purpose of fascism. On the other hand, they are useful for the formulation of revolutionary demands in the politics of art [Kunstpolitik].*[4]

More than 80 years later, Benjamin's 'prognostic requirements', made in the specific context of the 1930s, not only remain valid for our time but also acquire urgency. Transposing his diagnostic thesis to our present condition, where he says 'art', I add 'architecture'; and where he says 'fascism', I qualify it by employing the term 'democratic fascism'—a term I borrow from Alain Badiou—as the defining hegemonic political force in our time. In his analysis of the art of cinema, Benjamin situates film in the intersection of three trajectories: the ideology of art and aesthetics under industrial capitalism, the impact of technology on the perceptual apparatus of the human sensorium, and the political formation of masses. These are formative elements constitutive of the political crisis of modernity.[5]

The last 125 years—from the invention of film by the Lumière brothers in 1895 to our present time—can be conceived as a historical block forming a unity that I characterize as: 'Building in the Age of Cinema'. This unity comes under the jurisdiction of an altered *perceptual apparatus* brought about by the invention of cinema. Benjamin named it as *distraction* [*Zerstreuung*], a phenomenon arising fundamentally from an experience of what he called the 'big-city'. Put under this jurisdiction, it is the *non-art* of the 'art' of architecture that must be thought as the point of departure for theory and critique of architecture, and that I advance in analogical comparison to the '*non-art* of the art' of cinema in Badiou's presentation. We will come to this in a later chapter.

Benjamin wrote: 'Film corresponds to profound changes in the apparatus of apperception—changes that are experienced on the scale of private existence by each passerby in big-city traffic, and on a historical scale by every present-day citizen'.[6] In this work I contend that the theory, critique, and analysis of architecture must be restructured and rethought under the category of *apperception,* a term used by Benjamin and one he may have adopted from Kant's critical philosophy—the origin of which goes back to Leibniz—of whom he was an avid reader. I suggest that architecture as a technological *apparatus* (*dispositif*) must be studied with a view to a 'new task of apperception' for the individual, as Benjamin would say, affecting the *human sensorium.* In the center of this resides the 'theory of experience'. This theory is to be traced back to Kant's first Critique, the *Critique of Pure Reason*, and its transition to Hegel who called his 'Phenomenology' the *Science of Experience*.[7] On the basis of this philosophical theory of experience, I attempt to develop the thesis that there *cannot* be any thought of *an* architecture if it is not grounded in the philosophical theory of masses which, by logical inference, is *political* in nature. My aim is to accomplish a critique of the notion of 'semblance' in architecture in order to separate it from the *optical delusion* that permeates it today. The latter is an illusion produced solely by the senses. In Kantian terms, I make a distinction between illusion and *Schein*, the *necessity* or inevitability of the 'transcendental illusion', understood within the triadic structure of phenomenon, thing-in-itself, and *Schein*.[8]

Significantly, the invention of cinema coincided with two other notable events. It was in 1895 that Freud and Joseph Breuer published *Studies on Hysteria* with their epochal invention of psychoanalysis and the discovery of the *unconscious*, the same year that, as Todd McGowan instructively reminds us, Louis and Auguste Lumière screened their first film in the Grand Café in Paris. The coincidence of the discovery of psychoanalysis and the invention of cinema is not accidental. As McGowan notes: 'psychoanalysis makes its most important discoveries through the analysis of dreams, and to this day, the cinema remains a dream factory, a form of public dreaming'.[9] Now, the invention of these two was also simultaneous with the rise of the metropolis, which might better be termed the *cinemetropolis*. The big-city, as Benjamin called it, is a *cinematic* city or it is not at all. As Anton Kaes points out, cinema and metropolis 'are equally products of late capitalism and the technical-industrial revolution'.[10] Significantly, 'insofar as cinema is a part of metropolitan mass culture, the critique of cinema adopts some elements of the critique of the big city'.[11] In early cinema, 'the lightning-fast and disconnected physical movement characteristic of early silent film seemed to offer just what the big city dweller wanted to see', and, therefore, it was in the year 1910 that it was said:

> The psychology of the cinematographic triumph is metropolitan psychology. Not only because the big city constitutes the natural focal point for all manifestations of social life, but especially because the metropolitan soul, that ever-harried soul, curious and unanchored, tumbling from feeling impression to fleeting impression, is quite rightly the cinematographic soul.[12]

This confirms Georg Simmel's commentary in his famous 1913 essay, 'The Metropolis and Mental Life', where he wrote that the 'swift and continuous shift of external and internal stimuli' in the metropolis, bring about 'the intensification of emotional life', and further, 'The rapid telescoping of changing images, pronounced differences within what is grasped at a single glance, and the unexpectedness of violent stimuli'.[13] As Kaes notes, according to Simmel, these are 'constitutive conditions of perception in the big city and analogous to the perception of the rapid and jolting succession of cinematic images'.[14]

Together these three—the invention of cinema, the discovery of the *unconscious*, and the rise of the metropolis—are simultaneous with the rise of the *mass-mediated* society, later to be turned into a full-fledged *consumer society* by the early decades of the twentieth century, under the ideological hegemony of technological-industrial-liberal capitalism. In its center resides the phenomenon and reality of 'masses'. Fascism later came to usurp and manipulate this category through an effective manipulation of the same technological media. Politically speaking, every failure of liberal industrial capitalism—and it has not ceased to fail again and again—as we learned from Benjamin, paves the way for fascism. The term 'masses' itself has to be submitted to political, philosophical, and analytical scrutiny. In the age of cinema, there is a dialectical relation, as Benjamin put it, between technological '*mass reproduction*' and '*reproduction of mass*'. Fascism exploited it fully then, and 'democratic fascism' utilizes it now.

Now consider the following questions: In what terms should the relation of architecture to the 'masses' be defined? Is architecture a 'mass art'? What defines the *paradoxical* term 'mass art'? Is there an architecture that is not conditioned by the mass-mediated society and industrial capitalism? Can there be any theory of architecture worth considering that is not grounded in the *philosophy* of 'mass art'? Any theory of architecture on the Left must come to terms, first, with the Idea of 'masses' and, second, struggle with its political paradoxes. From Benjamin in the twentieth century to Alain Badiou in our time, we have a body of philosophy of 'mass art' in relation to cinema. In this work, I demonstrate the proximity of the two radical thinkers on the problem of 'mass art', and its fatal oblivion. Badiou in the twenty-first century has foregrounded the Idea of 'mass art' that Benjamin wrote of in the early decades of the twentieth century. At the core of the idea of 'masses' resides the notion of the *proletariat*. Both thinkers are aware of the centrality of its agency but had assigned different roles for it. The political and philosophical conceptual tools used by both thinkers relating cinema to 'mass art' can, as I will contend, lay the ground for a theoretical-philosophical and analytical way of thinking about an architecture that should be put under the aegis of the 'mass art'. I advance an idea of architecture by founding it on the *old* 'new, positive barbarism', a state of architecture that Benjamin positively explicated in his 'Experience and Poverty' in confrontation with the nascent rise of 'fascist barbarism' in 1933 that he saw presciently on the eve of his departure from Germany for Prague.[15] This 'new, positive barbarism' of Benjamin's can be turned into a *new* 'new, positive barbarism' in *confrontation* with the barbarism of 'post-fascist' capitalism or 'democratic fascism' of our time. When Benjamin discussed the 'poverty of experience', he was mainly thinking of *film* as the 'second technology' with his characteristic insistence on the 'investment in technology' while being aware of its destructive forces that, paradoxically, as Miriam Bratu Hansen has perceptively remarked, is reminiscent of Wagner's *Parsifal*: 'Only the spear that struck it heals the wound'.[16] The same 'second technology' governs architecture, in whose 'investment in technology' the same logic of *Parsifal* is discernable. While I contend that we must *own up* to Benjamin's *owning up* of the 'poverty of experience', I will nevertheless *recast* its philosophical foundation.[17] In a later chapter I come back to discuss this 'Poverty of Experience'.

Benjamin ends his Artwork essay, as is well known, with an 'Epilogue' that has kept scholars and commentators perplexed for well over half a century. The last paragraph of the 'Epilogue' reads as follows:

> 'fiat ars—pereat mundus', ['Let art flourish—and the world pass away'] says fascism, expressing from war, as Marinetti admits, the artistic gratification of a sense perception altered by technology. This is evidently the consummation of *l'art pour l'art*. Humankind, which once, in Homer, was an object of contemplation for the Olympian gods, has now become one for itself. Its self-alienation has reached the point where it can experience its own annihilation as a supreme aesthetic pleasure. *Such is the aestheticizing of politics, as a practice by fascism. Communism replies by politicizing art.*[18]

Susan Buck-Morss, one of the most astute scholars of Benjamin, wrote in 1992 that this paragraph 'haunted' her for over 20 years, and led her to perspicaciously advance an analysis of the 'Epilogue' with the notion of *anaesthetics*, in a dialectical relation with *aestheticization*.[19] While I consider this dialectical category to be useful for a critique of architecture's *aestheticization*, and, for that matter, cinema in contemporary society, my reading of the paragraph above will rather focus on Benjamin's use of the notion of 'communism'—with no perplexity or ambiguity. It is still 'haunting' us in spite of all efforts to conjure it away. I go against the ambivalences of certain of Benjamin's commentators on his reading of Marx, especially in relation to his use of the term *'politicizing art'*. My aim is to secure a position of *affinity* between Benjamin and the post-1989 discourse of the Left related to a re-reading of Marx, particularly *The Communist Manifesto* and *Capital*. This is long overdue and again bears witness to the contemporaneity of Benjamin.

Benjamin wrote that 'The function of film is to train human beings in the apperceptions and reaction needed to deal with a vast apparatus whose role in their lives is expanding always daily'.[20] And further: 'The most important social function of film is to establish equilibrium between human beings and the apparatus'.[21] As Hansen in her *Cinema and Experience* puts it, if Benjamin

> discerned the cinema as the foremost battleground of contemporary art and aesthetics, it was not because of a futurist or constructivist enthusiasm for the machine age, but because he considered film the only medium that might yet counter the devastating effects of humanity's 'bungled' [*verunglückte*] reception of technology.[22]

I come to pose this question: How can architecture, which in the Age of Cinema, or at the time of its 'death', faces even more devastating effects of the 'bungled reception of technology', perform the task of training *apperception* of the individual with its vast apparatus? To address this question I venture to construct theses grounded in Badiou's thoughts on cinema following his idea of 'philosophy *as* cinema' and 'cinema *as* philosophy'. In this effort I read Benjamin through Badiou and Badiou through Benjamin, while bearing in mind that Badiou, unlike Benjamin, never took up architecture for an analysis when he discussed cinema.

For Badiou, who thinks cinema *philosophically*, film is the *only* art that is 'really a mass art'. He goes so far as to say that 'There is no question that cinema is capable of being a mass art on a scale that brooks no comparison with any other art'.[23] And even more emphatically: 'It is quite simply beyond dispute that cinema is capable of being a mass art, unmatched by any other art'.[24] In my view, Badiou should have qualified his declarations by adding an amendment: *with the exception of architecture*. I must make it clear that by taking issue with Badiou on this point I am not asserting a narrow 'professional' and disciplinary prejudice, but rather, I am reiterating a historical statement made by Benjamin's vast observation and investigation on architecture from which we have yet to learn. But what is most instructive for us is Badiou's striking differentiation between the two words contained in the term 'mass art'. 'Mass art', he says, 'implies a paradoxical relationship. It is not at all an obvious relationship, because "mass" is a political category, a category of political activism, whereas, "art" is an aristocratic category'.[25] This is not a 'judgmental' statement, he insists, but rather a statement of fact. What is important is that 'art' for Badiou remains an 'aristocratic' category, while the term 'mass art' is a *democratic* category: 'In "mass art" you have the paradoxical relationship between a purely democratic element and a historically aristocratic element'.[26] I will return to this for more analysis in a later chapter. Here, it is pertinent to ask: Where should we locate architecture in this differentiation? Adolf Loos in the early twentieth century told us that architecture has nothing to do with 'art'. Only a very small part of it belongs to 'art': only when it deals with *death*—tombs and monuments. Art is *revolutionary*, he said, architecture is *conservative*. But, at the same time, we should consider this question: Is architecture *democratic* when it enters into a relation with 'masses'? As I will persistently claim, architecture *can no longer* be *thought* without thinking of cinema, the cinema that Badiou thinks *philosophically*. Cinema, Badiou tell us, is an *ontological* art. We therefore talk about its *being* and *appearance*. After Badiou, I want to declare that architecture too is an *ontological* 'art'. This means, among other things, that architecture in its essence must be thought *philosophically*, one might say *metaphysically* or *speculatively*.

For Benjamin, in contrast to Badiou, architecture is the '*prototype*' of mass art—well before the invention of cinema. He had a different idea of what constitutes 'mass art', and for that matter, what distinguishes 'masses' from 'art'. Benjamin, who is the only thinker in the twentieth century to think of cinema *with* architecture as the *only* two forms of mass art, recognized that film replaced building in mobilizing the masses. But a crucial difference governs over the two. While cinema, strictly speaking, is not a *necessary* or an *essential* art, architecture *is*.

Comparing architecture with all other forms of art, Benjamin acknowledged that, as I noted before, 'Many art forms have come into being and passed away', but as he says, 'the human need for shelter is permanent'.[27] Architecture, to repeat, 'has never had fallow periods. Its history is longer than that of any other art, *and its effect ought to be recognized in any attempt to account for the relationship of the masses to the work of art*'[28] (emphasis mine).

The *forgetfulness* of 'architecture' constitutes a blind spot in the thoughts of our radical philosophers. While I take issue with the most prominent of them in our time, I hasten to say that Badiou's philosophical writings on cinema as a 'mass art' that is an *impure* art contain enormous insights for rethinking architecture *also* as an *impure* mass art, with all the political implications that would entail.[29] Interestingly enough, when Badiou argues that 'cinema is a philosophical situation', he means to tell us that although the art of cinema is of recent invention, it is yet as ancient as philosophy. Interestingly, if we follow Badiou's contention, cinema is *as old as* architecture. Both are supposedly ancient—just imagine Plato making Socrates sit in the open *agora* surrounded by magnificent buildings watching films of Jean-Luc Godard or Abbas Kiarostami while engaging with his interlocutors in the dominant mode of *theatrical* dialogue! It is noteworthy to recall that, according to Badiou, the origin of philosophy is *theatrical*. Dialogue is a form of theater.

But in the center of the hazy idea of just who are the 'masses', there must be the notion of the 'proletariat', a point I will be raising repeatedly in this work. In this regard, what Benjamin wrote in a long footnote to the 'second version' of the Artwork essay is quite an illuminating exposition on the political notion of 'masses' in relation to 'proletariat' and 'class struggle' and unique in his entire work. It goes as follows:

> It should be noted in passing that proletarian class consciousness, which is the most enlightened form of class consciousness, fundamentally transforms the structure of the proletarian masses. The class-conscious proletariat forms a compact mass only from the outside, in the minds of its oppressors. At the moment when it takes up its struggle for liberation, this apparently compact mass has actually already begun to loosen. It ceases to be governed by mere reactions; it makes

transition to action. The loosening of the proletarian masses is the work of solidarity. In the solidarity of the proletarian class struggle, the dead, undialectical opposition between individual and mass is abolished; for the comrade, it does not exist. [...] But the same class struggle which loosens the compact mass of the proletariat compresses that of the petty bourgeoisie. [...] The petty bourgeoisie is not a class; it is in fact only a mass. And the greater the pressure acting on it between the two antagonistic classes of the bourgeoisie and the proletariat, the more compact it becomes. In *this* mass the emotional element described in mass psychology is indeed a determining factor. But for that very reason this compact mass forms the antithesis of the proletarian cadre, which obeys a collective *ratio*. In the petty-bourgeoisie mass, the reactive moment described in mass psychology is indeed a determining factor. But precisely for that reason this compact mass with its unmediated reactions forms that antithesis of the proletarian cadre, whose actions are mediated by a task, however momentary.[30]

And further, in reference to the German situation of the time:

The ambiguous concept of the masses, and the indiscriminate references to their mood which are commonplace in the German revolutionary press, have undoubtedly fostered illusions which have had disastrous consequences for the German proletariat. Fascism, by contrast, has made excellent use of these laws—whether it understood them or not. It realizes that the more compact the masses it mobilizes, the better the chance that the counterrevolutionary instincts of the petty bourgeoisie will determine their reaction. *The proletariat, on the other hand, is preparing for a society in which neither the objective nor the subjective conditions for the formation of masses will exist any longer.*[31]
(emphasis mine)

With regard to the term 'compact mass', Hansen points out that

As Benjamin himself knew, the collective assembled in the movie theaters was hardly that of the heroic proletariat; rather, he considered the cinema audience in tendency part of the 'compact mass'—the blind, destructive and self-destructive formation of the masses that were the object of political organization by fascism.[32]

19

Significantly, Theodor Adorno in his letter of 18 March 1936 to Benjamin in critically responding to the draft of the Artwork essay singles out Benjamin's footnote remarks for particular praise. He writes: 'I find your few sentences concerning the disintegration of the proletariat into "masses" through revolution to be amongst the most profound and most powerful statements of political theory I have encountered since I read *State and Revolution* [by Lenin]'.[33]

Earlier, in *One-Way Street,* published in 1928, Benjamin had brought up the problem of the term 'mass instinct'. In a section entitled 'Imperial Panorama' he expressed his pessimistic view of it:

> A curious paradox: people have only the narrowest private interest in mind when they act, yet they are at the same time more than ever determined in their behavior by the instincts of the mass. And mass instincts have become confused and enraged from life more than ever. Whereas the obscure impulse of the animal (as innumerable antecedents relate) detects, as danger approaches, a way of escape that still seems invisible, this society, each of whose members cares only for his own abject well-being, falls victim—with animal insensibility but without the insensate intuition of animals—as a blind mass, to even the most obvious danger, and diversity of individual goals is immaterial in face of the identity of the determining forces'.[34]

In the light of Benjamin's exposition above, we must subject the term 'masses' to scrutiny for its difficult and problematic political meanings. This is all the more important in the political conjuncture of our time with the rise of authoritarianism, right-wing populism, and what Enzo Traverso has characterized as 'post-fascism'.[35] And, as we will see, the term 'democracy', as Badiou has brought up, must be discussed when we examine the term 'masses'.

The point of departure of this investigation is my contention that Benjamin's Artwork essay, after almost a century since its first draft, is still a *work in progress*. This is attested to by Benjamin himself. As the editors of Benjamin's four volumes of Selected Writings have pointed out, Benjamin regarded his Artwork essay after its revised 'Third Version' (which actually was the fourth version) as 'a work in progress' rather than a completed work, up until 1939.[36] I go one step further and emphatically assert that insofar as we live in technological-industrial-capitalist society, which is in constant exposure to the imminent danger of the return of fascism—as the twentieth-century experience has shown us—Benjamin's Artwork essay will remain a *work in progress*. In the present conjuncture, it is the specific political instance, as I have pointed out above, of the notion of 'Communism' and its philosophical-political understanding in the work of Badiou with his reflections on cinema that significantly prompts a re-opening of the Artwork essay. This will attest to the fact that, in the twenty-first century, Benjamin's work is still 'a work in progress'. In this respect, the editors of *Mapping Benjamin: The Work of Art in the Digital Age* are too quick to express their ambivalence about Benjamin's theses in the Artwork essay when they say 'Finally many of us are no longer completely convinced that Benjamin's notorious political advice—his prescription to opt for a politicization of art against an aestheticization of politics—is pertinent or plausible in our time'.[37] They say this without bothering to offer a critical analysis of Benjamin's statement or to examine whether we have a sound understanding of it or not.[38] In fact, they have missed the whole point: Benjamin's theses in the Artwork essay, including the famous statement in the Epilogue, are ever more valid and urgent as they must be understood and studied as categories of radical critique against digital technology in contemporary global capitalism. Hansen echoes the same concern in confronting the assertion made by the editors of *Mapping Benjamin*. While alluding to the question of Benjamin's 'actuality', she perceptively writes:

> This question is inevitable at a time when our political, social, and personal lives seem more than ever to be driven by developments in media technology, and thus by an accelerated transformation, disintegration, and reconfiguration of the structures of experience. Indeed, if we pose the question of Benjamin's actuality in the light of tremendous changes associated with digital technology, it could easily be argued that his theses concerning the technological media, in particular their proclaimed revolutionary potential, belong to an altogether different period than ours, and that his major prognostications have been proven wrong, at the latest with the advent of digital and global consolidation of capitalism. But to reach such a conclusion is perhaps not the reason we read Benjamin today.[39]

In the Epilogue to this work, I will come back to this issue.

Notes

1. Walter Benjamin, 'The Work of Art in the Age of Its Technological Reproducibility', Third Version, in *Walter Benjamin: Selected Writings, Volume 4, 1938–1940*, general ed. Michael W. Jennings (Cambridge: The Belknap Press of Harvard University Press, 2003), 282, n. 47.
2. Alain Badiou, in *Cinema*, texts selected and introduced by Antoine de Baecque, trans. Susan Spitzer (Cambridge: Polity, 2013), 234.
3. Walter Benjamin, 'The Work of Art in the Age of Its Technological Reproducibility', Third Version, 282, n. 47.
4. Walter Benjamin, 'The Work of Art in the Age of Its Technological Reproducibility', Third Version, 251–252.
5. For more on these terms see Miriam Bratu Hansen, *Cinema and Experience: Siegfried Kracauer, Walter Benjamin, and Theodor W. Adorno* (Berkeley: University of Californian Press, 2011).
6. Walter Benjamin, 'The Work of Art in the Age of Its Technological Reproducibility', Third Version, 281, n. 42.
7. See Frederick Beiser, *Hegel* (New York: Routledge, 2005), 317.
8. I follow Kojin Karatani who explains this point in Kant:

    > Whereas older philosophy set as its task to critique a sensibility-based illusion by way of reason, Kant sought to critique the kind of illusion (*Schein*) that reason itself generates. This kind of illusion is actually indispensable for reason, and therefore reason cannot easily displace it. Kant called this world of illusion 'transcendental illusion'. Illusion of this sort is born of reason, and by the same token reason alone can critique it. Hence what Kant means by 'critique' is the critique of reason by reason itself.

    See Kojin Karatani, *Isonomia and the Origins of Philosophy* (Durham and London: Duke University Press, 2017), 94–95.
9. See Todd McGowan, *Psychoanalytic Film Theory and the Rules of the Game* (New York: Bloomsbury, 2018 [2015]), 1.
10. See Anton Kaes, 'The Debate about Cinema: Charting a Controversy (1900–1929)', in *New German Critique*, Special Issue on Weimar Film Theory, 40 (Winter 1987), 10.
11. Anton Kaes, 'The Debate about Cinema', 10.
12. Quoted in Anton Kaes, 'The Debate about Cinema', 12. Also see Hermann Kienzl's 'Theater und Kinematograph', in *Der Strom*, 1 (1911/1912), 219.
13. Quoted in Anton Kaes, 'The Debate about Cinema', 12. Also see Georg Simmel, 'The Metropolis and Mental Life', in *On Individuality and Social Forms: Selected Writings*, ed. Donald Lewis (Chicago: The University of Chicago Press, 1971), 325.
14. Anton Kaes, 'The Debate about Cinema', 12.
15. See Walter Benjamin, 'Experience and Poverty', in *Walter Benjamin: Selected Writings, Volume 2, 1927–1934*, ed. Michael W. Jennings, Howard Eiland, and Gary Smith, trans. Rodney Livingston and others (Cambridge: The Belknap Press of Harvard University Press, 1999).

16 See Miriam Bratu Hansen, *Cinema and Experience*, 321, n. 88.
17 I am referring to John McCole's excellent chapter in his *Walter Benjamin and the Antinomies of Tradition* (Ithaca: Cornell University Press, 1993), titled 'Owning up to the Poverty of Experience: Benjamin and Weimar Modernism'. I will come back to fully discuss this chapter in McCole in a later chapter in this book.
18 Walter Benjamin, 'The Work of Art in the Age of Its Technical Reproducibility', Third Version, 270. The editor notes that the phrase 'Let art flourish—and the world pass away' is a 'play on the motto of the sixteenth-century Holy Roman emperor Ferdinand I: "Fiat iustitia et perpeat mundus" ("Let justice be done and the world pass away")', 283.
19 See Susan Buck-Morss, 'Aesthetics and Anaesthetics: Walter Benjamin's Artwork Essay Reconsidered', in *October*, 62 (Autumn 1992), 3–41.
20 Walter Benjamin, 'The Work of Art in the Age of Its Technological Reproducibility', Second Version, in *Walter Benjamin: Selected Writings, Volume 3, 1935–1938*, ed. Howard Eiland and Michael W. Jennings, trans. Edmund Jephcott, Howard Eiland and others (Cambridge: The Belknap Press of Harvard University Press, 2002), 108.
21 Walter Benjamin, 'The Work of Art in the Age of Its Technological Reproducibility', Second Version, 117.
22 See Miriam Bratu Hansen, *Cinema and Experience*, 79.
23 Alain Badiou, *Cinema*, 234.
24 Alain Badiou, *Cinema*, 208.
25 Alain Badiou, *Cinema*, 208.
26 Alain Badiou, *Cinema*, 208.
27 Walter Benjamin, 'The Work of Art in the Age of Its Technological Reproducibility', Third Version, 268 (emphasis added).
28 Walter Benjamin, 'The Work of Art in the Age of Its Technological Reproducibility', Third Version, 268.
29 Amongst the essays collected in the book *Cinema* cited above two pieces stand out, namely 'Cinema as Philosophical Experimentation' and 'On Cinema as a Democratic Emblem'. Badiou has also written on the subject extensively elsewhere; see especially 'Philosophy and Cinema', in Alain Badiou, *Infinite Thought: Truth and the Return of Philosophy*, trans. and ed. Oliver Feltham and Justin Clemens (London: Continuum, 2005). Also, Badiou's writings on the relation between philosophy and art are related to my inquiry here; specifically see his 'The Common Preoccupation of Art and Philosophy', in *Badiou and His Interlocutors: Lectures, Interviews and Responses*, eds A. J. Bartlett and Justin Clemens (London: Bloomsbury Academic, 2018); 'Philosophy and Art', in *Infinite Thought*; and *Handbook of Inaesthetics*, trans. Alberto Toscano (Stanford: Stanford University Press, 2005).
30 Walter Benjamin, 'The Work of Art in the Age of Its Technological Reproducibility', Second Version, 129.
31 Walter Benjamin, 'The Work of Art in the Age of Its Technological Reproducibility', Second Version, 129.

32 See Mariam Bratu Hansen *Cinema and Experience*, 311, n. 66. See also Walter Benjamin and Theodor Adorno, *The Complete Correspondence, 1928–1940* (Cambridge: Harvard University Press, 1999), 145–146.
33 Cited in Miriam Bratu Hansen, *Cinema and Experience*, 311, n. 66. Also see Walter Benjamin and Theodor Adorno, *The Complete Correspondence, 1928–1940*, 132.
34 Walter Benjamin, 'One-Way Street', in *Walter Benjamin: Selected Writings, Volume 1, 1913–1926*, ed. Marcus Bullock and Michael W. Jennings (Cambridge: The Belknap Press of Harvard University Press, 1996), 451.
35 See Enzo Traverso, *The New Faces of Fascism, Populism and the Far Right* (London and New York: Verso, 2019).
36 See editor's note to 'The Work of Art in the Age of Its Technological Reproducibility', Third Version, 270.
37 See Hans Ulrich Gumbrecht and Michael Marrinan, *Mapping Benjamin: The Work of Art in the Digital Age* (Stanford: Stanford University Press, 2003), xiv. The editors further add that

> a realization that the central theses of Benjamin's Artwork essay have not come true—a situation that bears some resemblances to Hans Christian Andersen's tale of the 'Emperor's New Clothes'—was the starting point for the intellectual project materialized in this volume.
>
> xiv

38 Nowhere in their 'Preface' or in the whole collection do we see any reference to Susan Buck-Morss's ground-breaking analysis of the 'Epilogue' of the Artwork essay; see Susan Buck-Morss, 'Aesthetics and Anaesthetics'. I will come back to this essay later in this work.
39 Mariam Bratu Hansen, *Cinema and Experience*, 75.

Chapter 2

From the photographic moment of critical philosophy to the optical unconscious

> For it is another nature which speaks to the camera rather than to the eye.
> —Walter Benjamin, 'Little History of Photography'[1]

> 'The illiteracy of the future', someone has said, 'will be ignorance not of reading or writing, but of photography'.
> —Walter Benjamin, 'Little History of Photography'[2]

The invention of photography has been given far more significance than being just a technology of image production. Brought about by the technological apparatus of the *camera* that later became the foundation of *cinematography*, photography is elevated to a *notion* that can explain the revolution in philosophy inaugurated by Kant in his 'Copernican turn'. We can say that a technological invention *retroactively* has aided us to better understand the crux of Kantian critical philosophy, a technology not known to Kant himself. We owe our understanding of this to Kojin Karatani in his seminal *Transcritique: On Kant and Marx*.[3] Karatani explicates Kant's *transcendental* philosophy by a *curious* exemplification in the invention of photography. I want to characterize Karatani's insightful point as the 'Photographic Moment of the Critical Philosophy'.

As we know, the novel invention of photography was given to humanity in the nineteenth century by the famous French inventor Joseph Nicéphore Niépce (1765–1833) and his collaborator Louis-Jacques-Mandé Daguerre (1787–1851), long after Kant wrote his three *Critiques*. How can a technological invention, a 'photographic moment', be deployed to explain a complex philosophical corpus? Karatani traces this association in the key term 'pronounced parallax' that Kant had employed in a 'pre-critical' journalistic essay, entitled 'Dreams of a Visionary Explained with Dreams of Metaphysics', published in 1766. This is a rather weird essay that was prompted by the famous earthquake that struck Lisbon on 1 November 1755, on All Saints Day, causing the faithful who were in the church to question the Grace of God.[4] Kant wrote:

> Formerly, I viewed human common sense only from the standpoint of my own; now I put myself into the position of another's reason outside of myself, and observe my judgments, together with their most secret causes, from the point of view of others. It is true that the comparison of both observations results in *pronounced parallax*, but it is the only means of preventing the optical delusion, and of putting the concept of power of knowledge in human nature into its true place.[5]
>
> (emphasis mine)

Karatani clears up any misunderstanding that might arise from Kant's remarks above. He reminds us that Kant's saying is not a 'platitude' that 'one should see things not only from one's own point of view, but also from the point of view of others'. This would be a trite understanding. Rather, 'it is the reverse': 'If one's subjective view is an optical delusion, then the objective perspective or the viewpoint of the others cannot but be an optical delusion as well'.[6] The implication of this for philosophy is critical as Karatani sees it. If the history of philosophy 'is nothing but the history of such reflections, then the history of philosophy is itself nothing but optical delusion. The reflection that Kant brought about is the kind that reveals that reflections in the past were optical delusions'.[7] Karatani crucially remarks that 'This Kantian reflection as a critique of reflection is engendered by "pronounced parallax" between the subjective viewpoint and the objective viewpoint'.[8] It is here that Karatani incisively brings out the problem of 'reflection', first understood by way of a metaphor of seeing one's image in the mirror, but better explained in the invention of photography, which was not available in Kant's time. In a mirror or water surface or a painted portrait, we see the reflection of our own image, which too is *subjective*. While our mirror image can be seen and be identified with the image seen by others, there is nevertheless a 'complicity' with regard to one's own image, as Karatani surmises. Of course, the mirror image is not fixed and stable; it is an inverted left/right image and it is inside out. 'By contrast', Karatani notes, 'photography sustains a different, much more severe, *objectivity*'. Even though there is always a photographer, his or her subjectivity is less influential than the painter's. There being always a photographer taking the picture, his or her 'subjectivity' is not exactly the same as that of the painter, 'for there is an ineradicable, mechanical distance in the photographic image'.[9] Karatani goes on to put the whole point of the 'photographic image' specifically in Kantian categories:

> Strange as it may be, we cannot see our faces (read the thing-in-itself), except as an image reflected in the mirror (read phenomenon). And only thanks to the advent of photography, did we learn that fact. But again, photography is also an image, and, of course, people eventually get used to the mechanical image, so much so that they eventually come to feel that the image is themselves. But the crux here is the 'pronounced parallax'—that which people presumably experience when they 'first' see their photographic image.[10]

The crux, Karatani stresses, is the 'pronounced parallax'. It is what the observers presumably experience when they 'first' see their photographic image. Significantly, I must point out here that long before Walter Benjamin had made exactly the same observation. He wrote:

> It is very significant that our own body [*Leib*] is in so many respects inaccessible to us: we cannot see our face, our back, not even our whole head, that is, the most noble part of our body ... Hence the necessity that in the moment of pure perception the body transforms itself.[11]

I come back to Benjamin later in this chapter.

What Karatani wants to bring to our attention is that 'The philosophy that begins with introspection-mirror remains snared within the specular abyss of introspection. No matter how it seeks to introduce the other's stance, this situation never alters'.[12] He reminds us that philosophy begins with Socratic dialogues, but then quickly says that the dialogue is itself 'trapped within the mirror'. Karatani notes that

> Many have criticized Kant for having remained in a subjectivist-self-scrutiny, and have suggested that he sought an escape in his *Critique of the Power of Judgment* when he introduced a plural subject. But the truly revolutionary event in philosophy had already occurred in *Critique of Pure Reason*, after he was interrupted by Hume, where Kant attempted to implode the complicity inherent in introspection precisely by *confining* himself to the introspective framework. Here one can observe the attempt to introduce an objectivity (*qua* otherness) that is totally alien to the conventional space of introspection-mirror.[13]

Karatani arrives at a crucial conclusion regarding the *transcendental* in Kant:

> Though it is a self-scrutiny through and through, the transcendental reflection inscribes others' viewpoint. Said inversely, though it is impersonal through and through, the transcendental reflection is still self-scrutiny. One tends to speak of the transcendental stance as a mere method, and worse still, one speaks of the structure of faculties Kant discovered as a given.[14]

The crux of the matter is that

> The transcendental stance, however could not have appeared if not for the pronounced parallax. *Critique of Pure Reason* is not written in the mode of self-criticism as is 'Dreams of a Visionary', but the pronounced parallax is present, functioning therein. It came to take the form of 'antinomy', the device to reveal thesis and antithesis as optical illusion.[15]

We must understand that Kant, as Karatani points out, in his enterprise was addressing the question of the metaphysics and metaphysicians of his time. Metaphysicians 'treat thought *not* deriving from experience as substantial'.[16] They daydream that thought does not come from the *outside* by way of sense; they are 'visionary', which means they are *mad*. They are like the visionary Swedenborg, a first-rate scientist who was not demented when he said that he had anticipated the Lisbon earthquake, which Kant had to acknowledge but had also to negate. 'Although he called it a "psychosis"', as Karatani writes, 'he could not help taking "the dream of a visionary" seriously'. And yet he problematized his own seriousness:

> Therefore, by no means do I blame my readers, if they, instead of acknowledging the visionary as a half citizen of the other world, are quick to write him off as a hospital candidate and thereby shirk from all further inquiry.[17]

Insofar as the philosophers cannot get rid of metaphysics, they are by definition all mad! Put in Lacanian terms, they suffer from *psychosis*. There is always a dimension of *madness* in philosophy. Kant, opposing the illusions of the visionaries in his time and challenging their metaphysical delusion, was nevertheless not against metaphysics himself. But he introduced the problematic of the *otherness* (*qua* objectivity) in the notion of 'pronounced parallax', as Karatani argues. The *transcendental* stance in essence *is* the inscription of others' viewpoint. For that reason, Kant's 'Dreams of a Visionary Explained with Dreams of Metaphysics' is a self-critical scrutiny before coming to his *Critique of Pure Reason*, the first edition of which came out about ten years after, in which he would deny 'reason's expansion of knowledge beyond its limit'—a *critique of reason by reason*.

Now a single important implication of the 'pronounced parallax' in relation to photography, briefly discussed above, is for the distinction between 'phenomenon' and the 'thing-in-itself' in Kantian philosophy. This distinction has been debated, affirmed or dismissed when taken within a conventional duality (erroneously) of 'phenomenon' and 'essence', or surface and depth, as Karatani reflects. Those who reject the 'thing-in-itself' consider it to be mystical, and those who retain it, like Heidegger, Karatani points out, interpret it as the 'ontological depth or "abyss" [*Abgrund*]'. However, 'there are no mystical implications in the properly Kantian thing-in-itself. It is something like one's own face in the sense that it undoubtedly exists but cannot be seen except as an image (read *phenomenon*)'.[18] This sounds simple—but it is not. What is important to understand here, as Karatani remarks, is 'henceforth antinomy as a pronounced parallax—the sole thing that reveals what is more than an image (phenomenon)'.[19] And further,

> What is crucial here is the otherness, be it of the thing or of the other person. But this otherness is nothing mystical. What Kant implied by the thing-in-itself was the alterity of the other that we can never take for granted and internalize just on our whim or at our convenience.[20]

It was photography that brought us to think the 'thing-in-itself', but not to know it—except as phenomenon. Such is, therefore, the epochal effect of *photography* as the image of the *other* that retroactively comes to illuminate the foundation of the modern critical philosophy in Kant. I should stress, one more time, that we owe this insight to Karatani's exploration.

It must be pointed out that we can establish certain affinities between the 'thing-in-itself' and the psychoanalytical object, the Lacanian *objet petit a*, in relation to the notions of the *impossible* and the Real, or '*less than nothing*'. This would require an extended discussion of the notional differences between the terms 'thing-in-itself', 'transcendental object', and *noumena* in Kantian philosophy. This is a complicated notion that we cannot enter into here. What is important to note, though, is that in the center of the *transcendental* stance, grounded in 'parallax *qua* otherness', resides the Freudian discovery of the *Unconscious*, Freud's own 'Copernican revolution', after the Kantian one. As Karatani importantly remarks, *id, ego, and superego* in Freud's metapsychology are not the things that exist empirically. Rather, they are the things that methodologically are assumed to exist in the analysand's *disavowal* and *resistance* in the analytical setting. Karatani gives the most succinct definition of 'transcendental'—as opposed to 'transcendent'—specifically in relation to the 'unconscious': '*Simply stated, the transcendental approach seeks to cast light on the unconscious structure that precedes and shapes experience*'[21] (emphasis mine).

What is discussed above should serve as the point of entry to Benjamin's exploration of photography. Benjamin employed the Kantian term 'apperception' in the context of the *apparatus of perception* in his Artwork essay. Benjamin's use of this notion is not accidental given his early interest in Kant as evidenced in his 'On the Program of Coming Philosophy', written in 1918 but never published in his lifetime, in which he allegedly 'recast' Kantian philosophy.[22] The essay was written more than a century ago when neo-Kantianism, a reaction against the Hegelian speculative philosophical system, was the reigning philosophical school in German universities. Benjamin had rather an ambivalent attitude towards it, although he was impressed by its prominent representative Hermann Cohen.[23] Regardless of his take on Kant at the time, Benjamin is a thinker of *otherness*, as I would claim. This means that he had already an intuition of the notion of 'parallax' (*qua* other) in Kantian transcendental philosophy. Taking a Kantian gesture in his work, Benjamin must be recognized, I contend, as a *transcendental* thinker. This prompts a new 'recasting' of Kant based on a particular understanding of him in our time, specially the one informed by Karatani, grounded in the *antinomy* of the 'pronounced parallax' underlying the Transcendental stance. And, importantly, we must remind ourselves that Benjamin was a reader of Freud, taking the *unconscious* seriously. His singular notion of the 'optical unconscious' must be given a renewed meaning based on the 'photographic moment' underlying Critical Philosophy constructed on the concept of parallax.

Benjamin first introduced the term 'optical unconscious' in his 'Little History of Photography' published in 1931. He would later take it up again in the Artwork essay. The term appears after the comments he makes that I partially cited in the epigraph above. In full the section reads as follows:

> No matter how artful the photograph, no matter how carefully posed his subject, the beholder feels an irresistible urge to search such a picture for a tiny spark of contingency, of the here and now, with which reality has (so to speak) seared the subject, to find the inconspicuous spot where in the immediacy of the long-forgotten moment the future nests so eloquently that we, looking back, may rediscover it. For it is another nature which speaks to the camera rather than to the eye: 'other' above all in the sense that a space informed by human consciousness gives way to a space informed by the unconscious.[24]

There then follows this key sentence:

> Photography, with its device of slow motion and enlargement, reveals the secret. It is through photography that we first discover the existence

of this optical unconscious, just as we discover the instinctual unconscious through psychoanalysis.[25]

In the Artwork essay, third version, Section XIII, to support his analogy between the optical unconscious and the instinctual unconscious, Benjamin specifically refers to Freud's *Psychopathology of Everyday Life* (1901) and remarks that since the publication of this work 'things have changed'. He writes: 'This book isolated and made analyzable things which had previously floated unnoticed on the broad stream of perception'.[26] And further, by employing the term 'apperception', he adds that 'A similar deepening of apperception throughout the entire spectrum of optical—and now also auditory—impressions has been accomplished by film'. Now, there is no 'strangeness' in this analogy as Rosalind Krauss claims in her *The Optical Unconscious* where she comments on Benjamin.[27] Miriam Hansen follows it by her own incisive commentary on the 'optical unconscious' in *Cinema and Experience.* In my view, Krauss's negative comment on Benjamin's analogy remains pre-Kantian. It arises from the forgetfulness of the crucial dimension of 'otherness' of the *unconscious* in parallax. The *objectivity* in technology of the camera needs to be considered within the philosophical relation between subjectivity and objectivity beginning with Kant as discussed above.

Hansen acknowledges that Benjamin's resumption of the notion of the optical unconscious in the Artwork essay shifts his examples from 'the still to the moving image and even more decisively to the collective everyday shaped by the capitalist-industrial modernity'.[28] She adds that

> If in photography the optical unconscious harbored a revelatory and cognitive function, in film the kinetic dimension—the ability to record movement, to mobilize the image through camera movement, variable framing and rhythmic editing—augments this potential with a destructive, liberating, and transformative function in relation to the depicted world.[29]

She recalls that Howard Caygill characterizes the 'optical unconscious' as the 'possibility of creating an openness to the future'.[30] This definition is apt. Caygill writes: 'A space free from consciousness is charged with contingency if it is open to the future and to becoming something other than itself',[31] and goes on to cite the same passage I quoted above from 'Little History of Photography'. As Hansen points out,

> The political significance of this openness to the future, the possibility of things becoming something other than as what they are commonly perceived, is most strongly expressed in the beautiful passage from the artwork essay that attributes to film the ability to explode, with its 'dynamite of the split second', the 'prison world' of our urban-industrial environment.[32]

In Benjamin's own words:

> On the one hand, film furthers insight into the necessities governing our lives by its use of close-ups, by its accentuation of hidden details in familiar objects, and by its exploration of commonplace milieux through the ingenious guidance of the camera; on the other hand, it manages to assure us of a vast and unsuspected field of action [*Spielraum*]. Our bars and city streets, our offices and furnished rooms, our railroad stations and our factories seemed to close relentlessly around us. Then came film and exploded this prison-world with the dynamite of the split second, so that now we can set off calmly on a journey of adventure among its far-flung debris.[33]

Benjamin significantly refers to the debate that was raging around him at the time concerning the distinction between the 'aesthetic' and the 'social function' of photography, in moving out of the former into the realm of the latter. He encapsulates the debate in his own distinction between 'photography-as-art' and 'art-as-photography'. Benjamin quotes the photographer Sascha Stone, who said 'Photography-as-art is a very dangerous field'.[34] Benjamin further notes:

> Everyone will have noticed how much easier it is to get hold of a painting, more particularly a sculpture, and especially architecture, in a photograph than in reality. It is also tempting to blame this squarely on the decline of artistic appreciation, on a failure of contemporary sensibility. But one is brought up short by the way the understanding of great works was transformed at about the same time the techniques

of reproduction were being developed. They can no longer be regarded as the works of individuals; they have become a collective action, a corpus so vast it can be assimilated only through miniaturization. In the final analysis, mechanical reproduction is a technique of diminution that helps people to achieve control over works of art—a control without whose aid, they could no longer be used.[35]

For Benjamin, the Parisian photographer Eugène Atget was the first who initiated 'the emancipation of object from aura, which is the most signal achievement of the latest school of photography'.[36] Atget looked for what was 'unmarked, forgotten, cast adrift. And thus such pictures, too, work against the exotic, romantically sonorous names of the cities, *they suck the aura out of reality like water from a sinking ship*'[37] (emphasis mine). And then the famous question: 'What is Aura?' And the famous answer: 'A strange weave of space and time: the unique appearance of semblance of distance, no matter how close it may be'.[38] Bringing up the difference between the 'copy' and the 'original', Benjamin wrote: 'Uniqueness and duration are as intimately intertwined in the latter as are transience and reproducibility in the former. The peeling away of the object's shell, the destruction of the aura, is the signature of a perception whose sense for the sameness of things has grown to the point where even the singular, the unique, is divested of its uniqueness—by means of its reproduction'.[39] As will be seen later, when we come to discuss the question of 'masses', we should remember that 'reproduction' is the means by which we get closer to the 'masses', or they get closer to us.

In Atget's Paris photographs, like in surrealist photography, everything is 'remarkably' *empty*, Benjamin says. Buildings in his photographs

> are not lonely, merely without mood; the city in these pictures looks cleared out, like a lodging that has not yet found a new tenant [...] It gives free play to the politically educated eye, under whose gaze all intimacies are sacrificed to the illumination of details.[40]

Benjamin wonderfully brings to our attention that 'Atget's photographs have been likened to those of a crime scene', and this is not accidental, he says.[41] Benjamin astonishingly asks: 'But isn't every square inch of our cities a crime scene? Every passer-by a culprit? Isn't it the task of the photographer—descendant of the augurs and haruspices—to reveal guilt and to point out the guilty in his pictures?', and then '"The illiteracy of the future", someone has said, "will be ignorance not of reading and writing, but of photography"', as I cited in the epigraph above.[42]

In respect to Benjamin's last comment on Atget, concerning the likening of his photographs to a 'crime scene', I want to take the opportunity to say that in the last 200 years we can pinpoint two faithful *turning points* in modern architecture. That is, architecture *twice* took off as a *scene of crime* inspired by what happened in its outside. The first happened in the late eighteenth century, and the second, in the late nineteenth and early twentieth centuries. The first instance, as I have elsewhere discussed, was inspired by the 'blank wall' as exemplified in Jacques-Louis David's painting of *The Death of Marat* (1793).[43] And the second must be attributed to the accumulating perceptual effects of the invention of photography and ensuing *destruction of aura* in the 'age of technological reproducibility' that brought about the so-called 'cinematic city', or better, *cinemetropolis*, that can be exemplified, as we just saw, in Atget's photography of Paris. From *The Death of Marat* to Atget's photography, the *crime scene* has departed the scene of painting only to find a new abode in the space of the *cinematic city*. After the Paris photographs by Atget, *film noir* displayed over and over again the city and architecture as the *crime scene*.

How these two radical moments in depiction of the crime scene in modernity have been annulled in a regressive return to 'aura' in contemporary architecture and the city, the reasons behind this and political consequences of it, are questions that will all have to wait until we come to the Epilogue of this work.

Notes

1. Walter Benjamin, 'Little History of Photography', in *Walter Benjamin, Selected Writings, Volume 2, 1927–1934*, eds Michael W. Jennings, Howard Eiland, and Gary Smith, trans. Rodney Livingston and others (Cambridge: The Belknap Press of Harvard University Press, 1999), 510.
2. Walter Benjamin, 'Little History of Photography', 527.
3. See Kojin Karatani, *Transcritique: On Kant and Marx* (Cambridge: The MIT Press, 2005).

4   Karatani notes that the Lisbon earthquake 'shook all Europe at its root—the general populace and intellectual alike. It rent a deep crack between sensibility and understanding, as it were, which, right up to Leibniz, had maintained a relationship of remarkably seamless continuity'. Karatani further adds that 'The Kantian critique cannot be separated from this profound and multilayered crisis', Kojin Karatani, *Transcritique: On Kant and Marx*, 45.
5   In *The Philosophy of Kant*, ed. and intro. Carl, J. Friedrich (New York: The Modern Library, 1993), 15; also see Kojin Karatani, *Transcritique: On Kant and Marx*.
6   Kojin Karatani, *Transcritique: On Kant and Marx*, 1.
7   Kojin Karatani, *Transcritique: On Kant and Marx*, 1.
8   Kojin Karatani, *Transcritique: On Kant and Marx*, 1–2.
9   Kojin Karatani, *Transcritique: On Kant and Marx*, 48.
10 Kojin Karatani, *Transcritique: On Kant and Marx*, 48. Karatani further adds:

> The effect of parallax is evident also in Derrida's statement that consciousness is equivalent to 'hearing oneself speak [*s'entendre parler*]'. In regard to this claim, Hegel would say that it is speaking that objectifies (or externalizes [*entäußert*] the self; but this objectified voice (or utterance [*Äußerung*]) in the Hegelian sense is not objective at all—it is merely *my view*. To be objective, there must be the displacement or derangement one experiences when one first hears one's own recorded voice. The hideousness or uncanniness one experiences is due to the viewpoint of others that intervenes therein. When I see first my face and hear my voice from others' viewpoint, I think it is not my face nor my voice. In Freudian terms, this would be the 'resistance' of the analysand. Eventually, one comes to terms with the visual and audible images; one has to get used to them.
>
> 48

11 Cited in Miriam Bratu Hansen, *Cinema and Experience: Siegfried Kracauer, Walter Benjamin, and Theodor W. Adorno* (Berkeley: California University Press, 2012), n. 66, 311.
12 Kojin Karatani, *Transcritique: On Kant and Marx*, 49.
13 Kojin Karatani, *Transcritique: On Kant and Marx*, 49.
14 Kojin Karatani, *Transcritique: On Kant and Marx*, 49.
15 Kojin Karatani, *Transcritique: On Kant and Marx*, 49.
16 Kojin Karatani, *Transcritique: On Kant and Marx*, 46.
17 Kojin Karatani, *Transcritique: On Kant and Marx*, 46.
18 Kojin Karatani, *Transcritique: On Kant and Marx*, 50. Karatani mentions that Kant himself warned against finding mystical implications in the thing-in-itself and cites Kant from his *Prolegomena to Any Future Metaphysics* as having said:

> Idealism consists in the claim that there are none other than thinking beings; the other things that we believe we perceive in intuition are only representations in thinking beings, to which in fact no object existing outside these beings corresponds. I say in opposition: There are things given to us as

objects of our senses existing outside us, yet we know nothing of them as they may be in themselves, but are acquainted only with their appearances, i.e., with the representations that they produce in us because they affect our sense. Accordingly, I by all means avow that there are bodies outside us.

n. 33, 310–311

In Karatani's words,

> Kant thus acknowledges that both the world and other selves are not our products; they exist and become, irrespective of our being; in other terms, we are being-in-the world. He uses the thing-in-itself in order to stress the passivity of the subject.

reminding the reader of his analysis previously that 'vis-à-vis the Marxian turn, a proper materialism that is neither rationalist nor empiricist can come into existence only out of such a stance', 311.

19 Kojin Karatani, *Transcritique: On Kant and Marx*, 50.
20 Kojin Karatani, *Transcritique: On Kant and Marx*, 51.
21 Kojin Karatani, *Transcritique: On Kant and Marx*, 1.
22 See Walter Benjamin, 'On the Program of Coming Philosophy', in *Walter Benjamin, Selected Writings, Volume 1, 1913–1926*, eds Marcus Bullock and Michael W. Jennings (Cambridge: The Belknap Press of Harvard University Press, 1996). While I agree with Howard Caygill's statement, in his *Walter Benjamin: The Color of Experience* (London and New York: Routledge, 1998), that Benjamin's entire work must be seen in the light of what he said on Kant in his essay above, I, however, take my distance from Caygill's characterization of Benjamin's 'recasting' of Kant, by which he allegedly arrived at 'speculative philosophy'. Caygill writes: 'Benjamin's speculative recasting of Kant's transcendental account of experience involves the introduction of the absolute or infinite into the structure of forms of intuition—space and time—and the linguistic categories (*logoi*) of the understanding', 23.
23 For this see John McCole, *Walter Benjamin and the Antinomies of Tradition* (Ithaca and London: Cornell University Press, 1993).
24 Walter Benjamin, 'Little History of Photography', 510.
25 Walter Benjamin, 'Little History of Photography', 510–512.
26 Walter Benjamin, 'The Work of Art in the Age of Its Technological Reproducibility', Third Version, in *Walter Benjamin, Selected Writings, Volume 4, 1938–1940*, eds Howard Eiland and Michael W. Jennings, trans. Edmund Jephcott and others (Cambridge: The Belknap Press of Harvard University Press, 2003), 265.
27 See Rosalind Krauss, *The Optical Unconscious* (Cambridge: The MIT Press, 1993). Krauss writes that,

> Reading this ['Little History of Photography'], of course, we are struck by the strangeness of the analogy. True, the camera with its more powerful and even dispassionate eye can stand for the psychoanalyst, and hitherto unseen data

> can operate as a parallel to those slips of tongue or pen, those parapraxes through which the patient's unconscious surfaces into view. But what can we speak of in the visual field that will be an analogue of the 'unconscious' itself, a structure that presupposes first a sentient being within which it operates, and second a structure that only makes sense insofar as it is in conflict with the being's consciousness? Can the optical field—the world of visual phenomena: cloud, sea, sky, forest—*have* an unconscious.
>
> 178–179

28 Miriam Bratu Hansen, *Cinema and Experience*, 158.
29 Miriam Bratu Hansen, *Cinema and Experience*, 158.
30 See Howard Caygill, *Walter Benjamin*, 94.
31 Howard Caygill, *Walter Benjamin*, 94.
32 Miriam Bratu Hansen, *Cinema and Experience*, 159.
33 Walter Benjamin, 'The Work of Art in the Age of Its Technological Reproducibility', Third Version, 265.
34 Walter Benjamin, 'Little History of Photography', 526. As the editors of the volume mention, Sascha Stone, a pseudonym for Alexander Sergei Steinsapir (1895–1940), was a German Jewish photographer who was active on the margin of the group around the journal *G.*, which included László Moholy-Nagy, Ludwig Mies van der Rohe, Hans Richter, El Lissitzky, and Benjamin himself. He created the famous photomontage for the book jacket of Benjamin's *One-Way Street*, 530.
35 Walter Benjamin, 'Little History of Photography', 523.
36 Walter Benjamin, 'Little History of Photography', 518.
37 Walter Benjamin, 'Little History of Photography', 518.
38 Walter Benjamin, 'Little History of Photography', 518. Benjamin's statement is followed by the equally famous paragraph:

> While at rest on a summer's noon, to trace a range of mountains on the horizon, or a branch that throws its shadow on the observer, until the moment or the hour become part of their appearance—this is what it means to breathe the aura of those mountains, that branch. Now, to bring things *closer* to us, or rather to the masses, is just as passionate an inclination in our day as the overcoming of whatever is unique in every situation by means of its reproduction.
>
> 518–519

39 Walter Benjamin, 'Little History of Photography', 519. For an extended discussion of Benjamin's notion of 'aura' see Miriam Bratu Hansen, *Cinema and Experience*.
40 Walter Benjamin, 'Little History of Photography', 519.
41 Walter Benjamin, 'Little History of Photography', 527.
42 Walter Benjamin, 'Little History of Photography', 527.
43 See my *Architecture or Revolution: Emancipatory Critique After* Marx (Abingdon: Routledge, 2020).

Chapter 3

Mass art and impurity
Reading Benjamin with Badiou

> Cinema is unsurpassable as a mass art. But 'mass art' implies a paradoxical relationship.
> —Alain Badiou, 'Cinema as Philosophical Experiment'[1]

> *The technological reproduction of the artwork changes the relation of the masses to art.*
> —Walter Benjamin, 'The Work of Art in the Age of Its Technological Reproducibility'[2]

> At the cinema, we get to the pure from the impure.
> —Alain Badiou, 'On Cinema as a Democratic Emblem'[3]

Benjamin's notion of actuality [*Aktualität*]—applied to Benjamin himself—can be rethought in the light of Alain Badiou's singular philosophical thoughts on cinema in our time. This will go beyond its numerous accomplished readings pivoting on modernity and its contradictions.[4] Not just the political, or aesthetic, or technological, but also the *philosophical* imperative is the hallmark of this new *rethinking*: 'cinema *as* philosophy', or 'philosophy *as* cinema'—to cite Badiou's thought-provoking terms. At the crux is 'to think cinema as a mass art', as Badiou puts it, with the assertion that 'mass art' itself is a 'paradoxical' term. We will come back to this later. On the other hand, Benjamin's theses on cinema must be thought as *actual* only because they are both timely and *untimely*, to put it in Nietzschean terms.[5] As Miriam Bratu Hansen in her *Cinema and Experience* notes,

For Benjamin, actuality requires standing at once within and *against* one's time, grasping the 'temporal core' of the present in terms other than those supplied by the period about itself (as Kracauer put it) and above all in diametrical opposition to developments taken for granted in the name of 'progress'.[6]

We must grasp the 'temporal core' of our present time against the one supplied by the *phantasmagoria* of postmodern digital capitalism that has brought about the total disintegration of the structure of experience and has resulted in the numbing of the *human sensorium* and the robbing of the Subject of its political agency. It is against the ideology of 'technological progress' that we need to heed Benjamin's *antinomic* stance, or better, his productive *ambivalence*, facing the 'technological apparatus' today.

The core element that links Benjamin and Badiou, as I propose, is Political and Philosophical. Here I want to stress and insist that *both* are thinkers of 'Communism'. In the case of the former, it was the context of the political crisis surrounding the year 1936, and for the latter it is the Idea of Communism—an ancient idea as he puts it—ever more relevant in the present political conjuncture, bearing certain resemblances to the political crisis in the 1930s. Both thinkers are grounded in the *materialist* philosophy of Marx—with certain conceptual differences. Common in their philosophical theses on cinema is the category of 'the masses'— a *political* category exploited and manipulated by fascism, then and now. This political category is associated with the notion of 'mass art'. Benjamin explicated it in his Artwork essay, conceived in conjunction with *The Arcades Project*, and the last piece he wrote, 'On the Concept of History'.[7] As previously suggested, the Artwork essay was conceived as being a 'work in progress' in its 'final' Third Version in 1939 (which is actually the 'fourth version'), which by itself demanded its re-openings. The most recent attempt at a comprehensive 're-reading' of it is accomplished by Miriam Bratu Hansen in her brilliant *Cinema and Experience* mentioned above. We will come back to this later.

Badiou's philosophical engagement with cinema goes as far back as 1957 with his first publication on 'Cinema and Culture', now included in the collection entitled *Cinema*.[8] In this volume, two essays particularly stand out for my purpose. The longer one is entitled 'Cinema as Philosophical Experimentation' (2003), which I would call Badiou's 'manifesto on cinema', and the other is entitled 'On Cinema as a Democratic Emblem' (2005). Equally important are Badiou's recent reflections, entitled 'Cinema and Philosophy', included in a recent collection entitled *Badiou and His Interlocutors*.[9] Badiou's reflections on the relationship between philosophy and cinema in this piece and in another, 'The Common Preoccupation of Art and Philosophy', included in the same collection, are the most illuminating ones. Here I must point out that among the philosophers who have significantly written on cinema, including Gilles Deleuze, Jacques Rancière, Stanley Cavell, and more recently Robert Pippin, and Badiou himself, none has cared to take up Benjamin's Artwork essay for any meaningful inquiry.[10] As I mentioned before, Badiou refers to Benjamin's Artwork essay only in passing in his seminal *The Century*. References are mainly made to Henri Bergson and André Bazin. Badiou for his part has made a 'tribute' to Gilles Deleuze—with certain important reservations.[11] It is noteworthy that, unlike Benjamin, none of our prominent philosophers in their writings on cinema has anything to say about architecture.

Before proceeding further, it would be helpful to cite here a rough sketch of Benjamin's Artwork essay as concisely summarized by Hansen. It goes as follows:

> The technological reproduction of traditional works of art and, what is more, the constitutive role of technology in the media of film and photography have affected the status of art in its core. Evolving from the large-scale reorganization of human sense perception in capitalist-industrial society, this crisis is defined, on the one hand, by the decline of what Benjamin refers to as aura, the unique modality of being that has accrued to the traditional work of art, and, on the other, by the emergence of the urban masses, whose mode of existence correlates with the new regime of perception advanced by the media of technological reproduction.[12]

Furthermore, Benjamin places film at the 'intersection of three different strategies', namely 'the fate of art and aesthetics under industrial capitalism; technology and sense perception; mass politics'.[13] The last of the three, with which I am more concerned, deals with the political formation of masses and their exploitation by fascism. In the face of 'fascism's wedding of aestheticist principles to the monumental, particularly in the spectacular formations of the masses that give them an illusory expression', as Hansen notes,[14] Benjamin, confronting the situation of 'extreme emergency', concluded the Artwork essay with the famous—perplexing to many—statement: 'The logical outcome of fascism is an aestheticization of political life', to which 'Communism replies by politicizing art'.[15] I will come back to this 'problematic' conclusion in this work repeatedly. Before the famous statement above, Benjamin has a paragraph which is important for my purposes. He wrote:

> The increasing proletarianization of modern man and the increasing formation of masses are two sides of the same process. Fascism attempts to organize the newly proletarianized masses while leaving intact the property relations which they strive to abolish. It sees its salvation in granting expression to the masses—but on no account granting them rights.[16]

Benjamin added an equally important footnote after the paragraph above:

> A technological factor is important here, especially with regard to the newsreel, whose significance for propaganda purposes can hardly be overstated. *Mass reproduction is especially favored by the reproduction of masses.* In great ceremonial processions, giant rallies, and mass sporting events, and in war, all of which are now fed into the camera, the masses come face to face with themselves.[17]

In a further reflection, Benjamin said: 'The masses have a right to changed property relations; fascism seeks to give them *expression* in keeping these relations unchanged'.[18]

For Hansen, Benjamin's final conclusion 'raises more question than it answers'. She goes on to pose the following questions:

> What did communist art politics mean in 1936 (or for that matter, in 1939)? What did Benjamin mean by politics? What was his concept of revolution? Which 'masses' did he have in mind—a utopian collective, the proletariat, the moviegoing public, or the psychopathological mass mobilized by racist-nationalist politics? How does the dichotomous conclusion tally with his argument about the revolutionary role of film in relation to art, sense perception, and urban-industrial technology?[19]

We have to leave the answers to these questions suspended for now. Hansen, in the meantime, makes it clear that the Artwork essay

> is neither 'about' film as an empirical phenomenon nor, for that matter, about any other preconstituted, given object. Rather, it is concerned with the structural role Benjamin ascribes to film as a hinge between the fate of art under the conditions of industrial capitalism and the contemporary political crisis, which pivots on the organization of the masses.[20]

The 'political crisis' with its base in 'masses' is encoded in cinema as a technological apparatus that has an intimate relation to the 'crisis in perception'. This is why Benjamin analyzed cinema in conjunction with the 'theory of perception', which he took in the original Greek meaning of 'aesthetics', or *aisthesis*. With this very brief exposition of Benjamin's Artwork essay I now turn to Badiou and his philosophical thoughts on cinema. In the center of his thought resides the same question about 'the masses' associated with the notion of 'mass art'. But his real contribution, which I suggest to be an important supplement to Benjamin's ideas, is the notion of cinema as an 'impure art', or, as Alex Ling puts it, an 'Inessential' art.[21]

Impure art

'It is beyond dispute', Badiou says in his 'Cinema as Philosophical Experimentation', that cinema is 'capable of being a mass art, unmatched by any other art'.[22] It is an 'unsurpassable' art as a 'mass art'. He cites the case of Charlie Chaplin's great films as an 'indisputable example'. Chaplin's films 'were seen all over the world, even by the Eskimos'.[23] And, 'everyone instantly understood that these films were speaking about humanity, were speaking in a profound and crucial way about humanity, about what I call "generic humanity"—in other words, about humanity beyond its difference'.[24] Chaplin's character, therefore, is a representative of 'generic humanity'. Other genres like slapstick or even romantic films like Murnau's *Sunrise*, which Badiou considers a 'masterpiece' of all time, are in the same category. But there is a 'paradox', Badiou is quick to add. There is no obvious relationship in the term 'mass art'. 'Mass' is a 'political category', whereas art is an 'aristocratic category', Badiou tells us. This is a 'statement of fact', rather than a 'judgment', he further asserts. He notes: 'All this accounts for why "art" remains an aristocratic category, while "mass art" is typically a democratic category. In "mass art" you have a paradoxical relationship between a purely democratic element and a historically aristocratic element'.[25] Thus we have a relationship between two 'tenuous' terms in 'mass art': 'Art and Masses. Aristocracy and democracy'.[26] And this *is* why philosophy is concerned with cinema, Badiou stresses.

Elsewhere, earlier than his above piece on cinema, in 'Third Sketch of a Manifesto of Affirmationist Art', Badiou discusses 'Affirmationist Art' after the avant-garde of the twentieth century, criticizes formalist 'neo-romanticism' as the dominant mode of contemporary art that he calls *l'art pompier*, and puts forward the paradoxical term '*proletarian aristocratism*'. He writes: 'Art is made, and says what it does, according to its own discipline, and without considering anybody's interest. That is what I call its proletarian aristocratism: an aristocratism exposed to the judgment of all'.[27] Citing the French theater director Antoine Vitez, Badiou writes that he would say that the theater is '*elitism for everyone*' and asserts that the term '*proletarian*' 'designates that which, in everyone, and through the discipline of work, co-belongs to generic humanity', and further, the term '*Aristocratic*' names 'that which, in everyone, is subtracted from every evaluation carried out in terms of average, minorities, resemblance, or imitation'.[28] Some years later, in his further reflections on the question of 'art' in his lecture on 'Fifteen Theses on Contemporary Art', resonating with the paradox of 'mass art', Badiou said: 'So the question of art today is a question of political emancipation, there is something political in art itself. There is not only a question of art's political orientation, like it was the case yesterday, today it is a question in itself. Because art is a real possibility to create something new against the abstract universality that is globalization'.[29]

Paradoxically, cinema as a 'mass art' is an art of the twentieth century, which was *the century* of the avant-garde arts. As I have discussed before, Badiou in his magisterial *The Century* explored the twentieth century as the century of avant-gardes, artistically and politically.[30] It is noteworthy to mention that Benjamin, while appreciating the avant-gardists in the twentieth century, nevertheless took issue with their techniques in paintings and poems. In section XIV of the Artwork essay he targeted Dadaism in particular. He wrote: 'Dadaism attempted to produce with the means of painting (or literature) the effects which the public today seeks in film'.[31] In a paragraph at the end of the section he judged Dadaism by these words: 'By means of its technological structure, film has freed the physical shock effect—which Dadaism had kept wrapped, as it were, inside the moral shock effect—from this wrapping'.[32] In the footnote Benjamin makes some severe remarks. He writes:

> Film proves useful in illuminating Cubism and Futurism, as well as Dadaism. Both appear as deficient attempts on the part of art to take into account the pervasive interpretation of reality by the apparatus [...]. Unlike film, these schools did not try to use the apparatus as such for the artistic representation of reality, but aimed at a sort of alloy of represented reality and represented apparatus. In cubism, a premonition of the structure of this apparatus, which is based on optics, plays a dominant part; in futurism, it is premonition of the effects of the apparatus—effects which are brought out by rapid coursing of the band of film.[33]

Cinema is not always a mass art, Badiou asserts: 'There are avant-garde films, there is an aristocratic cinema, there is a difficult cinema which presupposes knowledge of the history of cinema', but 'there is always the possibility of a mass art in cinema'.[34] This is why for Badiou these paradoxical aspects of cinema make cinema become an object of philosophical thoughts. We will come back to this. Later, in 'On Cinema as a Democratic Emblem', Badiou takes up again the question of mass art to further elaborate on the same paradoxical relationship between 'democratic' and 'aristocratic' in the term 'mass art'. This is the reason why philosophy is concerned with cinema, because 'it imposes a vast and obscure complex of paradoxical relationships'.[35] He reasons that there are five ways to 'think cinema as mass art' around this paradoxical relationship. Topically they are: 1. The question of the image, 2. The question of time, 3. Comparing cinema with the other arts, 4. The relation of art to non-art, and 5. Its ethical significance. Among these, the fourth category, 'Impurity', is the one that Badiou had already discussed extensively in 'Cinema as Philosophical Experimentation', in the section 'Cinema, an absolutely impure art', the one with which I am more concerned. The reason why cinema is an *absolutely impure art* from its moment of conception is because 'the system of its condition of possibility is an impure material system'.[36] It is a well-known fact, Badiou reminds us, that cinema is all about money: 'cinema requires money, a lot of money. Money is what unites things that are totally different from one another, everything from the actors' salaries to set construction, from technical equipment to editing rooms, from distribution to publicity—all those hundreds of completely disparate things'.[37] It is the factor of money that convinces Badiou that there is no purity in cinema. Citing Malraux as having said, 'In any case, the cinema is an industry', Badiou makes his point emphatically that 'In actual fact, the cinema is *first and foremost* an industry', and therefore, *money* combined with *industry* affirms that 'cinema begins with an impure infinity'.[38] The task of 'art' in cinema is to wrest a purity out of impurity. And, thus, Badiou infers that the art of cinema is basically a 'work of purification'. The major struggle in cinema for Badiou is the struggle with the 'infinite'; a struggle to 'purify the infinite', as he puts it.

In further scrutiny of this impurity, Badiou examines in more detail the notion of *non-art* in art. To affirm cinema as a 'mass art' is to say it is 'always at the edge of non-art'. Badiou continues:

> Cinema is an art particularly *laden with* non-art. An art that is always full of trite forms [...]. It could be argued that, at every stage of its brief existence, cinema has explored the border between art and what is not art. It is located on this border. It incorporates the new forms of existence, be they art or non-art, and it makes a certain selection among them, albeit never a complete one. And so in any film, even a pure masterpiece, you can find a great number of banal images, trite materials, stereotypes, images seen a hundred times elsewhere, completely trivial things.[39]

We therefore enter into the art of cinema from what is *not art*, according to Badiou. The reverse is true in all the other arts. We must enter their non-artistic part,

> their flaws, from art, from the grandeur of art. You could say that with cinema *you have the possibility of rising*. You can start with your most common ideas, your most nauseating sentimentality, your vulgarity,

even your cowardice. You can be an absolutely ordinary film viewer. You can have bad taste in your access, in your entry, in your initial attitude. But that doesn't prevent the film's allowing you to rise. You may arrive at powerful, refined things.[40]

In other arts one is always in danger of falling, as Badiou thinks, which is the great 'democratic advantage' of the art of cinema. Badiou cites Aristotle as having said 'if we do good, pleasure will come "as a bonus"', but then he adds, 'When we see a film, it is often the other way around: we feel an immediate pleasure, often suspect (owing to the omnipresence of non-art), and the good (of art) comes as a bonus'.[41] At the cinema, we go from the pure to the impure. This is not the case with the other arts, Badiou tells us. There are bad paintings that we do not go deliberately to see. We won't rise with a bad painting, we are rather a bunch of fallen aristocrats seeing bad paintings, losing ourselves in them, as Badiou amazingly puts it. Whereas, you are 'more or less a democrat on the rise' at the cinema.

> Therein lies a paradoxical relationship, the paradoxical relationship between aristocracy and democracy, which is ultimately an internal relationship between art and non-art. And this is also what counts for cinema's political significance: cinema achieves a cross between ordinary opinion and the work of thought. A subtle cross, which you won't find in the same guise elsewhere [...]. Cinema is a mass art because it democratizes the process whereby art uproots itself from non-art by turning that process into a border, by turning impurity into the thing itself.[42]

In his 'Philosophy and Cinema', an essay that was included in *Infinite Thought*, Badiou took up the doctrine of the 'essential impurity of cinema' to expand his thesis on 'impurity'.[43] He proposes the following principle:

> The cinema is a place of intrinsic indiscernibility between art and non-art. No film, strictly speaking, is controlled by artistic thinking from beginning to end. It always bears absolutely impure elements within it, drawn from ambient imagery, from the detritus of other arts, and from conventions with a limited shelf life. Artistic activity can only be

discerned in a film as a *process of purification of its own immanent non-artistic character*. This process is never completed.[44]

Badiou further remarks that 'Cinema's artistic operations are incompletable purification operations, bearing on current non-artistic forms, or indistinct imagery. The result of all of this is that the dominant forms of non-art are immanent to art itself, and make up part of its intelligibility'.[45] He formulates the main principle in the following way: 'A film is contemporary, and thus destined for everyone, inasmuch as the material whose purification it guarantees is identifiable as belonging to the non-art of its time'.[46] This is, he claims, what makes cinema 'intrinsically and not empirically' a mass art.

In his *The Handbook of Inaesthetics*, while discussing the idea of 'movement' as the 'poetic of cinema', Badiou notes that it is impossible not to think cinema in relation to other arts and writes that

> Cinema is the seventh art in a very particular sense. It does not add itself to the other six while remaining on the same level as them. Rather, it implies them—cinema is the 'plus-one' of the arts. It operates on the other arts, using them as its starting point, in a movement that subtracts them from themselves.[47]

Further, 'if we turn to the impure movement of the arts, we see that the poetics of film is really to be sought in the manner that the poetics supposed to underlie the poem is wrested from itself'.[48] Badiou implicitly poses a challenge to Hegel when he declares that

> The entire effect of this poetics is to allow the Idea to visit the sensible. I insist on the fact that the Idea is not incarnated in the sensible. Cinema belies the classical thesis according to which art is the sensible form of the Idea. The visitation of the sensible by the Idea does not endow the latter with a body. The Idea is not separable—it exists only for cinema in its passage. The Idea itself is visitation.[49]

Noting that, therefore, 'the poetics of film is the passage of an idea that is not itself simple', he evokes Plato to say that 'genuine ideas are a mixture. Every attempt at univocity signals the defeat of the poetic'.[50]

Alex Ling in his reflections on Badiou's philosophical thought on cinema examines the same notions of 'impurity' and 'non-art' discussed above and perceptively observes that

> in the case of cinema, non-art is immanent to art *as a rule*. Not only is every film, in the final analysis, a commodity circulating in a global market, which is produced by a certain number of labourers, and manufactured within a specific system of economic and ideological relations; moreover, the voracious relation of camera to the real means that no film can truly shield itself from the stock images of the time.[51]

It is within this notion that Badiou can proclaim: 'with only slight exaggeration cinema could be compared to the treatment of waste'.[52] 'Indeed', Ling remarks,

> insofar as cinema figures as something of a grey area between art and non-art, Badiou contends that any properly artistic activity in cinema—that is, the effective passage of a cinema-Idea—can only be discerned as a 'process of purification of its own immanent non-artistic character'. Which is today that, for a film to be truly artistic, an (effectively interminable) process of *purging* must first take place.[53]

Ling further notes that, as Badiou sees it, 'an absolute purification of cinema's non-artistic content would actually work to *suppress* its artistic capacity, inasmuch as it is precisely through its inherent non-artistry that a film is able to find its "mass address"'.[54] For Badiou, the inherent non-artistry character of cinema assures its *universality*, as Ling notes, which gives it its 'mass' appeal, makes it a 'mass art'. At the end, as Ling succinctly puts it, 'cinema *purifies* non-art at the same time as it *impurifies art*'.[55] We will come back to this point in a later chapter.

In conclusion, I want to mention that Hansen, who wants to make Adorno's thinking on music 'productive' for cinema, also argues for fundamental 'heterogeneity' and 'impurity' of film by deploying a set of other categories. She writes that this character arises from 'not only its promiscuous borrowing from the other arts and entertainment forms', but also 'its constitutive combination of heterogeneous visual, graphic, and acoustic material of expression, each with its own registers of temporality and mobility, organized to varying degrees of integration, continuity, balance, and closure or, conversely, tension, dissonance, disjunction, and openness'.[56]

Notes

1. Alain Badiou, 'Cinema as Philosophical Experimentation', in Alain Badiou, *Cinema*, texts selected and introduced by Antoine de Baecque, trans. Susan Spitzer (Cambridge: Polity, 2013), 208.
2. Walter Benjamin, 'The Work of Art in the Age of Its Technological Reproducibility', Third Version, in *Walter Benjamin, Selected Writings, Volume 4, 1938–1940*, trans. Edmund Jephcott, ed. Howard Eiland and Michael W. Jennings (Cambridge: The Belknap Press of Harvard University Press, 2003), 264.
3. Alain Badiou, 'On Cinema as a Democratic Emblem', in Alain Badiou, *Cinema*, texts selected and introduced by Antoine de Baecque, trans. Susan Spitzer (Cambridge: Polity, 2013).
4. As Miriam Bratu Hansen explains 'The notion of actuality was a shared concern between Kracauer and Bloch and other Weimar intellectuals, signaling the epistemology and political imperative to engage with modernity and its contradictions. The term was revived, and applied to Benjamin himself'; see Miriam Bratu Hansen, *Cinema and Experience: Siegfried Kracauer, Walter Benjamin, and Theodor W. Adorno* (Berkeley: University of California Press, 2012), 305, n.3. In the last three decades many attempts have been made to re-read Benjamin's *actuality* in reference to his Artwork essay. Hansen's attempt in her *Cinema and Experience* is an exceptional achievement. She explains her re-reading of Benjamin as follows: 'One of my goals is to defamiliarize the artwork essay, rethink its claim more generally, and make it available for different readings', 83. She further explains that

   > The other, larger goal is less a faithful reconstruction of what Benjamin said about film and technological media (though that, too) than an attempt to extrapolate from his observations and speculations elements of a Benjaminian theory of cinema, of a media aesthetics and politics in his expanded sense of both terms, that might still claim actuality.
   >
   > 83

   For an excellent exposition of 'actuality' in Benjamin see Irving Wolfarth's 'The Measure of the Possible, the Weight of the Real and the Heat of the Moment: Benjamin's Actuality Today', in *The Actuality of Walter Benjamin*, eds Laura Marcus and Lynda Nead (London: Lawrence and Wishart, 1998). I quote here Wolfarth's 'provisional conclusion':

   > Benjamin is perhaps the last halfway theological thinker whose voice still speaks today to the disenchanted. The question of his actuality is, I am claiming, inseparable from the question—the *Gretchenfrage*—that our actuality asks of us. Where we stand in relation to Benjamin depends on where

> we stand vis-à-vis the present—assuming that we are still standing and not merely wobbling about. Just as Kierkegaard defined his concept of irony with constant reference to Socrates, so we may best define our actuality with constant reference to Benjamin. Far from merely belonging on today's agenda as a preliminary item to the real business at hand, the question is that of today's agenda. Somewhat like Kant's 'I think' which 'must accompany all my representation', and somewhat like the operations of Benjamin's hunchback dwarf, the present conjuncture is the synthesizing a priori which—whether we know it or not—effectively organizes everything we think. All this is to be learned from Benjamin. The question that remains is whether we can actually seize this specific historical now. Nothing seems more elusive, yet nothing is surely closer to hand.

34 We must note that these remarks are made post-1989, after the Fall of the Berlin Wall and the collapse of the 'communist' camp, and 'really existing socialism'. Also see Sigrid Weigel's *Body- and Image-Space: Re-reading Walter Benjamin* (London and New York: Routledge, 1996), especially Chapter 1.
5 As noted by Miriam Bratu Hansen in *Cinema and Experience*. Accordingly, the editors of *Mapping Benjamin: The Work of Art in the Age of Digital Technology* go a little too fast when they reach the conclusion that Benjamin's theses on technological media are not applicable to current digital technology and that his prognostications have been proven wrong. By making this claim, they blunt the revolutionary potential of Benjamin's thought and its possible implications for thinking our present conjuncture with a total disintegration of the structure of experience—that had already begun going back to the1930s in Benjamin's time. See Hans Ulrich Gumbrecht and Michael Marrinan, eds, *Mapping Benjamin: The Work of Art in the Digital Age* (Stanford: Stanford University Press, 2003).
6 In Miriam Bratu Hansen, *Cinema and Experience*, 75–76.
7 See Walter Benjamin, 'The Work of Art in the Age of its Technological Reproducibility', Third Version. See also Walter Benjamin, *The Arcades Project*, trans. Howard Eiland and Kevin McLaughlin, ed. Rolf Tiedmann (The Belknap Press of Harvard University Press, 1999); and Walter Benjamin, 'On the Concept of History', in *Walter Benjamin, Selected Writings, Volume 4, 1938–1940*, trans. Edmund Jephcott, ed. Howard Eiland and Michael W. Jennings (Cambridge: The Belknap Press of Harvard University Press, 2003).
8 See Alain Badiou, *Cinema*, texts selected and introduced by Antoine de Baecque, trans. Susan Spitzer (Cambridge: Polity, 2013).
9 See A. J. Bartlett and Justin Clemens, eds, *Badiou and His Interlocutors: Lectures, Interviews and Responses* (London: Bloomsbury, 2018). This collection includes Badiou's 'The Common Preoccupation of Art and Philosophy', in which Badiou touches on cinema. It should be mentioned here that prior to these pieces on cinema, Badiou in his various philosophical works drew on cinema for his reflections, mainly in 'Philosophy and Cinema', in Alain Badiou, *Infinite Thought: Truth and the Return of Philosophy*, trans. and ed. Oliver Feltham and Justin Clemens

(London: Continuum, 2005). To date, the only book-length study that has brought to our attention the significance of Badiou's thoughts on cinema within the general context of his complex philosophy is Alex Ling's *Badiou and Cinema* (Edinburgh: Edinburgh University Press, 2013 [2010]). Also see Alex Ling, 'Thinking Cinema with Alain Badiou', in *Film as Philosophy*, ed. Bernd Herzogenrath (Minneapolis and London: University of Minnesota Press, 2017), and his informative 'An Inessential Art?: Positioning Cinema in Alain Badiou's Philosophy', included in the volume *Badiou and His Interlocutors* mentioned above.

10 See especially Jacques Rancière, *Film Fables*, trans. Emiliano Battista (Oxford and New York: Berg, 2006), and Jacques Rancière, *The Intervals of Cinema*, trans. John Howe (London and New York: Verso, 2014). Also see Stanley Cavell, *The World Viewed: Reflections on Ontology of Film, Enlarged Edition* (Cambridge: Harvard University Press, 1971), and Robert B. Pippin, *The Philosophical Hitchcock: Vertigo and the Anxieties of Unknowingness* (Chicago and London: The University of Chicago Press, 2017).

11 See André Bazin's two volumes on cinema, *What Is Cinema?*, Volume 1, essays selected and translated by Hugh Gray, foreword by Jean Renoir, with new foreword by Budley Andrew (Berkeley: University of California Press, 1967, 2005) and *What Is Cinema?*, Volume II, essays selected and translated by Hugh Gray, foreword by François Truffaut (Berkeley: University of California Press, 1971). See Gilles Deleuze's two volumes on cinema, *Cinema 1: The Movement-Image*, trans. Hugh Tomlinson and Barbara Habberjam (Minneapolis: Minnesota University Press, 1986), and *Cinema 2: The Time-Image,* trans. Hugh Tomlinson and Robert Galeto (Minneapolis: Minnesota University Press, 1994). Also see Jacques Rancière, *Film Fable*, and Jacques Rancière, *The Interval of Cinema*.

12 Miriam Bratu Hansen, *Cinema and Experience*, 85.
13 Miriam Bratu Hansen, *Cinema and Experience*, 89.
14 Miriam Bratu Hansen, *Cinema and Experience*, 85.
15 See Walter Benjamin, 'The Work of Art in the Age of Its Technological Reproducibility', Third Version, 269–270.
16 Walter Benjamin, 'The Work of Art in the Age of Its Technological Reproducibility', Third Version, 269.
17 Walter Benjamin, 'The Work of Art in the Age of Its Technological Reproducibility', Third Version, 282, n. 57. It reads in its entirety as follows:

> The technological factor is important here, especially with regard to the newsreel, whose significance for propaganda purposes can hardly be overstated. *Mass reproduction is especially favored by the reproduction of masses.* In great ceremonial processions, giant rallies, and mass sporting events, and in war, all of which are now fed into the camera, the masses come face to face with themselves. This process, whose significance need not be emphasized, is closely bound up with the development of reproduction and recording technologies. In general, mass movements are more closely apprehended by the camera than by the eye. A bird's eye view best captures assemblies of hundreds of thousands. And even when this perspective is no less accessible to the human eye than to the camera, the image formed by the eye cannot be enlarged in the

same way as a photograph. This is to say that mass movements, including war, are a form of human behavior especially suited to the camera.

282, n. 47

18 Walter Benjamin, 'The Work of Art in the Age of Its Technological Reproducibility', Third Version, 269.
19 Miriam Bratu Hansen, *Cinema and Experience*, 85.
20 Miriam Bratu Hansen, *Cinema and Experience*, 85.
21 See Alex Ling, 'An Inessential Art?: Positioning Cinema in Alain Badiou's Philosophy', in *Badiou and His Interlocutors: Lectures, Interviews and Responses*, eds A. J. Bartlett and Justin Clemens (London: Bloomsbury, 2018).
22 Alain Badiou, 'Cinema as Philosophical Experimentation', 208.
23 Alain Badiou, 'Cinema as Philosophical Experimentation', 207.
24 Alain Badiou, 'Cinema as Philosophical Experimentation', 207.
25 Alain Badiou, 'Cinema as Philosophical Experimentation', 208.
26 Alain Badiou, 'Cinema as Philosophical Experimentation', 208.
27 See Alain Badiou, 'Third Sketch of a Manifesto of Affirmationist Art', in *Polemics*, trans. and intro. Steve Corcoran (London and New York: Verso, 2006), 147.
28 Alain Badiou, 'Third Sketch of a Manifesto of Affirmationist Art', 147.
29 See Alain Badiou, 'Fifteen Theses on Contemporary Art', in *Lacanian Ink*, 23 (2004), 107.
30 See Alain Badiou, *The Century* (Cambridge: Polity, 2007). Also see my *An Architecture Manifesto: Critical Reason and Theories of a Failed Practice* (Abingdon: Routledge, 2019).
31 Walter Benjamin, 'The Work of Art in the Age of Its Technological Reproducibility', Third Version, 266.
32 Walter Benjamin, 'The Work of Art in the Age of Its Technological Reproducibility', Third Version, 267.
33 Walter Benjamin, 'The Work of Art in the Age of Its Technological Reproducibility', Third Version, 282, n. 43.
34 Alain Badiou, 'Cinema as Philosophical Experimentation', 208.
35 Alain Badiou, 'On Cinema as a Democratic Emblem', 235.
36 Alain Badiou, 'Cinema as Philosophical Experimentation', 226. Badiou, comparing film with painting a picture or writing a poem, states that

> the condition of the production of the movement-image and time-image [Deleuze's terms] involves a unique assemblage of materials. You need technical resources, but you also need to marshal extremely complex and, above all heterogeneous materials. For example, you need locations, either natural or constructed ones; you need spaces; you need a text, a screenplay, dialogue, abstract idea; you need bodies, actors; plus you'll need chemistry, and editing equipment. And so you need to make use of a whole collective apparatus, a whole collection of different materials, which you'll have to master, at least to some extent, through the resources of their inscription within the image.
>
> 225–226

37   Alain Badiou, 'Cinema as Philosophical Experimentation', 226.
38   Alain Badiou, 'Cinema as Philosophical Experimentation', 226.
39   Alain Badiou, 'On Cinema as a Democratic Emblem', 238. Badiou adds that, 'Owing to a large number of its ingredients, cinema is always *beneath* art. Even its most obvious artistic successes include an immanent infinity of shoddy ingredients, of blatant bits of non-art', 238.
40   Alain Badiou, 'On Cinema as a Democratic Emblem', 239.
41   Alain Badiou, 'On Cinema as a Democratic Emblem', 239.
42   Alain Badiou, 'On Cinema as a Democratic Emblem', 239.
43   See Alain Badiou *Infinite Thought*. The article was first printed in *L'Art du Cinéma*, 24 (March 1990).
44   Alain Badiou, *Infinite Thought*, 84.
45   Alain Badiou, *Infinite Thought*, 84–85.
46   Alain Badiou, *Infinite Thought*, 86.
47   See Alain Badiou, *Handbook of Inaesthetics*, trans. Alberto Toscano (Stanford: Stanford University Press, 2005), 79.
48   Alain Badiou, *Handbook of Inaesthetics*, 80.
49   Alain Badiou, *Handbook of Inaesthetics*, 80.
50   Alain Badiou, *Handbook of Inaesthetics*, 81. Badiou further remarks,

> But does this impurity, like that of the Idea, not oblige us—if we wish simply to speak of film—to undertake some strange detours, these same 'long detours' whose necessity Plato established long ago? It is clear that film criticism is forever suspended between the chatter of empathy, on the one hand, and historical technicalities, on the other. Unless it is just a question of recounting the plot (the fatal novelistic impurity) or of singing the actors' praises (the theatrical impurity). Is it really so easy to speak about a film?
>
> 83

51   See Alex Ling, 'An Inessential Art?', 136. Also see Alex Ling, 'Thinking Cinema with Alain Badiou'.
52   Quoted in Alex Ling, 'An Inessential Art?', 136.
53   Alex Ling, 'An Inessential Art?', 136. Ling further observes that

> Badiou quickly concedes, such an absolutely purificatory process can of course never actually be achieved. At best, such a 'pure' cinematic idea might only be approached *asymptotically*. This 'impossibility', Badiou declares, 'is the real of cinema, which is a struggle with the infinite, a struggle to purify the infinites'.
>
> 136

54   Alex Ling, 'An Inessential Art?', 137.
55   Alex Ling, 'An Inessential Art?', 137.
56   See Miriam Bratu Hansen, *Cinema and Experience*, 240. Hansen mentions that she is borrowing the term '*materialist expression*' from Christian Metz, in his *Language and Cinema*, trans. Donna Jean Umiker-Sebeok (The Hague and Paris: Mouton, 1974).

Chapter 4

In and out of Plato's cave

> We cannot escape cinema.
> —Alain Badiou, 'Cinema and Philosophy'[1]

> It will not be a disaster if cinema disappears.
> —Alain Badiou, 'Cinema and Philosophy'[2]

> The Proletarians have nothing to lose but their chains. They have a world to win.
> —Karl Marx and Friedrich Engels, *The Communist Manifesto*[3]

It is a familiar parable. Cinema is the allegory of Plato's cave. It has been cited numerous times by film critics. For example, Jean-Louis Baudry once said that 'the allegory of the cave … haunts the invention of cinema and the history of its invention'.[4] But the treatment of this allegory from the *Republic* by Alain Badiou, with which I am mainly concerned here, is quite extraordinary. The crux in this allegory for Badiou is the question of the relationship between cinema and philosophy. Before we come to this, we should first refresh our memory. In Book VII, Socrates, who is in dialogue with Plato's brother Glaucon, starts with the matter of 'education' and goes on to describe the state of prisoners in the underground cave. It goes as follows:

> Imagine human beings living in an underground, cavelike dwelling, with an entrance a long way up, which is both open to the light and as wide as the cave itself. They've been there since childhood, fixed in the same place, with their necks and legs fettered, able to see only

in front to them, because their bonds prevent them from turning their heads around. Light is provided by a fire burning far above and behind them. Also behind them, but on higher ground, there is a path stretching between them and the fire: Imagine that along this path a low wall has been built, like the screen in front of puppeteers above which they show their puppets.

I'm imagining it.

Then also imagine that there are people along the wall, carrying all kinds of artifacts that project above it—statues of people and other animals, made out of stone, wood, and every material. And, as you'd expect, some of the carriers are talking, some are silent.
  It is a strange image you're describing, and strange prisoners. (514)
  [...]
  Then the prisoners would in every way believe that the truth is nothing other than the shadows of those artifacts.
  They must surely believe that. (515)
  [...]
  This whole image, Glaucon, must be fitted together with what we said before. The visible realm should be likened to the prison dwelling, and the light of the fire inside it to the power of the sun. And if you interrupt the upward journey and study of things above as the upward journey of the soul to the intelligible realm, you'll grasp what I hope to convey, since that is what you wanted to hear about. Whether it's true or not, only the god knows. But this is how I see it: In the knowable realm, the form of the good is the last thing to be seen, and it is reached only with difficulty. Once one has seen it, however, one must conclude that it is the cause of all that is correct and beautiful in anything, that it produces both light and its sources in the visible realm, and that in the intelligible realm it controls and provides truth and understanding, so that anyone who is to act sensibly in private or public must see it.
  I have the same thought, at least as far as I'm able. (517)[5]

Badiou has produced a famous 'translation' of Plato's *Republic* from its original Greek entitled *Plato's Republic: A Dialogue in 16 Chapters*.[6] With this landmark 'translation' in our twenty-first century, we no longer have one *Republic* belonging to Plato. As Badiou himself claims, 'I think in the end we don't know what is exactly the *Republic* of Plato. It is possible that I say, finally, that in fact the *Republic* of Plato is a book of Badiou. *It is the sign maybe of the end of philosophy*'[7] (emphasis mine). I will come back to the last sentence later. Meanwhile, Badiou claims that his translation is not at all a pure imitation of Plato but 'a prolongation of Plato, something after Plato, and naturally, in my opinion, better than Plato!'[8] In this imaginative and humorous 'translation', Badiou reorganizes the ten books of Plato into 16 chapters and, more significantly, 'transforms' Plato's cave into 'a contemporary cinema'. In the Preface he explains the way he has treated the text with the changes he has brought, including changing 'soul' to 'Subject' and the famous 'Idea of the Good' to the 'Idea of the True', along with introducing certain 'general techniques' as he puts it, including '*Introducing a female character*', 'Adeimantus became Amantha', and more importantly, there was the '*Updating of the Images*. The Cave of the famous myth is so like an enormous movie theater that it only takes describing that movie theater and having Plato's prisoners become spectator-prisoners of the contemporary sphere of media for it to be the same thing, only better'.[9] In the following, I cite the passages that 'correspond' to the paragraphs in Plato's *Republic* quoted above. In Chapter 11, entitled 'What is An Idea (502c–521c)', Badiou, setting the stage for the dialogue between Glaucon, Amantha, and Socrates, and after reconfiguring the vertical line diagram in the original Book VI, ties the conversation to his own Platonic preoccupation of the 'mathematical ontology' leading to his notion of 'cinema':

> The existence of mathematical idealities is in turn assumed in analytical thought. But we're certain of the universality of the ideal principles to which dialectical thinking leads us. This order can also be expressed thus: the more a being is given in the element of Truth, the more the Subject can think in its own clarity.
>
> —Which would mean that objective truth and subjective clarity, *Amantha mused aloud*, are two aspects of the same process.
>
> —You're making me sound a little too much like Descartes! But since you mentioned light, I'll try and paint you a picture, with shadow and light intermingled.
>
> —After the matheme, it's back to the poem! *Said Glaucon playfully.*

—Well, why not, imagine an enormous movie theater. Down front, the screen, which goes right up to the ceiling (but it's so high that everything up there gets lost in the dark) blocks anything other than itself from being seen. It's a full house. For as long as they've been around, the audience members have been chained to their seats, with their eyes staring at the screen and their heads held in place by rigid headphones covering their ears. Behind these tens of thousands of spectators shackled to their seats there's an immense wooden walkway, at head level, running parallel to the whole length of the screen. Still further back are enormous projectors flooding the screen with an almost unbearable white light.

—What a strange place! *said Glaucon.*

—Hardly any more than our Earth ... All sorts of robots, dolls, cardboard cut-outs, puppets, operated and manipulated by invisible puppeteers or guided by remote control, move along the walkway. Animals, stretcher-bearers, scythe-bearers, cars, storks, ordinary people, armed soldiers, gangs of youths from the *banlieues*, turtle doves, cultural coordinators, naked women, and so forth go back and forth continuously in this way. Some of them shout, others talk, others play the cornet or the concertina, while others just hurry silently along. On the screen can be seen the shadows of this chaotic parade thrown by the projectors. And through their headphones the immobilized crowd can hear sounds and words.

—My God! *Amantha burst out.* That's one weird show and even weirder audience!

—They're just like us. Can they see anything themselves, of the people sitting next to them, of the movie theater, and of the bizarre scenes on the walkway other than the shadows projected onto the screen by the flood of lights? Can they hear anything other than what their headsets deliver to them?

—Not a thing, for sure, *exclaimed Glaucon*, if their heads have always been prevented from looking anywhere but at the screen and their ears have been blocked by the headphones.

—And that *is* the case. So they have no perception of the visible other than through the mediation of the shadows, and none of what's being said other than through the mediation of those sound waves. Even assuming they could figure out ways of talking among themselves, they'd necessarily equate the shadow, which they *can* see, with the object, which they *can't* see, which that shadow is the shadow of.

—Not to mention, *added Amantha*, that the object on the walkway, whether it's a robot or a puppet, is already a copy itself. We could say that all they see is a shadow of a shadow.[10]

Two years after the publication of his 'translation' of Plato's *Republic*, Badiou gave two public lectures in November 2014, entitled 'Cinema and Philosophy' and 'The Common Preoccupation of Art and Philosophy'.[11] In these astonishing talks, Badiou returns to his 'translation' of the allegory of Plato's cave as cinema and offers an extended analysis. Badiou begins by posing six questions, namely: 'What is cinema?'; 'What is the relationship between philosophy and cinema?'; 'Is cinema an art?'; if cinema is an art, 'What is its relation to all sequences of arts?'; 'Is the relation between cinema and philosophy singular?'; and finally, 'Is it possible that cinema becomes a form appropriate to philosophy?' In relation to the second question, he further asks 'why a relationship between philosophy and cinema?'[12] He proposes two hypotheses. First, there is an 'opposition between philosophy and cinema, a contradiction': 'If cinema is composed of images, if cinema is a form of imaginary relationship to the world', then cinema is exposed to

> a fundamental critique from the point of view of philosophy, a very old critique, which is the suspicion concerning images and the opposition, in some sense, to the potency of images in the names of concepts, thinking and rationality.[13]

Badiou claims that in Plato we find a critique of cinema precisely because of the same allegory of the cave, which is a representation, the most important one, in both philosophy and cinema. This is why in his 'translation', as he tells us, he transformed the cave into 'contemporary cinema'. 'It was clear', he says,

> It was the presence of images in the place of the Real and the humanity in the cave is seeing some images in the conviction that these images are the unique reality and philosophy is to organize the possibility of going outside the cave, to escape the dictatorship of images.[14]

We are now more in the cave than in the time of Plato, Badiou claims, because of the 'complexity of the world' beyond anything Plato might ever have imagined. So, the allegory of the cave is 'properly a contradiction between philosophy and cinema [...]. Philosophy is finally something that is against the potency of images, against cinema in the end'.[15] But then Badiou says that if we cannot reduce cinema to images, then 'cinema is not the cave of Plato'. So images are like an illusion. But Badiou asserts that

> this illusion, the illusion of the cinema, is not a negative function of images in the sense of Plato because for Plato images are something that is a false reality. But cinema is not a false reality. Cinema is a new relationship to the real itself.[16]

So the situation is completely different, Badiou states, from the prisoner of the cave, 'who has the conviction that images are the only form of the real'.[17]

The conclusion that Badiou wants to arrive at is that, at the end, strictly speaking, there is no contradiction between cinema and philosophy. On the contrary, as he says, cinema is a condition of philosophy:

> I name condition of philosophy an activity, a form of creation, a form of thinking which is in some sense the horizon of philosophical activity. So a condition is what is present in the world and which is really a sort of new possibility for philosophical thinking,

and further, 'In this direction, my position is that today we cannot do philosophy without any relationship to cinema'.[18] Addressing the third question, 'Is cinema an art', Badiou extends his point about the 'impurity' of cinema that we saw in the previous chapter and further remarks that the

> fight against the cave of cinema is inside the cinema itself, if cinema is not the production of images but the war against bad images and to affirm what is a true image. Not as a substitute to reality but the true image as an image.[19]

Asking '*What is a true image?*', he refers to Godard, for whom an image is not a representation of something but an image as 'something that by itself is a new thinking of the real'. To have this true image we get into the fight inside the image itself. So Badiou says that for Godard 'a true image is always an image when we find two things that have no relation between them'.[20]

Cinema is an *impure* art, as we have seen. It is the art of *non-art*, partly aristocratic and partly democratic. And for this very reason, for Badiou, cinema is a form of a conflict that cannot disappear:

> It is a new conflict, a possibility to have a form of art so impure, so horrible (in some sense) that what can be inscribed in this form is all the possible fictions of the fundamental conflict of our existence. So cinema is a recollection of all contradictions inside aesthetic creation, but also more generally.[21]

Further, cinema poses the question of 'democracy', Badiou says. 'It is the only democratic art in some sense. All forms of art today are aristocratic, exceptional'.[22] Cinema harbors inside itself a contradiction, Badiou insists. It is a contradiction between what is 'pure creativity' and what is 'horrible materials'. And so 'cinema has two qualities: it is dialectics, because it is an art of contradiction, and it is democratic. *And so the cinema is a democratic dialectics. It is something exceptional*'[23] (emphasis mine).

In respect to the relationship of cinema to philosophy, Badiou argues that 'cinema is an important symptom', a 'fundamental symptom', it is a 'place where all the contradictions of the world are really assumed',[24] as philosophy also has the

> function of creating a space of thinking to examine the contradiction of the contemporary world and to propose an orientation. Philosophy finally is the search for a true life. [...] And Plato was saying to do that we must escape the potency of the image, the allegory of the cave.[25]

But surprisingly, Badiou suggests that, today,

> we must go to the cinema. So we must go into the cave, in the modern cave where the spectacle of image is more elaborate. If we say something concerning the relationship between cinema and philosophy we must say that the cinema is for philosophy today the new allegory of

the cave which is 'go to the cave, go to the cave'. It's only by going to the cave that we can find the new means to go outside, because precisely the cinema is the immanent conflict between what is the bad presentation of images, the troubled fascination of images on the one side, but on the other side the possibility of clear vision by images themselves of the possibility to an orientation in the real. So to go to the cave, which is today the cinema, is also to participate in the democratic dialectics. And so it's part of our modern education.[26]

Badiou comes to Plato's 'paradox' and the problematic relationship of art to philosophy. Plato's position in philosophy is a 'curious' one, Badiou suggests. On the one hand, art was dangerous for Plato, art is an imitation and removed from the truth, but paradoxically his dialogues are themselves in 'theatrical' form, in an *art form*. The current meaning of philosophy, Badiou says, goes back to Plato, but his writings are not in classical form. Badiou informs us that after Plato practically no philosophers used the 'theatrical' form invented by Plato, the form of the dialogues.[27] As he claims:

> Now we must understand that the paradox of Plato, to be in some sense an enemy of art but inside art in another sense—because after all Plato is a very great writer in the Greek language, practically a poet in prose of the Greek language—is precisely not of an aesthetic nature. Plato does not say that tragedy is not a pleasure or a beautiful thing or weak and without interest—not at all. It is because tragedy is a very profound pleasure and a magnificent thing that the philosopher must be suspicious. Because for Plato philosophy is not a knowledge, and there is no aesthetic in the relationship to tragedy.[28]

And further Badiou stresses the point that he has elsewhere insisted upon:

> Philosophy is a movement, the goal of which is to transform subjectivity, a subjectivity which is corrupted by the dominant opinion. And you know that if Socrates was sentenced to death for the corruption of the youth, the definition of philosophy must be, effectively, the corruption of the youth: to destroy the true corruption of youth by the ordinary world and to corrupt the corruption.[29]

Returning to Plato's cave, Badiou reiterates that Plato created cinema in the allegory of the cave:

> Plato in the allegory of the cave presents the world, the real world, as a very big cinema, where all humanity is seeing images and these images are confused because nobody can distinguish between the images and the real because there are only images and so we are in the big cosmic cinema. [...] But for Plato there are bad caves, which is precisely the domination of false opinion, and the domination of corruption. And so the philosophical effort is to transform the subject by rational means.[30]

This rational means is practical rather than a 'pure theoretical transmission'. Therefore:

> The goal is to go out of the cave, to find the sun and the light, to find the real in the place of images and this public action, this necessity to educate in how to come out of the cave is the true definition of philosophy and Plato knows that theatre and more generally art also transform subjectivity.[31]

The ultimate goal is then to transform subjectivity—through art and philosophy. But the philosophy is in a 'conflict' or 'fight' and not in 'difference', since for Plato, Badiou tells us, the relation between theater and philosophy cannot be reduced to a 'difference'. These two forms compete with each other to transform the subjectivity. Theater is the 'invention of a split in the One', Badiou says. 'It is the way out of the cave of the One'.[32] It is, therefore, the 'invention of dialectics':

> And maybe the difficult relationship between philosophy and theatre, properly, but practically all forms of art concerns the question of dialectics. Because philosophy too is the invention of dialectics, philosophy too is the examination of the question of negativity. And this is why we have the presence of theatre in the entire philosophical history of dialectics. In Hegel—the contradiction between Antigone and Creon in Sophocles: universality against particularity. Or in Aeschylus, the opposition of Athena and the Erinyes: the creation of an objective trial and political rights against revenge and so on. Finally, the question of the

relationship between art and philosophy is the question of dialectics; the question of the presentation of what is dialectical thinking that is also a critical thinking, thinking which is able to develop negativity.[33]

There is much more to be said about Badiou's relation to philosophy, and for that matter to Plato and art, which is outside of the narrow concern here exclusively related to the allegory of Plato's cave and cinema.[34] There is admittedly a larger number of ideas that can be connected to the idea of Plato's cave. Below I briefly reflect only on one, closely related to my purpose in this work.

What if Plato's cave is the place of the capitalist world in which we are trapped? Aren't we under its dark shadow? Aren't we chained to it without the hope of unchaining ourselves? Is not Plato's cave the 'cinema of capitalism'? It is a horror movie. Badiou in his remarkable explorations of cinema does not address this question of 'capitalist cinema'. Frank Ruda in his 'Marx in the Cave' ingeniously addresses it.[35] But, Ruda, who had previously written an important book on Badiou,[36] does not cite Badiou's 'translation' of his *Platonic Republic*, nor his extensive writings on cinema and the relationship between cinema and philosophy. Ruda is rather concerned with Marx and the myth of Plato's cave in relation to the notion of 'emancipation'. He begins with the often-cited claim that the whole history of philosophy is nothing but a 'footnote to Plato'. By extending it, he asks whether we might not claim that the history of 'emancipatory thought' is *also* a footnote to the allegory of Plato's cave. He remind us that in fact the cave allegory is a 'pre-enlightenment enlightenment critique of mythical thinking and action', and thereby it 'directly addresses emancipation'.[37] In light of this, Ruda proposes a hypothesis that he sets out to examine: 'What if modern—that is, capitalist—society, in a sense to be specified, resembles a version of Plato's cave? And what if Marx can be read "experimentally", yet consistently in this vein?'[38] Yet, 'Unchaining man—from whatever chains, real or metaphorical—', Ruda says, is an 'intricate' task, especially if, quoting Alfred Sohn-Rethel, 'the social being in which we live exists in such a way that it exudes deceptions and nobody, even a Marxist[!], can withdraw from their influences'.[39]

What, after all, is the cave, Ruda asks. It is not only the cultural but also the natural 'cave-state' of man that cannot be 'entirely abolished'.

And, 'does not Plato already speak of the need to return to the cave after exiting it? Where does this (regressive) desire come from?'.[40] Is the cave an 'artificial set-up', an 'efficient device for domination', Ruda further asks. If yes, 'who set it up'? These questions are persistent in modern philosophy. Descartes 'dialectized the different options':

> The Cartesian 'cave' is neither a natural human condition (we are not deceived by nature) nor simply cultural (we are not in a metaphorical cave, imprisoned by others' opinions, unable literally to think outside the box). Rather, a *genius malignus*, an evil spirit, constructed a false world that appears completely natural to us. Only by traversing this fantastic cave scenario does Descartes reach a point of absolute certainty (the 'I think' about which even an evil cave-maker cannot deceive me).[41]

The early Marx in fact 'revamps this scenario', Ruda continues,

> when he depicts the alienation imposed on human beings by capitalism's *genius malignus* and its disciplinary regime of labor in terms of human pre-history: a state that must be exited through the revolutionary activity of those 'who have nothing but their chains'.[42]

It can be exited only because of another 'shadowy existence', that is, the 'specter of communism', Ruda reminds us. The enchainment in the cave 'fettered in chains' and 'riveted by shadow' in Plato originates from either nature or the struggle of rational with irrational forces, or it was caused by the 'sophists' and the 'poets'. Recall that in Book X of the *Republic* Plato has harsh words for the poets who are in the business of 'shadowy representations', in mimesis, producing copies of the copies of the real, enticing the rational human being, making it lose orientation towards the Idea, art as a 'factory of shadows' generating illusions, much like ideology in Marx. Equally,

> the sophists are 'enticing image-makers' who 'do magic … by producing images through words' that capture and direct our thought and action into inconsistent directions. They generate a 'mere satisfaction' by presenting shadows of insights, knowledge, and arguments, mere 'moving images' that especially capture those unfamiliar with the truth, and thereby, ultimately, 'semblance becomes the master over the happiness of human beings'.[43]

'Can Marx be read as presenting a critique of one of the most sophisticated productions of shadows—that is, capitalism?' is how Ruda ingeniously poses the question. He sets for himself the task of 'read[ing] capitalism as a naturalizing realm of shadows'. He reminds us that Marx knew that in capitalism everyone, capitalist or not, succumbs to the 'inversion of reality'. As Slavoj Žižek in *Living in the End Times* writes: 'what Marx discovered with his problematic of "commodity fetishism" [in *Capital*] is a phantasmagoria or illusion which cannot simply be dismissed as a secondary reflection, because it is operative at the very heart of the "real production process" [...]'.[44] The everyday practical reality of capitalism then entails a constitutive 'religious', 'mythical', or 'metaphysical moment', Ruda adds. *Capital* presents us with a

> critical analysis of capitalism's logic of appearance. In this, shadowy entities capture and determine those who produce them, since 'just as man is governed in religion by the products of his own brain, so in capitalist production, he is governed by the product of his own hand.' [...] Not only are the workers themselves producing the chain that binds them to the system; critically representing the economic laws of movement of modern societies also implies depicting the function of this practical self-enchainment.[45]

Citing Marx in *Capital*, Volume 3, where he wrote of a 'bewitched, distorted and upside-down world haunted by Monsieur le Capital and Madame la Terre, who are at the same time social characters and mere things', Ruda says that 'critical engagement with the science that, without understanding it articulate its constitutive assumption, is therefore similar to what one experiences at "the entrance to hell"— itself, maybe, a very specific kind of cave'.[46] The question that must be raised, he says, is obviously 'what it means to exit the cave'. He goes on to pose these questions:

> How can one conceive of the beginning of emancipation (being freed from the chains)—and who would be free? What kind of coercion is needed to 'force us to think' (Deleuze)? Why is it not enough, as Heidegger noted, to take off the chains for the prisoners to be ready to leave the cave? What must be added to this? How can one even begin

to imagine the outside of the cave? What would it mean to leave and return to the cave, given that, for Plato, the very idea of the good is linked not only to 'events' of turn(ing away from the shadows) but also to the return (to the cave)? And what does one do with the problem that occurs when one does return—namely, that the other cave prisoners do not want to be liberated? How can one transmit to them what is not knowledge but something else—an idea?[47]

We have to leave Ruda with these thought-provoking questions that we cannot address here.

In conclusion: I return to Badiou and the question of the 'end'—in philosophy and in cinema. Recall that Badiou said, and I quote again:

> I think in the end we don't know what is exactly the *Republic* of Plato. It's possible that I say, finally, that in fact the *Republic* of Plato is a book of Badiou. It is the sign maybe of *the end of philosophy* (emphasis mine).
>
> Alain Badiou, 'The Common Preoccupation of Art and Philosophy', 31

Badiou is our Plato! Badiou is the name for *philosophy after the death of philosophy*. The same goes for the pronouncement of the death of cinema by Godard. Recall again what Badiou said: 'Cinema is finished, except maybe the cinema of Godard because it's cinema of the death of cinema'. Maybe, only maybe, cinema as an *inessential art* will disappear—unlike the art of building, which will never and cannot go away. But what remains, what is not *dead*, is the idea of 'negativity' as a means by which to transform *subjectivity*, in thought and philosophy. We must return to *dialectics*, and we will.

Notes

1. Alain Badiou, 'Cinema and Philosophy', in *Badiou and His Interlocutors: Lectures, Interviews and Responses*, ed. A. J. Bartlett and Justin Clemens (London: Bloomsbury, 2018), 28.
2. Alain Badiou, 'Cinema and Philosophy', 25.
3. Karl Marx and Friedrich Engels, *The Communist Manifesto* (Lexington: SoHo Books, 2010), 64.
4. Jean-Louis Baudry, 'The Apparatus: Metaphysical Approaches to Impression of Reality in Cinema', in *Narrative, Apparatus, Ideology: A Film Reader*, ed.

Philip Rosen, trans. Jean Andrews and Bernard Augst (New York: Columbia University Press, 1968), 299–318. On this also see Alex Ling, *Badiou and Cinema* (Edinburgh: Edinburgh University Press, 2011, 2013). More recently, the film critic Jonathan Rosenbaum, discussing the films of Abbas Kiarostami, notes that 'There's a parable by Plato that sees the shadows on the wall of a cave as representations of reality. It can be read as a kind of metaphor about cinema', in Mehrnaz Saeed-Vafa and Jonathan Rosenbaum, *Abbas Kiarostami*, Expanded Second Edition (Urbana: University of Illinois Press, 2003, 2018), 114.

5   Plato, *Complete Works*, ed., intro., and notes, John M. Cooper (Indianapolis and Cambridge: Hackett, 1977), 1132–1135.
6   Alain Badiou, *Plato's Republic: A Dialogue in 16 Chapters*, trans. Susan Spitzer, intro. Kenneth Reinhardt (New York: Columbia University Press, 2012).
7   See Alain Badiou, 'The Common Preoccupation of Art and Philosophy', in *Badiou and His Interlocuters: Lectures, Interviews and Responses*, ed. A. J. Bartlett and Justin Clemens (London: Bloomsbury, 2018), 31. The entire paragraph in Badiou's humorous words goes as follows:

> I have produced an excellent translation of Plato's *Republic* from Greek into French, and after that Susan Spitzer has made an excellent translation into English of my French translation of the Greek. At the last level, the Chinese are to realize an excellent translation in Chinese of the excellent translation of English, of my translation in French of the Greek original. If the Japanese take the Chinese translation to do an excellent translation into Japanese, and so on … I think in the end we don't know what is exactly the *Republic* of Plato. It's possible that I say, finally, that in fact the *Republic* of Plato is a book of Badiou. It is the sign maybe of the end of philosophy.
>
> 31

8   Explaining that he is on the side of Plato and his 'theatrical' form of the dialogues rather than on the side of the classical or 'academic' style of Aristotle, Badiou says that

> this is why in my translation of the *Republic* I was obliged to introduce some ameliorations, some modifications, some points where Plato is not taking the 'right line' and so my translation is not at all a pure imitation of Plato but a prolongation of Plato, something after Plato, and naturally, in my opinion, better than Plato!
>
> Alain Badiou, 'The Common Preoccupation of Art and Philosophy', 33

9   Alain Badiou, *Plato's Republic*, xxxiii.
10 Alain Badiou, *Plato's Republic*, 211–213.
11 Both are included in *Badiou and His Interlocuters*.
12 Alain Badiou, 'Cinema and Philosophy', 19.
13 Alain Badiou, 'Cinema and Philosophy', 19.

14 Alain Badiou, 'Cinema and Philosophy', 19.
15 Alain Badiou, 'Cinema and Philosophy', 19.
16 Alain Badiou, 'Cinema and Philosophy', 20.
17 Alain Badiou, 'Cinema and Philosophy', 20.
18 Alain Badiou, 'Cinema and Philosophy', 20. Naming other contemporary philosophers who have written on cinema, prominently Deleuze and Rancière, Badiou says that

> from Bergson to myself, if you accept this narcissistic consideration, we find a growing interest in cinema for the philosophers with the books of Deleuze, the books of Rancière, the books of many contemporary philosophers concerning cinema. And this is because cinema, which is an essential component of our world. Is also something new and something like a new lesson for the philosophical possibility.
>
> 20

19 Alain Badiou, 'Cinema and Philosophy', 23.
20 Alain Badiou, 'Cinema and Philosophy', 23.
21 Alain Badiou, 'Cinema and Philosophy', 26.
22 Alain Badiou, 'Cinema and Philosophy', 26.
23 Alain Badiou, 'Cinema and Philosophy', 26–27.
24 Alain Badiou, 'Cinema and Philosophy', 27.
25 Alain Badiou, 'Cinema and Philosophy', 27.
26 Alain Badiou, 'Cinema and Philosophy', 27.
27 Badiou explains that

> we have the strange situation that the creation of philosophy, of the contents of philosophy, is made in a form which has no future. It is an artistic form, and Plato is a writer, but it's an artistic form that after has no descendants. [...] But in fact the dominant form of philosophy, all along its history, is not at all the dialogue, but the academic treatise, and academic treatise is not an invention of the first philosopher Plato. The academic treatise is invented by Aristotle, the second philosopher. But Aristotle is not at all an enemy of theatre, so you see the enemy of theatre writes dialogues, and the friend of theatre writes academic treatises. The situation is a really a complex one.
>
> Alain Badiou, 'The Common Preoccupation of Art and Philosophy', 32

28 Alain Badiou, 'The Common Preoccupation of Art and Philosophy', 33.
29 Alain Badiou, 'The Common Preoccupation of Art and Philosophy', 33.
30 Alain Badiou, 'The Common Preoccupation of Art and Philosophy', 34.
31 Alain Badiou, 'The Common Preoccupation of Art and Philosophy', 34.
32 Alain Badiou, 'The Common Preoccupation of Art and Philosophy', 36. Badiou further remarks that

the beginning of theatre is the invention of the second person, speaking on the stage. So it's the invention of a ceremony, certainly—the old theatre is a ceremony—which presents the opposition between two subjects, two opinions and two contradictory convictions. So in theatre, in relation to religious ceremony, the two comes after the One. And so theatre, before philosophy, is the appearing of negation; the artistic appearing of the potency of division and negation.

33 Alain Badiou, 'The Common Preoccupation of Art and Philosophy', 36–37.
34 Among the vast literature see, for example, A. J. Bartlett, *Badiou and Plato: An Education by Truths* (Edinburgh: University of Edinburgh Press, 2011, 2015).
35 See Frank Ruda, 'Marx in the Cave', in Slavoj Žižek, Frank Ruda, and Agon Hamza, *Reading Marx* (Cambridge: Polity, 2018).
36 See Frank Ruda, *For Badiou: Idealism without Idealism*, with a preface by Slavoj Žižek (Evanston: Northwestern University Press, 2015).
37 Frank Ruda, 'Marx in the Cave', 62.
38 Frank Ruda, 'Marx in the Cave', 65.
39 Frank Ruda, 'Marx in the Cave', 65.
40 Frank Ruda, 'Marx in the Cave', 65.
41 Frank Ruda, 'Marx in the Cave', 65–66.
42 Frank Ruda, 'Marx in the Cave', 66.
43 Frank Ruda, 'Marx in the Cave', 66–67. Ruda adds that

> Both produce disorientation in people's practical and theoretical conduct. And we might recall that more recently Badiou partially revamped this criticism when, after the decline of communist states and the worldwide victory of capitalism, he stated that sophists are arising everywhere, pretending to be philosophers, offering fake orientation in political matters and inaugurating a 'phony way of thinking'. They thereby prevent any real (political) thought from becoming effective—by, inter alia, undermining the distinction between truth and opinion, criminalizing all political action that relies on this distinction, and ultimately not only offering wrong solutions, but—worse—fake problems.
>
> 67

44 Slavoj Žižek, *Living in the End Times* (London and New York: Verso, 2010), 190.
45 Frank Ruda, 'Marx in the Cave', 70.
46 Frank Ruda, 'Marx in the Cave', 70.
47 Frank Ruda, 'Marx in the Cave', 71.

Chapter 5

Theory of distraction
Tactile and optical

> The relation of distraction to absorption must be examined.
> —Walter Benjamin, 'Theory of Distraction'[1]

> The laws of Architecture's reception are highly instructive.
> —Walter Benjamin, 'The Work of Art in the Age of Its Technological Reproducibility'[2]

As Gilloch remarks, 'Chance configurations of traffic and crowds in motion, fleeting constellations and conjunctures, the physical fabric of the cityscape in perpetual transformation, Berlin subject to time—these spatio-temporal, *cinematic* aspects of modernity fascinate Kracauer'. In the city 'everything moves, everything stirs, and only "film is adequate to this sense of motion"'.[3] Before I turn to Benjamin, who is my main concern in this chapter, it must be noted that, as Gilloch remarks, for Kracauer 'film and the city are manifestations of the modern unconscious. This is the key to their elective affinity'.[4]

In Section XV of the Artwork essay (third version), Benjamin wrote: 'Architecture has always offered the prototype of an artwork that is received in a state of distraction and through the collective'. Earlier, in Section XII, Benjamin made painting face up to the model of architecture before coming to cinema. He begins the section by making an incisive declaration: 'The technological reproducibility of the artwork changes the relation of the masses to art. The extremely backward attitude toward a Picasso painting changes into a highly progressive reaction to a Chaplin film'.[5] In the second paragraph he takes painting to task: 'Painting, by its nature, cannot provide an object of

71

simultaneous collective reception, as architecture has always been able to do, as the epic poem could do at one time, and as film is able to do today'.[6] In these claims it is the political and philosophical notion of 'masses' that occupies the center for Benjamin. I come to this point later.

Here I am mainly concerned with Section XV and the final section, the Epilogue in the third version of 'The Work of Art in the Age of Its Technological Reproducibility'.[7] In both sections there is a constellation of categories and concepts that I will discuss in relation to the central thesis regarding the exemplary model of architecture for cinema in the epoch of technology and the impact of the new structure of experience in the newly emerging mass-mediated society. While working on the Artwork essay, Benjamin penned a fragment labeled 'Theory of Distraction' that was published posthumously. In this piece Benjamin reflects that 'The value of distraction should be defined with regard to film, just as the values of catharsis are defined with regard to tragedy'.[8] He argues that just as the art of the Greeks was 'geared to lasting, so the art of the present is geared toward becoming worn out', and this 'may happen in two different ways: through consignment of the artwork to fashion or through the work's refunctioning in politics'.[9] Another important piece with relevance to the theses in the Artwork essay is the one Benjamin wrote in November to December 1936, entitled 'Letters from Paris (2): Painting and Photography'.[10] It should be mentioned here that these short essays written in conjunction with the Artwork essay are all on the margin of *The Arcades Projects* and its two Exposés of 1935 and 1939, in which, as is well known, architecture of the city, urban culture, technology, politics and masses in the nineteenth century, among other topics, constitute major themes in Benjamin's investigations. These issues come to a culminating point in the Epilogue of the Artwork essay, on 'fascism' and 'communism', to which I come later.

Howard Caygill, who discuss Benjamin's Artwork essay at length, importantly points out that Benjamin, in departing from a discussion of André Gide, sees the

> achievement of fascist theory and practice of art to consist in bringing together 'the decadent theory of art with monumental practice'. The self-contained work of art for art's sake was fused with mass self-presentation into a 'monumental design', incarnating an aestheticized

philosophy of history and politics which froze history and made the present into an impenetrable work of art for mass contemplation.[11]

He continues by noting that

> The monumental fusion of aestheticism and self-presentation of the mass has two salient characteristics: first it monumentalized existing social relations, and second, it put the producers as much as the recipients under a spell in which they must appear to themselves as monumental, that is, as incapable of considered and independent action.

The crucial link in Benjamin's aesthetics and politics argument was supplied by technology, since for Benjamin fascism was a response to a crisis which was 'both social and technological'.[12] He cites Benjamin from his 'Letters from Paris': 'The development of productive forces which includes, besides the proletariat, technology, has led to a crisis which pushes towards the socialization of the means of production. This crisis is above all a function of technology'.[13]

Before I proceed further, I want to pause here and parenthetically remind ourselves that the twentieth century is marked by the appearance of two major *anti-fascist* pieces of writing. The first one is, of course, Benjamin's Artwork essay and the other is by Jacques Lacan in his famous 'The Mirror Stage as Formative of the I Function as Revealed in Psychoanalytical Experience', simply known as the 'Mirror Stage'.[14] Lacan attended the International Psychoanalytical Association's meeting in Marienbad in 1936 to present his paper. He was interrupted by Ernest Jones, the biographer of Freud, who was Chair of the session, before being able to finish reading his presentation. The next day Lacan took the train to go to Berlin to observe the Olympics being held under the Nazis.[15] His paper was later published in 1949. I do not have space here to go into as detailed an analysis of Lacan's article with its complex history as it deserves. Suffice it to say here that any psychoanalytical discussion of fascist ideology and mass politics must reckon with Lacan's 'Mirror Stage'. Recognizing the affinities between Lacan and Benjamin in this respect, Miriam Bratu Hansen points out that 'fascism has perfected a method of mobilizing the masses that at once paralyzes their practical, moral, and political judgement and provides a collective imaginary that would overcome the experience—individual as well as national—of fragmentation, loss and defeat', and thus 'the masses join their oppressors in "[Experiencing their] own destruction as a supreme aesthetic pleasure"'.[16] I can now resume reading Section XV of the Artwork essay where I left off.

I first take up the concept of 'Distraction'. The word is the translation of *Zerstreuung* in German, which also means 'entertainment'. Distraction and concentration, *Zerstreuung* and *Sammlung*, Benjamin tells us, form an antithesis. Formulating it, Benjamin importantly informs us that a 'person who concentrates before a work of art is absorbed by it; he enters into the work of art', which is like a Chinese painter who, according to legend, 'entered his complete painting while beholding it'.[17] 'By contrast', Benjamin continues, '*the distracted masses absorb the work of art into themselves*'[18] (emphasis mine). It is here that Benjamin enters the notion of 'building' to affirm the latter case of the 'distracted masses' absorbing the work of art, which he says is the most obvious. He crucially affirms, as cited above, that 'Architecture has always offered the prototype of an artwork that is received in a state of distraction and through the collective', further adding that 'The laws of Architecture's reception are highly instructive'.[19] Should we consider that many forms of art in the history of humanity have come into existence and then disappeared, architecture has persisted, because, as Benjamin asserts, and I repeat again, 'the human need for shelter is permanent'.[20] The history of building is longer than that of any other form of art and, as Benjamin claims, 'its effects ought to be recognized in any attempt to account for the relationship of the masses to the work of art'.[21] Benjamin comes to formulate his thesis on the modes of reception in architecture by making the following remarks:

> Buildings are received in a twofold manner: by use and by perception. Or, better: tactilely and optically. Such reception cannot be understood in terms of the concentrated attention of a traveler before a famous building. On the tactile side, there is no counterpart to what contemplation is on the optical side. Tactile reception comes about not so much by way of attention as by way of habit.[22]

Benjamin further argues that the latter, the mode of 'tactility', 'largely determines even the optical reception of architecture, which spontaneously takes the form of casual noticing, rather than attentive observation. Under certain circumstances, this form of reception shaped by architecture *acquires canonical value*'[23] (emphasis mine). This is followed by a crucial paragraph in which the notion of 'habit' is foregrounded. Benjamin writes:

For the task which faces the human apparatus of perception at historical turning points cannot be performed solely by optical means—that is, by way of contemplation. They are mastered gradually—taking their cue from tactile reception—through habit.[24]

In further reflections on what is facing the human sensory apparatus, that is, 'the ability to master certain tasks in a state of distraction', which proves that their 'performance has become habitual', Benjamin brings out the notion of 'apperception' and continues: 'The sort of distraction that is provided by art represents a covert measure of the extent to which it has become possible to perform new tasks of apperception'.[25] What is important to mention is that for film to perform this task, it must follow the model of architecture in order to be able to 'mobilize the masses'. Benjamin writes:

Reception in distraction—the sort of reception which is increasingly noticeable in all areas of art is a symptom of profound changes in apperception—finds in film its true training ground. Film, by virtue of its shock effects, is predisposed to this form of reception. It makes cult value recede into the background, not only because it encourages an evaluating attitude in the audience but also because, at the movies, the evaluating attitude requires no attention. The Audience is an examiner, but a distracted one.[26]

Caygill, who pays due attention to the distinction Benjamin draws between architecture and cinema, makes particular reference to the same Section XV in the Artwork essay, that in the first version had been titled 'Tactile and Optical Reception', and reminds us that Benjamin described the task of art in the epoch of technology to be one of reorientation 'with respect to a new condition of experience'. The model for this new condition and for the 'future art of the technological epoch', Caygill reminds us, 'is architecture, the art which responds most readily to changes in the structure of experience'.[27] This point had been established by Benjamin in a footnote to Section XV, where he sets up the architectural setting in relation to film for the experience of technology by deploying the same term 'apperception': 'Film is the art of form corresponding to the increased threat to life that faces people today. Humanity's need to expose itself to shock effects presents an adaptation to the dangers threatening it. Film corresponds to profound changes in the apparatus of apperception—changes that art experienced on the scale of private existence by the passerby in big-city traffic, and on a historical scale by every present-day citizen'.[28] Caygill points out that this aspect of film 'had already been anticipated by architecture, whose form cannot easily be separated from technique and which is for this reason close to the structure of technological experience'.[29] Here it is important to remember that 'all experience for Benjamin is technological, since the term technology designates the artificial organization of perception; as such, experience changes with the development of technology'.[30] Architecture, as a technological apparatus, is the prime locus of this organization of perception which changes the human sensorium. In this relation, as Caygill states, the experience of film fundamentally remains 'optical'. Although its cathartic effect is 'tactile', it nevertheless 'lacks the overwhelmingly tactile character of architecture'.[31] As we saw, on the basis of modern experience, Benjamin told us that the 'mass audience' does not enter into but rather 'absorbs the work of art'. This absorption can 'take place either through "inoculation" in the case of film, or, through "tactile appropriation" in the case of architecture'.[32] The key to the durability of architecture, therefore, does not only lie in its 'porosity' but resides in its 'canonical value' in a specific 'mode of appropriation', which is both 'tactile and optical':

> Architecture provides the main site for the interaction of technology and the human, a negotiation conducted in terms of touch and use. It is both a condition and object of experience, the speculative site for the emergence of the 'technological *physis*'.[33]

Caygill further writes that

> the speculative status of architecture for Benjamin is not defined in terms of transcendence, but in terms of porosity and flexibility. As the

locus of modern experience, architecture both establishes the parameters of perception in space and time while being itself subject to constant transformation.[34]

This is why Benjamin ends his Artwork essay by identifying architecture as, as Caygill puts it, 'concrete a priori', or an art form with 'canonical value'. In this respect, we must remember that architecture, the city, and urban masses were massively present not only in *The Arcades Project* but also in all of Benjamin's explorations on the city, from Naples to Berlin, from Moscow to Paris. As forms of possible experience they 'cast ambivalently as both promise and threat'.[35] As Gilloch in his *Myth and Metropolis* points out, photography and cinema provided models for 'the depiction of the urban complexes'. In fact, 'Benjamin exhorts writers to start taking photographs, and to deploy themselves "at important points in the sphere of imagery"'.[36]

In 'On Some Motifs in Baudelaire' Benjamin brings out the connection between the 'figure of shock' and 'contacts with urban masses' in Baudelaire's prose poem. He writes: 'For another, it tells us what is really meant by these masses. They do not stand for classes or any sort of collective; rather, they are nothing but the amorphous crowd of passers-by, the people in the street'.[37] Benjamin importantly notes that this amorphous crowd of which Baudelaire was always aware is not directly addressed, but rather, 'it is imprinted on his creativity as a hidden figure'.[38] As Miriam Bratu Hansen remarks, Benjamin registers the urban crowd in Baudelaire's poetry as a 'hidden figure' or 'moving veil' through which the urban shock is staged. Significantly, Hansen writes, 'As in Baudelaire, Benjamin sees the epochal turn towards the masses encoded in the architecture, fashions, events, and institutions of high-capitalist culture'.[39] Benjamin sees the phenomenon of the modern urban masses as manifesting the factor of reception and consumption of the commodity in capitalist-industrial society, and as a key factor of the empirical reality of the twentieth century in its ongoing political crisis. In a draft note for the Artwork essay Benjamin wrote: 'the mass reproduction of the artwork is not only related to the mass production of industrial goods but also to the mass reproduction of human attitudes and activities'.[40]

In Hansen's view,

> Whether we consider Benjamin's insight into an optically mediated tactility as a restoration of polarity of distance and nearness (which had been sundered into dichotomy earlier in the essay), or whether we extrapolate from it a model counter to the spiral of shock, anaesthetics, and aestheticization, suffice it to suggest that in view of the complexity of these questions and the political claims made for distraction seem indeed 'mild', if not inadequate.[41]

Acknowledging the 'progressive potential' that Benjamin ascribes to distraction as a habitual—and habituating—mode of attention, Hansen nevertheless believes that Benjamin

> retreats from the more far-reaching implications of an aesthetics of mediated tactility and instead resumes his earlier assumption of a testing, evaluating, quasi-expert disposition at work in cinematic representation and reception: 'the audience is an examiner, but a distracted one'.[42]

Hansen critically remarks that reading the Artwork essay, especially in its third version, 'reveals a culturally conservative strand in Benjamin's thinking, a segregation of the critical intellectual from the masses as object of formation', and further, 'More specifically, it gives us a sense of the conceptual cost incurred within Benjamin's own thinking by the tactical dichotomization of the term *aura* and *masses* with regard to the cinema'.[43] Hansen further brings up an important point:

> By conceiving of the relationship between cinema and masses primarily in terms of a structural affinity based in a nonauratic perceptual regime, and by muting the ambivalent and dialectical dimensions in his concept of masses, Benjamin ends up placing the cinema on the side of 'experiential poverty' (*Erfahrungsarmut*) and the 'new, positive concept of barbarism' he had espoused in his programmatic essay of 1933.[44]

In the next chapter I come to discuss this 'experiential poverty' in relation to architecture. For my part, I take a positive stand on this 'poverty of experience' in Benjamin.

Now I want to proceed to examine the final section, the 'Epilogue', in the third version of the Artwork essay. Benjamin's reflection on the problematic of the 'masses' comes to a turning point here. He begins the section with the following remarks bringing up the question of the 'proletariat':

> The increasing proletarianization of modern man and the increasing formation of masses are two sides of the same process. Fascism attempts to organize the newly proletarianized masses while leaving intact the property relations which they strive to abolish. It sees its salvation in granting expression to the masses—but on no account granting them rights.[45]

In the footnote for the above paragraph Benjamin explains that the technological factor is important with special reference to the 'newsreel' so effectively used for propaganda purposes. As he succinctly maintains: '*Mass reproduction is especially favored by the reproduction of the masses*. In great ceremonial procession, giant rallies, and mass sporting events, and in war, all of which are now fed into the camera, the masses come face to face with themselves. This process, whose significance need not be emphasized, is closely bound up with the development of reproduction and recording technology. In general, mass movements are more clearly apprehended by the camera than by the eye. A bird's eye view best captures assemblies of hundreds of thousands. And even when this perspective is no less accessible to the human eye than to the camera, the image formed by the eye cannot be enlarged in the same way as a photograph. This is to say that mass movements, including war, are a form of human behavior especially suited to the camera'.[46] Benjamin asserts that the masses have the 'right to change property relations', but 'fascism seeks to give *expression* in keeping these relations unchanged', and therefore, he concludes that '*The logical outcome of fascism is an aestheticizing of political life*'.[47] And, ominously, '*All efforts to aestheticize politics culminate in one point. That one point is war*'.[48] The Epilogue ends by stating that as Marinetti, the futurist, himself admits, fascism expects from war the 'artistic gratification of a sense perception altered by technology', which results in humankind becoming an object of its own contemplation, and hence 'Its self-alienation has reached the point where it can experience its own annihilation as a supreme aesthetic pleasure'.[49] And, famously, and as cited previously, Benjamin concludes in declaring that *'Such is the aestheticization of politics, as practiced by fascism. Communism replies by politicizing art'*.[50]

As I have already mentioned, Buck-Morss analyzed Benjamin's 'perplexing' declaration above under a dialectical term, 'anaesthetics and aestheticization', as Miriam Bratu Hansen notes, a dialectics in which technology is implicated, whether in industrial warfare, or rationalized labor, or urban living. In this regard, Hansen writes that in Benjamin's view the 'reception of technology had miscarried', mainly because the 'capitalist and imperialist exploitation of technology, in his rendition of the familiar Marxian argument, had turned this productive force from its potential as a "key to happiness" into a "fetish of doom"'.[51] These terms come from the essay Benjamin published in 1930 on 'Theories of German Fascism' devoted to a critical review of the collection of essays on *War and Warriors* edited by Ernst Jünger.[52] There Benjamin wrote that 'one might say that the harshest, most disastrous aspects of imperialist war are in part the result of the gaping discrepancy between the gigantic means of technology and the minuscule moral illumination it affords', and further added that 'Indeed, according to its economic nature, bourgeois society cannot help insulating everything technological as much as possible from the so-called spiritual [*Geistigen*], and it cannot help resolutely excluding technology's right of determination in the social order. Any further war will also be a slave revolt on the part of technology'.[53]

Going back to the technological dimension of 'anaesthetization', Benjamin, like Georg Simmel and other theorists of modernity,

> was interested in the nexus between the numbing of the sensorium in defense against technologically caused shock and the emergence of ever more powerful aesthetic technique, thrills, and sensations in the nineteenth-century industries of entertainment and displays (world exhibitions, panoramas, and viewing/moving machines)—the phantasmagoria of the nineteenth century he explored in *The Arcades Project*.[54]

As Hansen importantly notes, 'By the 1930s, this dialectics of anaesthetics and aestheticization had impaired human faculties of experience, affects, and cognition on a mass scale, thereby paralyzing political agency and the collective ability to prevent the deployment of technology toward self-destructive ends'.[55]

I will later come back again to the last sentence of Benjamin in his Artwork essay to take up the question of 'fascism' and 'communism'.

Notes

1. In 'Theory of Distraction', in *Walter Benjamin, Selected Writings, Volume 3, 1935–1938*, trans. Edmund Jephcott and others, eds Howard Eiland and Michael W. Jennings (Cambridge: The Belknap Press of Harvard University Press, 2002), 142.
2. Walter Benjamin, 'The Work of Art in the Age of Its Technological Reproducibility', Third Version, in *Walter Benjamin, Selected Writings, Volume 4, 1938–1940*, trans. Edmund Jephcott and others, eds Howard Eiland and Michael W. Jennings (Cambridge: The Belknap Press of Harvard University Press, 2003), 268.
3. Graeme Gilloch, *Siegfried Kracauer* (Cambridge: Polity, 2015), 86.
4. Graeme Gilloch, *Siegfried Kracauer*, 200. The 'unconscious' manifests itself in the category of 'phantasmagoria'. As Gilloch points out, the dreamlike quality of film

    > returns us for the last time to the notion of phantasmagoria. For all his emphasis in *Theory of Film* on 'Camera reality', Kracauer was under no illusion as to the illusory character of film. If film disenchants modernity it does so not because it is inimical to the phantasmagoria of the city but rather because it is part of enchantment itself. Film *is* phantasmagoric. Film is the ultimate phantasmagoria of modernity—this insight is surely what lies at the heart of Kracauer's fascination with the medium.
    >
    > 200

    For more on the notion of phantasmagoria see Libero Andreotti and Nadir Lahiji, *The Architecture of Phantasmagoria: Specters of the City* (Abingdon: Routledge, 2017).
5. Walter Benjamin, 'The Work of Art in the Age of Its Technical Reproducibility', Third Version, 264.
6. Walter Benjamin, 'The Work of Art in the Age of Its Technical Reproducibility', Third Version, 264.
7. These sections correspond to Sections XVIII and XIV in the Second Version, respectively. See 'The Work of Art in the Age of Its Technical Reproducibility', Second Version, in *Walter Benjamin, Selected Writings, Volume 3, 1935–1938*, trans. Edmund Jephcott and others, eds Howard Eiland and Michael W. Jennings (Cambridge: The Belknap Press of Harvard University Press, 2002).
8. Walter Benjamin, 'Theory of Distraction', 141.
9. Walter Benjamin, 'Theory of Distraction', 142. As the editors of Volume 3 of Benjamin's writings explain, the term 'Refunctioning' translates *Umfunktionierung*, 'a term taken from Brecht', 142.
10. Walter Benjamin, 'Letters from Paris (2)', in *Walter Benjamin, Selected Writings, Volume 3, 1935–1938*, trans. Edmund Jephcott and others, eds Howard Eiland and Michael W. Jennings (Cambridge: The Belknap Press of Harvard University Press, 2002).

11 See Howard Caygill, *Walter Benjamin: The Color of Experience* (London and New York: Routledge, 1998), 96.
12 Howard Caygill, *Walter Benjamin*, 96–97.
13 Quoted in Howard Caygill, *Walter Benjamin*, 97.
14 See Jacques Lacan, 'The Mirror Stage as Formative of the *I* Function as Revealed in Psychoanalytical Experience', in *Écrits: The First Complete Edition in English*, trans. Bruce Fink (New York and London: W. W. Norton, 2002, 2006). Other commentators have also noted the relationship that can be established between the two, including Susan Buck-Morss in her 'Aesthetics and Anaesthetics: Walter Benjamin's Artwork Essay Reconsidered', in *October*, 62 (Autumn 1992), and Miriam Bratu Hansen in her *Cinema and Experience: Siegfried Kracauer, Walter Benjamin, and Theodor W. Adorno* (Berkeley: University of California Press, 2012).
15 For more on this see David Macy, *Lacan in Context* (New York: Verso, 1988).
16 Miriam Bratu Hansen in her *Cinema and Experience*, 99.
17 Walter Benjamin, 'The Work of Art in the Age of Its Technical Reproducibility', Third Version, 268.
18 Walter Benjamin, 'The Work of Art in the Age of Its Technical Reproducibility', Third Version, 268.
19 Walter Benjamin, 'The Work of Art in the Age of Its Technical Reproducibility', Third Version, 268.
20 Walter Benjamin, 'The Work of Art in the Age of Its Technical Reproducibility', Third Version, 268.
21 Walter Benjamin, 'The Work of Art in the Age of Its Technical Reproducibility', Third Version, 268.
22 Walter Benjamin, 'The Work of Art in the Age of Its Technical Reproducibility', Third Version, 268.
23 Walter Benjamin, 'The Work of Art in the Age of Its Technical Reproducibility', Third Version, 268.
24 Walter Benjamin, 'The Work of Art in the Age of Its Technical Reproducibility', Third Version, 268. He quickly adds that 'Even the distracted person can form habit'. Here I suggest that the notion of 'habit' corresponding to 'tactility' in the last phrase above should be given an analysis to endow it with a new meaning beyond its employment in Benjamin.
25 Walter Benjamin, 'The Work of Art in the Age of Its Technical Reproducibility', Third Version, 268.
26 Walter Benjamin, 'The Work of Art in the Age of Its Technical Reproducibility', Third Version, 269.
27 In Howard Caygill, *Walter Benjamin*, 114.
28 Walter Benjamin, 'The Work of Art in the Age of Its Technical Reproducibility', Third Version, 281, n. 42.
29 Howard Caygill, *Walter Benjamin*, 115.
30 Howard Caygill, *Walter Benjamin*, 96.
31 Howard Caygill, *Walter Benjamin*, 115.
32 Howard Caygill, *Walter Benjamin*, 115.

33 Howard Caygill, *Walter Benjamin*, 116.
34 Howard Caygill, *Walter Benjamin*, 116.
35 Howard Caygill, *Walter Benjamin*, 116.
36 See Graeme Gilloch, *Myth and Metropolis: Walter Benjamin and the City* (Cambridge: Polity Press, 1996), 18. Gilloch aptly observes that 'It is film, however, which is most important for Benjamin in this visualization of urban environment. He notes that "only film commands optical approaches to the essence of the city"', 18.
37 See Walter Benjamin, 'On Some Motifs in Baudelaire', in *Walter Benjamin, Selected Writings, Volume 4, 1938–1940*, trans. Edmund Jephcott and others, eds Howard Eiland and Michael W. Jennings (Cambridge: The Belknap Press of Harvard University Press, 2003), 320–321.
38 Walter Benjamin, 'On Some Motifs in Baudelaire', 321.
39 Miriam Bratu Hansen, *Cinema and Experience*, 95.
40 Quoted in Miriam Bratu Hansen, *Cinema and Experience*, 95.
41 Miriam Bratu Hansen, *Cinema and Experience*, 101.
42 Miriam Bratu Hansen, *Cinema and Experience*, 101–102. Hansen writes that

> the emphasis on the critical, testing function of distraction overshadows the elements of play and humor that Benjamin had considered key to film's political task of redressing the pathological imbalance between human and technology in the essay's earlier versions—key precisely to the imperative of diffusing and disarming destructive forms of intoxication within the masses.

She further remarks that

> an even greater inconsistency, if not antinomy, within Benjamin's politics of distraction opens up in relation to the 1935 exposé for the Arcades Project, 'Paris, the Capital of the Nineteenth Century'. In the section on world expositions, distraction is explicitly linked to the Marxian category of self-alienation. Here the etiology of self-alienation is less the technologically altered sense perception (as in the artwork essay) than a Lukácsian logic of reification. The nineteenth-century world exhibitions, with their enthronement of the commodity, inaugurate 'a phantasmagoria which the human being enters in order to be distracted. The entertainment industry facilitates this by elevating [the spectator] to the level of commodity. He surrenders to its manipulations while enjoying his alienation from himself and others'. In this context, capitalist mass culture, rather than the fascist spectacle of mass destruction, provides the dystopian vanishing point of self-alienation.
>
> 102–103

43 Miriam Bratu Hansen, *Cinema and Experience*, 103.
44 Miriam Bratu Hansen, *Cinema and Experience*, 103. Hansen continues her critical remarks pointing out that

the liquidationist agenda makes the distinction between *Bild* (auratic, aesthetic image) *and Abbild* (copy, facsimile, reproduction) congeal into an opposition. Relegated to the latter side of that opposition, a politically progressive cinema would thus offer a training ground for an enlightened barbarism, rather than—as in the second version—a medium for a new kind of mimetic experience, a '*Spiel-Raum*' or room-for-play for trying out an alternative innervation of technology. With the undialectical surrender of the auratic image in favor of reproduction, it could be argued, Benjamin denies the masses the possibility of aesthetic experience, in whatever form or medium (and thus, like the communist cultural politics he opposed, risks leaving sensory-affective needs to be exploited by the right). At the same time, the liquidationist gesture disavows a crucial impulse of his own thinking—his lifelong concern with the fate of experience in the age of its declining transmissibility, a concern in which the concept of the aura plays a central if precarious part.

103

45 Walter Benjamin, 'The Work of Art in the Age of Its Technical Reproducibility', Third Version, 269.
46 Walter Benjamin, 'The Work of Art in the Age of Its Technical Reproducibility', Third Version, 282, n. 47.
47 Walter Benjamin, 'The Work of Art in the Age of Its Technical Reproducibility', Third Version, 269.
48 Walter Benjamin, 'The Work of Art in the Age of Its Technical Reproducibility', Third Version, 269.
49 Walter Benjamin, 'The Work of Art in the Age of Its Technical Reproducibility', Third Version, 270.
50 Walter Benjamin, 'The Work of Art in the Age of Its Technical Reproducibility', Third Version, 270.
51 Miriam Bratu Hansen, *Cinema and Experience*, 79.
52 See Walter Benjamin, 'Theories of German Fascism', in *Walter Benjamin, Selected Writings, 1927–1934*, trans. Rodney Livingston and others, eds Michael W. Jennings, Howard Eiland, and Gary Smith (Cambridge: The Belknap Press of Harvard University Press, 1999).
53 Walter Benjamin, 'Theories of German Fascism', 312.
54 Miriam Bratu Hansen, *Cinema and Experience*, 79–80.
55 Miriam Bratu Hansen, *Cinema and Experience*, 80.

Chapter 6

Poverty of experience

> Barbarism? Yes, indeed. We say this in order to introduce a new, positive concept of barbarism.
>
> —Walter Benjamin[1]

As we are reminded, *modernity* impoverished *experience*. Benjamin called for 'owning up to it'.

Not only that, as John McCole informs us, he radically professed it.[2] Benjamin penned a short text entitled 'Experience and Poverty' in 1933 on the eve of his departure from Nazi Germany for Prague. By departing his homeland, Benjamin refused the conventional claim 'to have brought the heritage of the "good German" with him into exile as part of his cultural baggage'.[3] For Benjamin, McCole writes, 'The order of the day was rather to collaborate in the work of destruction' and, in anticipating the charge against it, he defiantly embraced the term 'Barbarism': 'Yes, indeed'—the 'good kind'—the 'new, positive' barbarism.[4] As McCole explains, the programmatic statements in 'Experience and Poverty' represent 'an abiding liquidationist moment in Benjamin's thinking'.[5] Rather than being a 'personal idiosyncrasy' in Benjamin, they are attempts to 'steal the idea of decline of experience from cultural conservatives, the energies of barbarism from the fascists, and to reverse the conventional valuation of creativity and destruction'.[6] Underlying Benjamin's thinking at this period was a new theory of technology to which we will come later.

Benjamin asked: 'For what does poverty of experience do for the barbarians?'[7] His answer goes as follows:

> It forces him to start from scratch; to make a new start; to make a little go a long way; to begin with a little and build up further, looking neither left nor right. Among the great creative spirits, there have always been the inexorable ones who begin by clearing a tabula rasa. They need a drawing table; they were constructors. Such a constructor was Descartes, who required nothing more to launch his entire philosophy than the single certitude, 'I think, therefore I am'. And he went on from there.[8]

The crux of Benjamin's statement is this: Let us '*begin from the beginning*'. And this would bring Benjamin surprisingly close to what Lenin once said. In 1922, after winning the Civil War, Lenin wrote a short piece entitled 'On Ascending a High Mountain'. He wrote,

> Communists who have no illusions, who do not give way to despondency, and who preserve their strength and flexibility 'to begin from the beginning' over and over again in approaching an extremely difficult task, are not doomed (and in all probability will not perish).[9]

Slavoj Žižek argues that this is Lenin at his 'Beckettian best'. It has echoes of *Worstward Ho*: 'Try again. Fail again. Fail better'.[10] Lenin here is not advocating, as Žižek tells us,

> slowing down progress in order to fortify what has already been achieved, but rather, of *descending back to the starting* point: One should 'begin from the beginning', not from the peak one may successfully have reached in the previous effort. In Kierkegaard's terms, a revolutionary process is not a gradual progress, but a repetitive movement, a movement of *repeating the beginning* again and again.[11]

For Benjamin, this 'begin from the beginning' amounted to a defense of a 'new, positive barbarism' *against* the fascist barbarism. For us, it must be a 'movement of *repeating the beginning*'. I claim that we must own up to 'Benjamin's owning up to the poverty of experience'. We must not only profess but *repeat modernity*. Against the doxa of 'postmodernity', we must not mourn the poverty of experience in this modernity. Benjamin said: 'our poverty of experience is not merely poverty on the personal level, but poverty of human experience in general. Hence a new kind of barbarism'.[12] We must, once again, become a *'constructor'* of this 'new kind of barbarism'.

In 'Experience and Poverty' Benjamin famously favored architectural manifestations of this 'positive barbarism' in the work of avant-garde architects. For him architecture at this time not only expressed this new structure of experience [*Erfahrung*] but directly affirmed it and contributed to it.[13] He aligned Bertolt Brecht with Adolf Loos. The former said that 'Communism is the just distribution of poverty, not of wealth', and the latter stated that 'I write only for people who possess a modern sensibility ...'[14] Through Sigfried Giedion and Adolf Behn, Benjamin came to learn about the new materials of iron and glass and the rationality of the building industry in the nineteenth century. He particularly read Giedion's *Bauen in Frankreich*, later translated as *Building in France*,[15] with enthusiasm and learned from it about 'transparency' in the work of Le Corbusier dissolving the hard distinction between the inside and the outside. He appreciated the Bauhaus Building and admired the Dutch architect J.-J. P. Oud. He saw them as 'the naked man of the contemporary world who lies screaming like a newborn babe in the dirty diapers of the present'[16]. Paul Scheerbart exemplified the figure who 'greeted this present' and whose 'dream of glass building' Benjamin came to appreciate: 'Do people like Scheerbart dream of glass building because they are spokesmen of a new poverty?', he asked. Affirmatively he declared: 'Objects made of glass have no "aura"'.[17] Living in a 'glass house' is not just 'revolutionary virtue' but a way of life. But this way of life did not become widespread for a collective life as had been expected. Far from it. The idea of the 'glass house' as a model of technological revolution that would transform the collective mode of perception was rather reserved for a private bourgeois client and was famously designed and built by the architect Mies van der Rohe in an excess of aestheticism in the middle of the twentieth century. This was a case in which Scheerbart's 'utopia' would descend into 'reality'. Alas, technical revolution in building, that in Benjamin's mind was supposed to abolish the generalized private life, as he had observed in his trip to Moscow, was bound never to materialize.

Benjamin came into contact with avant-garde artists and architects from different countries who would gather in Berlin and meet regularly. He frequented the meetings of the group that between 1923 and 1926 published the famous journal *G. Material zur elementaren Gestaltung* (material for elementary shaping, forming, or construction) that was founded by Hans Richter. This group included, among others, Mies van der Rohe, Ludwig Hilberseimer, El Lissitzky, Naum Gabo, Theo van Doesburg, Raoul Hausmann, Hans Arp, Tristan Tzara, Adolf Behn, and Benjamin's wife, Dora Sophie Pollak. As Hansen informs us, the journal published articles on a wide range of topics, including 'industrial architecture and design, urban planning, recording technology, film, photography, theater, poetry, painting and fashion'.[18] It is noteworthy to mention that Benjamin praised the photographer László Moholy-Nagy, who was briefly a member of G group, in a review article and quoted the photographer as having said that 'It is not the person ignorant of writing but the one ignorant of photography who will be the illiterate of the future'.[19]

Benjamin liked Brecht's 'neat phrase' that would instruct: 'Erase the traces!' We must not leave any traces. Glass does not leave any traces. And, for that matter, we have nothing to do with stuffy bourgeois private *intérieurs*. There is absolutely no sense in vainly attempting a redemptive idea of a 'unified experience'. We must rather live this 'crisis of experience'. As noted by Miriam Bratu Hansen, reflecting on the antinomic structure of Benjamin's thinking and his thesis in 'Experience and Poverty', Benjamin, turning his back on 'decaying aura, the medium of beautiful semblance that cannot be salvaged anyway', espoused the 'new, positive barbarism' which is consistent with the 'vernacular' of *Neue Sachlichkeit* or New Objectivity.[20] Interesting in this relation is Benjamin's characterization of aura as *ornament*, as Hansen notes. She comments that 'The characterization of aura as ornament or ornamental halo may sound odd in light of Benjamin's concurrent endorsement of Neue Sachlichkeit (New Objectivity), including Adolf Loos and his famous attack on ornament in architecture and design', and she then notes that 'However, the term names an important epistemological trope in other contexts'.[21] The notion of ornament, she notes, is associated with the writing of Kracauer. The latter, interestingly enough, rejected the 'tabula rasa mentality', which came to be associated with the 'hegemonic modernity', as Hansen tells us. Unlike his friend Benjamin, Kracauer 'remained skeptical throughout of aesthetic efforts to ground visions of social change in the model of technology, in particular as elaborated by the functionalist school of modern architecture'.[22] Hansen writes:

> The 'culture of glass', that Benjamin so desperately welcomed as the deathblow to bourgeois culture (and attendant concepts of 'interiority', 'trace', 'experience', 'aura') leaves Kracauer, an architect by training, filled with 'scurrilous grief' over the historical-political impasse that prevents the construction of housing responsive to human needs.[23]

Kracauer thus countered the functionalist school against ornament, and, in a manner consistent with his idea of 'mass ornament', showed how the 'repressed ornament returns in the very aesthetics of technology that ordains the mass spectacle of chorus lines, sport events, and party rallies'.[24] But Kracauer missed the element of the technological 'unconscious' in building construction with no ornament that Benjamin had learned from Giedion. In *The Arcades Project*, Benjamin affirmatively cites Giedion as saying 'In the nineteenth century construction plays the role of the subconscious', to which Benjamin adds, 'Wouldn't it be better to say "the role of bodily process"—around which "artistic" architectures gather, like dreams around the framework of physiological processes'.[25] We should here replace Giedion's term 'the subconscious' by the correct term, 'the unconscious'. As McCole puts it, the nineteenth-century glass and iron construction buried under ornamental motifs 'played the role of a repressed unconscious'.[26] The space experienced through building collectively, that is, *unconsciously*, 'would become Benjamin's model for other forms of aesthetic reception, including film'.[27] As McCole perceptively observes,

> 'As if out of fear', however, nineteenth-century architects had felt compelled to disguise their forward-looking constructions in 'historicizing masks', ornamental embellishments drawn from the styles of past eras. Giedion interpreted this fear as the reflex of a more general social process: the 'collective apparatus of industry' had unleashed vast new productive forces, but the benefits had been diverted for the consumption of only a few. His reading of modern architectural history gave substance to Benjamin's intuitive sense that technology anticipated new collective needs, and his plea against the distortion of construction by

historicist embellishment resonated with Benjamin's avowal of parsimony demanded by the new poverty of experience.[28]

McCole rightly observes that 'What Benjamin saw in the architectural avant-garde, then, was not a model of rationalization and efficiency but the constructive anticipation of a form of social practice that breaks with bourgeoise society'.[29]

In the center of 'poverty of experience', we must note, is a special conception of technology and its social control. In 'One-Way Street', published in 1928, the final section is entitled 'To the Planetarium'. There Benjamin wrote: 'But because the lust for profit of the ruling class sought satisfaction through it, technology betrayed man and turned the bridal bed into a bloodbath'.[30] He rails against the 'imperialists' for whom the 'mastery of nature' is the sole purpose of technology. Benjamin further wrote:

> technology is the mastery not of nature but of the relation between nature and man. Men as a species completed their development thousands of years ago; but mankind as a species is just beginning his. In technology, a *physis* is being organized through which mankind's contact with the cosmos takes a new and different form from that which it had in nations and families.[31]

Towards the end of 'One-Way Street' Benjamin reminds us of the 'nights of annihilation of the last war' and the 'revolt that followed it' by which mankind first attempted to 'bring the new body under its control'. He ends by saying: 'The power of the proletariat is the measure of its convalescence. If it is not gripped to the very marrow by the discipline of this power, no pacifist polemics will save it'.[32] Thus the problem for Benjamin was the capitalist *misuse* of technology. Technology was fundamentally to be understood as the balance and regulation in the 'interchange between humankind and nature'.[33] Benjamin put the problem in the Marxist terms that 'technology's vast potential is fettered by the existing relation of production', and the agent who would correct this misuse is the proletariat.[34] The problem thus is not with technology itself, it is not by itself bound with domination, but rather, 'the misbegotten reception of technology'.[35]

In the years before 1933, Benjamin had broadened his earlier concept of *Technik* and brought it to the center of his thinking about technology. The German word *Technik* covers both 'technique' and 'technology' in English.[36] Discussing this distinction, Hansen reflects that the German words *Technik* and *Technologie* do not correspond to the English terms of *technique* and *technology*—that is, 'If we take the former to refer to artistic mastery of the formal aspects of a work, or any artisanal method and skill, and the latter to denote an ensemble of mechanical and industrial tools and procedures'.[37] She adds that in both languages *technology* 'retains its distinction as the "branch of knowledge" that comprises individual techniques. But the German word *Technik* far exceeds the term technique; it refers to both artistic and extra-artistic, industrial and preindustrial practice'.[38]

Equipped with this notion of *Technik* and facing the ideology of technology in his time, and witnessing the Left putting too much faith into the affirmation of technology with its fascination in machines, Taylorism and Fordism, a naïve faith in rationalization and efficiency that ended up espousing the industrial capitalism, Benjamin adopted an *antinomic* stance distinguishing himself from reactionary modernism and simple faith in rationalization and progress. He sought, as McCole aptly puts it, what may be called the 'paradox of antiinstrumental affirmation of technology'.[39]

In conclusion we return to 'Experience and Poverty'. Benjamin wrote there:

> Poverty of experience. This should not be understood to mean that people are yearning for new experience. No, they long to free themselves from experience; they long for a world in which they can make such pure and decided use of their poverty—their outer poverty, and ultimately also their inner poverty—that it will lead to something respectable.[40]

Notes

1 Walter Benjamin, 'Experience and Poverty', in *Walter Benjamin, Selected Writings, Volume 2, 1927–1934*, trans. Rodney Livingstone and others, ed. Michael W. Jennings, Howard Eiland, and Gary Smith (Cambridge: The Belknap Press of Harvard University Press, 1999), 732.

2. See John McCole, *Walter Benjamin and the Antinomies of Tradition* (Ithaca: Cornell University Press, 1993), 156. For much of my exploration in this chapter I am indebted to this book, especially the excellent 'Chapter Four: Owning up to the Poverty of Experience: Benjamin and Weimar Modernism'.
3. John McCole, *Walter Benjamin and the Antinomies of Tradition*, 156. McCole quotes Benjamin: 'For who can seriously assume that humanity will ever get across the narrow pass that lies before it if burdened with the baggage of a collector or an antique dealer?', 156.
4. John McCole, *Walter Benjamin and the Antinomies of Tradition*, 156.
5. John McCole, *Walter Benjamin and the Antinomies of Tradition*, 157.
6. John McCole, *Walter Benjamin and the Antinomies of Tradition*, 157.
7. Walter Benjamin, 'Experience and Poverty', 732.
8. Walter Benjamin, 'Experience and Poverty', 732. Benjamin goes on to say,

   > Einstein, too was, such a constructor; he was not interested in anything in the whole wide world of physics except a minute discrepancy between Newton's equation and the observation of astronomy. And this same insistence on starting from the very beginning also marks artists when they followed the example of mathematicians and built the world from stereometric forms, like the Cubists, or modeled themselves on engineers, like Klee.
   >
   > 732–733

9. Quoted in Slavoj Žižek, 'How to Begin from the Beginning', in *The Idea of Communism*, eds Costas Douzinas and Slavoj Žižek (London and New York: Verso, 2010), 210. Also see V. I. Lenin, 'Notes of a Publicist: On Ascending a High Mountain ...', in *Collected Works*, vol. 33 (Moscow: Progress Publishers, 1965), 204–211.
10. Slavoj Žižek, 'How to Begin from the Beginning', 210.
11. Slavoj Žižek, 'How to Begin from the Beginning', 210.
12. Walter Benjamin, 'Experience and Poverty', 732.
13. See Howard Caygill, *Walter Benjamin: The Color of Experience* (London and New York, 1998).
14. Walter Benjamin, 'Experience and Poverty', 733.
15. Sigfried Giedion, *Building in France: Building in Iron, Building in Ferroconcrete*, trans. J. Duncan Berry (Los Angeles: The Getty Center for the History of Art, 1995). Benjamin had cited Giedion's book and quoted him extensively in *The Arcades Project*, trans. Howard Eiland and Kevin McLaughlin (Cambridge and London: The Belknap Press of Harvard University Press, 1999).
16. Walter Benjamin, 'Experience and Poverty', 733.
17. Walter Benjamin, 'Experience and Poverty', 234.
18. See Miriam Bratu Hansen, *Cinema and Experience: Siegfried Kracauer, Walter Benjamin, and Theodor W. Adorno* (Berkeley: University of California Press, 2012), 134.
19. Quoted in Miriam Bratu Hansen, *Cinema and Experience*, 134.
20. See Miriam Bratu Hansen, *Cinema and Experience*, 81.

21　Miriam Bratu Hansen, *Cinema and Experience*, 120.
22　Miriam Bratu Hansen, *Cinema and Experience*, 67.
23　Miriam Bratu Hansen, *Cinema and Experience*, 67.
24　Miriam Bratu Hansen, *Cinema and Experience*, 67. Hansen furthermore notes that Kracauer criticized the 'Bauhaus style of *Neue Sachlichkeit* in the Berlin entertainment malls and picture palaces for its secret complicity with the business of distraction and social repression of the fear of ageing and death', 67.
25　Walter Benjamin, *The Arcades Project*, 391 [K1a, 7].
26　John McCole, *Walter Benjamin and the Antinomies of Tradition*, 193.
27　John McCole, *Walter Benjamin and the Antinomies of Tradition*, 193.
28　John McCole, *Walter Benjamin and the Antinomies of Tradition*, 185.
29　John McCole, *Walter Benjamin and the Antinomies of Tradition*, 185. McCole echoes the concerns of Kracauer by noting that

> But if the motif he prized in Giedion and Loos were undoubtedly central to the avant-garde movement, other elements were curiously absent. Perhaps the most striking omission was the movement for settlement architecture, or *Siedlungsbau*, which designed and built innovative modernist housing for low-income families on the fringes of major cities. Benjamin could hardly have overlooked this, since Frankfurt am Main was one of the most active centers for such work in the 1920s.
>
> 　　　　　　　　　　　　　　　　　　　　　　　　　　　　　　185

30　See Walter Benjamin, 'One-Way Street', in *Walter Benjamin, Selected Writings, Volume 1, 1913–1926*, eds Marcus Bullock and Michael Jennings (Cambridge: The Belknap Press of Harvard University Press, 1996), 487.
31　Walter Benjamin, 'One-Way Street', 487.
32　Walter Benjamin, 'One-Way Street', 487.
33　John McCole, *Walter Benjamin and the Antinomies of Tradition*, 186–187.
34　John McCole, *Walter Benjamin and the Antinomies of Tradition*, 187.
35　Quoted in John McCole, *Walter Benjamin and the Antinomies of Tradition*, 188.
36　See John McCole, *Walter Benjamin and the Antinomies of Tradition*; also see Miriam Bratu Hansen, *Cinema and Experience*. For my reflection on the concept of 'technology' in Benjamin here I heavily rely on the insights of these two authors.
37　In Miriam Bratu Hansen, *Cinema and Experience*, 211. Hansen discusses this distinction extensively in the section of her book on Adorno that I do not need to enter in this work.
38　Miriam Bratu Hansen, *Cinema and Experience*, 211. Hansen adds, 'Thus, throughout *Dialectic of Enlightenment* [by Max Horkheimer and Theodor Adorno] the term *Technik* denotes the principles and means of controlling nature, be they industrial-capitalist, artisanal, or archaic-magical', 211. Suffice it to say here that this notion would come close to Benjamin's own conception of *Technik*.
39　John McCole, *Walter Benjamin and the Antinomies of Tradition*, 182.
40　Walter Benjamin, 'Experience and Poverty', 734.

Chapter 7

Dialectics and mass art

> In 'mass art' you have the paradoxical relationship between a purely democratic element and a historically aristocratic element.
> —Alain Badiou, 'Cinema as Philosophical Experimentation'[1]

> So the question of art today is a question of political emancipation. There is something political in art itself.
> —Alain Badiou, 'Fifteen Theses on Contemporary Art'[2]

Cinema, according to Badiou, is nothing but the art of 'cut', 'shot', and 'take', and, of course, 'montage'. The former categories lead us specifically to the philosophical principle of 'scission' and its process. 'Scission', taken as an ontological-dialectical principle, is a 'fundamental split'. We are, therefore, in Hegelian territory standing on the ground of 'dialectics'. This is why Badiou can argue that cinema has the quality of 'dialectics because it is an art of contradiction'. It is in this domain that Badiou could go so far as to provocatively proclaim: 'philosophy *as* cinema'. In this chapter, I want to examine the idea of *dialectic* in 'mass art', for which we necessarily need to discuss Badiou's *materialist* intervention into Hegelian dialectics. But before I come to it, I want briefly to examine again the term 'mass art'.

As we saw in previous chapters, central to Badiou's argument is that 'mass art' is a paradoxical term; that is, 'art' is *aristocratic* and 'mass' is *political* and democratic. And further, cinema, as mass art, is an '*impure*' art. There is a *non-art* of art in cinema. In his *Handbook of Inaesthetics*, Badiou talks about 'the element of an incurable impurity' in cinema.[3] Further, 'Cinema is an impure art. Indeed, it is the "plus-one" of the arts, both parasitic and inconsistent'.[4] Later I will come to the specific meaning of the term 'Inaesthetics'. In his *Infinite Thought*, in the chapter on 'Philosophy and Cinema', Badiou says that 'cinema is a place of intrinsic indiscernibility between art and non-art', and that cinema 'always bears absolutely impure elements within it, drawn from ambient imagery, from the detritus of other arts, and from conventions with a limited shelf life'.[5]

Alex Ling in his *Badiou and Cinema* incisively expands on the main categories and concepts in Badiou, complementing them with his analysis, which it would be instructive to reiterate here.[6] In a key chapter labeled 'The Castle of Impurity', Ling offers a summary of 'fifteen theses'. I only mention those that I am concerned with here, which, in abbreviated forms, go as follows: 1. *Cinema as an inessential art*. 'Cinema has no essence'. It is 'immaterial', 'in that it has no base material that is its and its alone'.[7] 2. *Cinema as a superficial art*. It is an art of surfaces, of appearances. 3. *Cinema as a subtractive art*. The term 'subtractive' in Badiou's philosophy has a special meaning. Here it is taken to mean the determination of 'cinema's power to lie in the dis-appearances of space, in the subtractive movement which directs image towards the void'.[8] 4. *Cinema as an onto-logical art*. Cinema is an art that illustrates best 'being' and 'appearance'. 5. *Cinema as an unexpected art*. Cinema is not meant to be '*artistic*'; If cinema, as Badiou says, is indeed a 'Saturday night art', 'then this is equally a "great democratic advantage"', namely that, as Badiou puts it, 'you can go there on a Saturday evening to rest and rise unexpectedly'.[9] 6. *Cinema as an impure art*. This thesis, as we have seen, is central to Badiou's cinematographic writings. In its confirmation, Ling cites André Bazin as having said, against film's 'puritan detractors', that 'to be annoyed by this is as ridiculous as to condemn the opera on behalf of theatre and music'.[10] 7. *All the arts are impure*. Ling writes: 'While cinema is doubtless an absolutely impure art, this in no way means that the other arts are by contrast "pure"'.[11] He affirmatively cites Jacques Rancière, who 'substitutes his own "aesthetic regime of art" for the 'incoherent label "modernity"'.[12] He goes on to say that even the most 'modern' of 'modernist works would appear to be hopelessly complicated with non-art'.[13] One of Marcel Duchamp's 'readymades', famously the 1917 *Fountain*, is an exemplary case, which clearly demonstrates an 'indiscernibility between art and non-art, an acknowledgement that the very material of art is first and foremost non-artistic'.[14] This is why, as Ling reminds us, and as we have seen before, Badiou can hold that 'the real of art comprises an ideal impurity as the immanent process of its purification'.[15] 8. *Nothing is pure.* This thesis goes back to Badiou's Platonic philosophy regarding the question of 'truth' as 'pure impurity'. This is too complicated to get to here. 9. *Cinema is the most impure of the arts.* Ling writes that 'it is from its absolute impurity that film derives both its power and its purpose. In a word, the generic address of the other arts loses out to cinema for the simple fact that *they are not impure enough*'.[16] 10. *Cinema is a mass art.* This is the central thesis I have been most concerned with, which goes back to the division between 'aristocratic' and 'democratic' elements. As Ling puts it, while the arts in general are

> inescapably tied to what Badiou designates a 'proletarian aristocratism'—namely, 'an aristocratism exposed to the judgment of all', absolutely indifferent to its 'clientele'—only cinema constitutes a truly 'mass art', at once aristocratic and proletarian, obstinate and universal, *which can and must take its public into consideration*.[17]

'Moreover', he adds, 'cinema's being a *mass* art equally necessitates a certain political responsibility. Simply, cinema must never forget its obligation to the masses'.[18] Here I quote Ling's conclusion in full:

> To conclude on a polemical note, we cannot help but observe that the contemporary films that really live up to their political responsibility—such as the work of Udi Aloni or Abbas Kiarostami (to take but two examples singled out by Badiou)—paradoxically do not carry with them the mass appeal that less immediately political films do (just as truly artistic films do not find the mass audience they deserve while 'popular' films almost invariably neglect their political responsibilities). Thus our one and only cinematic prescription: cinema must truly become, not only in address but also in form, a *mass art*, an art of and for the masses. For, politically (as much as artistically) speaking, it is only in really embracing its democratic nature that cinema might live up to its true potential.[19]

At the end of his book, Ling says: 'This cinema—*the* cinema—has not yet appeared. Only when it does will cinema finally be able to leave the Kingdom of Shadows once and for all and enter the Castle of Impurity'.[20]

While in principle I endorse Ling's argument, I do not assume, like he does, that cinema is the *only* 'mass art'. I therefore superimpose my own 'polemical note' over his to claim that: While we must indeed subscribe to 'cinematic prescription' for cinema to 'truly become, not only in address, but also in form, a *mass art*, an art of the masses', and this after its (in)famous *end*, as Jean-Luc Godard proclaimed, we must not *forget* that it is the *art of building* that, in *essence,* has been *always-already* 'a *mass art*, an art of and for the masses'—by *necessity*. 'But human need for shelter is permanent', as Walter Benjamin said and I have reiterated again and again. Cinema is not *permanent* in human society. There is an *essence* in shelter, as opposed to essenceless cinema, the *essence of the essential living, of existence*. If cinema is an *inessential* art, architecture is essence-full. The thought of 'shelter' in the act of building is a '*living category*', a 'transcendental lived reality'. If cinema 'potentially' must, politically and artistically, embrace its 'democratic nature', as Ling envisions, it is rather the *actual* art of building, indeed ever more *impure* than cinema, on fundamental *material* ground, that must live up to its democratic social norms and ethical imperatives. When talking about 'mass art', it seems that architecture remains a blind spot in the thoughts of the philosopher. As has been remarked: 'every eye has its *camera obscura*'.[21]

I can now return to my main concern of discussing Badiou's intervention on the subject of *dialectics* that he places at the center of his philosophy of cinema without expanding on it. In the last paragraph of 'The Common Preoccupation of Art and Philosophy' Badiou says this: 'Finally, the question of the relationship between art and philosophy is the question of dialectics; the question of the presentation of what is dialectical thinking that is also a critical thinking, thinking which is able to develop negativity'.[22]

In his 'Cinema and Philosophy' Badiou notes:

Cinema is a form of conflict and this conflict cannot disappear. It is a new conflict, a possibility to have a form of art so impure, so horrible (in some sense) that what can be inscribed in this form is all the possible fictions of the fundamental conflict of our existence. So cinema is a recollection of all contradictions inside aesthetic creation, but also more generally. It is why cinema, and the derivative of cinema, television and all that, is today the only artistic activity that is really mass art, for everybody. Everybody has access to cinema.[23]

He continues with: 'so cinema is also the question of democracy. It's only democratic art in some sense. All forms of art today are aristocratic, exceptional'.[24] He makes it clear to us that he is not being 'judgmental' in this statement, but rather 'it is a fact'. Cinema is the *only* art that can be experienced by millions of people. Though, as he insists, there are excellent cinematic products that are, at the same time, popular and vulgar. This is because, Badiou reiterates, 'the cinema is, inside itself, a contradiction, the movement of the contradiction between what is pure creativity and what is in fact horrible material'.[25] And this makes it possible to have an internal critique of it. From here Badiou goes on to make an extremely cogent statement:

> Not to separate the critiques but to create the critiques inside what is criticized. And so cinema has two qualities: it is dialectics, because it is an art of contradiction, and it is democratic. *And so the cinema is a democratic dialectics. It is something exceptional.*[26]
>
> (my emphasis)

Nowhere in his writings on cinema does Badiou explicate the terms 'dialectics', 'contradiction', and 'democracy', nor 'negativity', for that matter. Yet, these terms are invoked so forcefully in his praise of cinema. He assumes that his 'cinema audience' is already familiar with his highly complex philosophical conception of dialectics. We know that he initially intervened into the Hegelian system, which goes back at least fifty years earlier, beginning with the 'red years' (*Les années rouges*) when he and his colleagues discussed the matter in *The Rational Kernel of the Hegelian Dialectics*, originally published in 1978, which came out in English translation in 2011 and was simultaneous with his *Theory of the Subject*.[27] That engagement continued in the intervening years, leading to the publication of *Logics of Worlds*—all before the latest two talks on cinema philosophy that Badiou actually delivered in 2014.[28] We need an understanding, albeit a rough one, of the aforementioned two qualities of the cinema, in order to appreciate what Badiou says, which is the crux of his claim of 'philosophy *as* cinema'. We must consult, therefore, the central question of 'dialectic' in his other philosophical writings as specifically related to his critical, more accurately *materialist*, intervention in Hegel's philosophical system. In so doing I will confine myself in the limited space available in this chapter to making some short remarks, and hope I do not oversimplify the topic of dialectics that is in itself a massively complex and much abused and misunderstood subject that is moreover compounded by the complexity of Badiou's thought about it. I will then follow this up by discussing art in relation to philosophy within the same Hegelian system in Badiou's work, after which I return to cinema again, and from there pass to architecture. In this itinerary, my leading concern is to examine how the reframing of 'dialectic' plays out in Badiou's concept of art in general and cinema in particular. My intention here is to claim that Badiou's thesis on cinema, within the specific terms he uses quoted above, teaches us an enormous lesson and carries promises for a conceptualization of the same notion of dialectic for critique of architecture as 'mass art'. In fact, I go one step further and argue that Badiou's insights on dialectics in cinema are more *things* in the nature of architecture before belonging exclusively to the art of cinema. I must point out in advance that Badiou stops short of carrying 'dialectic' and 'contradiction' over to the fundamental category of *dialectical contradiction* in the capitalist system which adversely affects both cinema *and* architecture—architecture more than cinema—that must serve as a *supplement* to any future critical thought on cinema.

Dialectics

First, one or two words here by way of a short exposition of this complex concept named 'dialectic'. We should know that dialectics in its most developed philosophical form comes to us from Hegel and his systematic philosophy, which is ultimately the philosophy of identity. But it must be immediately noted that the dialectic is also the moment of *negation*, the non-identical in the identical. Now, as is known, philosophy initially posits that *thought* and *being* are identical, that they are One. As we will see later, Badiou famously contests this One, or the 'Whole'. At the most fundamental level, a concern for Hegel is at the foundation of his thought on dialectics, prompted as a response to Kant. As Frederick Beiser informs us, 'Hegel saw his metaphysics not only as a *possibility* but as a *necessity* of the critical philosophy itself'.[29] Further, 'For Hegel the problem of justifying metaphysics was essentially one of discovering and following the right philosophical method',[30] and this because, as has been said, 'Hegel is the most methodologically self-conscious of all philosophers in the Western tradition'.[31] Beiser, affirming this statement, adds that it is especially true of Hegel during his Jena years, when he was in desperate search for the proper methodology to justify his new metaphysics. *The eventual fruit of this search was his dialectic*'[32] (emphasis mine). As Beiser appropriately warns us, the Hegelian term dialectic itself is often misunderstood.[33] One major misconception is the popular, if not vulgar, schema of 'thesis–antithesis–synthesis', which Hegel himself never used, and therefore has to be abandoned.[34]

Fredric Jameson makes a tremendous effort in his rather encyclopedic *Valences of the Dialectic*, over 600 pages long, to revive the thinking on dialectics. In his philosophical exploration he takes a stand against the contemporary regression from the notion of the 'negative'.[35] Early on in this text, Jameson cites Engels from *The Dialectic of Nature* on the 'three laws of the dialectic' in confirmation of 'dialectical materialism', which in Jameson's judgment is 'far from being outmoded':

The law of the transformation of quantity into quality and vice versa;
The law of the interpretation of the opposite;
The law of the negation of the negation.[36]

Covering a vast field from art, literature, philosophy, and psychoanalysis to politics and theory to examine 'dialectic', Jameson goes back and forth between Hegel and Marx. From the beginning, he makes a distinction between 'the dialectic', with the definite article, and plural dialectics, distinguishing dialectical from non-didactical or anti-dialectical modes of thinking. He repeatedly reminds us of 'the older commonsense empirical thought' in what 'Hegel called *Verstand* (or Understanding) and what Marx called reification'.[37] At one point, Jameson instructively points out that from a 'formal perspective, modernism itself is dialectical to the degree to which it is obliged to posit its own formal oppositions and to navigate them by way of invention and differentiation'.[38] This is a useful reminder because it is precisely the notion of 'dialectical opposition' which is an operative term in cinema and architecture, in different ways, as the two forms of 'mass art' in the era of 'mass-mediated modernity' around the turn of the twentieth century.

For Jameson there are two thinkers who are 'two of the most brilliant dialecticians in the history of philosophy' that the contemporary world has produced: namely, Theodor Adorno and Slavoj Žižek. He praises the former by constructing what he calls the 'dialectic of Adorno', rather than 'Adorno *on* dialectic'. This is significant as, at the time Jameson published his *Valences of the Dialectic* in 2009, Adorno's *An Introduction to Dialectics* had not yet come out. It was only published in German in 2011.

Adorno gave a series of introductory lectures in 1958 on theoretical explication and interpretation of 'dialectics'. These lectures were given after his *Dialectic of Enlightenment* (with Max Horkheimer) and before his *Negative Dialectics*. Published in English in 2017 as *An Introduction to Dialectics*, these lectures delivered in a lucid language—not typical of Adorno— are quite accessible and pedagogically illuminating.[39] In 'Lecture 1', Adorno tells that in a conversation with Goethe, Hegel described dialectics as 'the organized spirit of contradiction'.[40] In the same lecture Adorno informs us that at the point in philosophy where the concept of dialectics first emerges in Plato, it names a 'disciplined form of thought which is meant to protect us from all sophistic manipulation', as exemplified by Plato, who used its against his opponents, the Sophists, and claimed that 'we can say something rational about things only when we understand something about the matter itself'.[41] As a 'method of thinking', Adorno points out that Hegel in *Phenomenology of Spirit* spoke 'expressively' about 'the movement of the concept', where 'concept' has a double sense:

> on the one hand, it is the concept which we bring to things—that is to say, the methodically practiced manner in which we grasp the relevant conceptual 'moments'—yet, on the other hand, it is also the life of the matter itself.[42]

Thus, the dialectical method is a 'procedure for explaining an object in accordance with the necessary movement of its contradiction'.[43] But, 'in the whole', which the philosophy of Hegel is said to be—'The true is the whole', in Hegel's *Phenomenology*—these contradictions are 'living moments', as Adorno tells us, which are 'sublated' (*aufgehoben*), 'at once superseded and preserved, in philosophy as a whole'.[44] Adorno also takes issue with the vulgar understanding of a dialectic schema mentioned above and quotes a passage from The Preface of *Phenomenology of Spirit* to show how Hegel clarifies the issue:

> Of course, the *triadic form* must not be regarded as scientific when it is reduced to a lifeless schema, a mere shadow, and when scientific organization is degraded into a table of terms. Kant rediscovered this triadic form by instinct, but in his work it was still lifeless and uncomprehended; since then it has, however, been raised to its absolute significance, and with it the true form in its true content has been presented, so that the concept of Science has emerged.[45]

Citing again what he calls a 'celebrated passage' from the Preface of *Phenomenology*, Adorno tells his audience that it gives the 'essential' character of dialectic. It is actually 'passage 20' in the Preface, which runs as follows:

> The true is the whole. But the whole is nothing other than the essence consummating through its development. Of the Absolute [which can here be equated with truth in the emphatic sense] it must be said that it is essentially a *result*, that only in the *end*, is it what truly is; and that precisely in this consists its nature … Though it may seem contradictory that the Absolute should be conceived essentially as result, it needs little pondering to set this show of contradiction in its true light. The beginning, the principle, or the absolute, as a first immediately enunciated, is only the universal. Just as when I say '*all* animals', this expression cannot pass for zoology, so it is equally plain that the words 'the divine', 'the Absolute', 'the Eternal', etc., [and perhaps I might add 'Being' to the list here] do not express what is contained in them; and only such words, in fact, do express the intuition as something immediate. Whatever is more than such a word, even the transition to a mere proposition, contains a *becoming-other* that has to be taken, or is a mediation.[46]

Adorno actually omits the last paragraph of the passage in his citation which goes as follows: 'But it is just this that is rejected with horror, as if absolute cognition were being surrendered when more is made of mediation than in simply saying that it is nothing absolute, and is completely absent in the Absolute'.[47] Here I should mention that it is of course proper for Adorno to make reference to the *Phenomenology* as the source of dialectic in Hegel, as scholars of Hegel have abundantly pointed out to us that dialectic first appeared in its mature form in Hegel's 1807 *Phenomenology of Spirit*, and that dialectic was never meant to be a '*formal* logic'.[48] It was rather Hegel's response and a solution to the Kantian antinomies:

> The proper solution in the antinomies is not to divide but to unite the noumenal and the phenomenal, unconditioned and conditioned, by showing how both form necessary parts of a single indivisible whole; it was necessary to show, in other words, that the noumenal is within the phenomenal, the unconditioned within the conditioned.[49]

When Hegel uses the term dialectic, 'it usually designates the "self-organization" of the subject matter, its "inner necessity" and "inherent movement"'.[50] As Beiser informs us,

> The dialectic arises from an inevitable contradiction in the procedure of the understanding [...] Although Hegel often distinguishes between reason (*Vernunft*) and understanding (*Verstand*), these terms do not designate completely independent functions of faculties. Reason is simply the necessary result of the immanent movement of understanding.[51]

Adorno's paraphrase of the quoted passage is that

> expressed in other words, the moment you take a word like the 'Divine', the 'Absolute', the 'Eternal'—a word by which you can understand absolutely everything, and indeed only when you do so does it fulfill that claim to absoluteness with which the word itself addresses you—the moment you explicate such a word through a sentence or proposition, when you say, for example, that 'the Absolute is what remains immutably identical with itself', or 'the Absolute is the identity of thought and being', in that moment you already qualify that which precisely signified everything and to which the pathos of such a word,

its claim to absolute validity, effectively clings, and in doing so you alter the concept itself.[52]

'You have here', Adorno goes on to say, 'an explanation of the principle of dialectic and an exemplary case of the dialectic developed with reference to a specific concept'.[53] And by going back to the beginning of the passage he cited in Hegel, he encapsulates the point in the claim that 'the true is the whole', and he is quick to make it clear that we do not 'necessarily need to defend the claim that the whole is the true, if we wish to awaken the concept of truth in the first place, if we wish to uphold the concept of truth'.[54]

By 'Lecture 9' Adorno comes to distinguish the 'idealist dialectic'—Hegel—from the 'materialist dialectic'—Marx—and promises to take up the latter for more explications later—a promise that he does not fulfill. He limits himself to bringing up again the question of the identity of thought and being and the 'non-identical' in relation to the notion of 'totality', noting that dialectics is a kind of thought in which 'in spite of all the non-identity in the particular moments, non-identity is ultimately turned into something identical within the whole'.[55] He then offers to reflect on the 'materialist dialectic' only by saying that a dialectic is not

> a merely intellectual process, but a process of reality itself—that dialectical tendency to make the moment of non-identity, of contradiction, into the decisive factor does not imply that we must assert some final or conclusive identity of thought and being in the world as it is, that is, in the object of knowledge.[56]

In other words, 'being' has a primacy over 'thought'. It is in this same 'Lecture 9' that Adorno brings up the controversy he had with his friend Walter Benjamin more than 20 years ago on the latter's writing on Charles Baudelaire. At that time, in his famous letter, Adorno took Benjamin to task on account of the claim that his materialist dialectic supposedly lacked 'mediation'.[57]

At this point I leave Adorno, hoping that my cursory investigation into the theory of dialectic has succeeded in conveying its complexity. Things get far more complicated—unfortunately!—when we come to

Badiou's intervention into the Hegelian dialectic, to which I now turn. I cannot enter into the complexity of his philosophical intervention in any comprehensive way, and will therefore limit my discussion to those aspects that will directly help us understand his philosophical remarks about the 'dialectical' character of cinema.

Badiou and dialectics

In light of Adorno's criticism of Hegel's dialectic in *Negative Dialectics*, for the 'ethical consequences of maintaining the reality of the whole over the possibility of diverse multiplicity', as Adriel Trott succinctly phrases it, for Badiou 'Hegel's whole is not only morally and politically unjust', but more crucially, 'the whole is not'.[58] What underlies this statement is that, as Trott points out, Badiou himself takes up a dialectical method in his systematic philosophy, thus 'situating himself in the same philosophical lineage as Hegel', and 'uses dialectic to think the relation between the one and the many, difference and identity'.[59] Trott writes,

> Badiou perpetuates the dialectic by making contradiction, not identity, the driver of his dialectic, producing a divergent rather than convergent dialectic. Not that being is a contradiction, but that the effort to speak of it as whole results in contradiction. Badiou's dialectic attempts to follow the separating moments of what is driven apart on pain of contradiction. By contrast while Hegel affirms contradiction and seems to privilege negation, his speculative dialectic thinks the identity of identity and contradiction; Hegel thus supposes he can resolve the contradiction into a whole resulting in 'circular completion'.[60]

In the section on Hegel in *Logics of Worlds* Badiou writes:

> Hegel is without the shadow of a doubt the philosopher who has pushed furthest the interiorization of Totality into even the slightest movement of thought. One could argue that whereas we launch a transcendental theory of worlds by saying 'there is no whole', Hegel guarantees the inception of the dialectical odyssey by positing that 'There is nothing but the Whole'.[61]

Comparing the 'axiom' of his philosophical system with that of Hegel, Badiou continues:

> But this interest cannot reside in a simple extrinsic comparison, or in a comparison of results. What is decisive is following the Hegelian idea in its movement, that is at the very movement in which it explicitly governs the method of thinking. This alone will allow us, in the name of the materialist dialectic, to do justice to our father: the master of 'idealist' dialectic.[62]

Badiou further writes:

> Ultimately the Hegelian challenge can be summed up in three principles:
>
> - The only truth is that of the Whole.
> - The Whole is a self-unfolding, and not an absolute-unity external to the subject,
> - The Whole is the immanent arrival of its own concept.
>
> This means that the thought of the Whole is the effectuation of the Whole itself. Consequently, what displays the Whole within thought is nothing other than the path of thinking, that is its method. Hegel is the methodical thinker of the Whole. It is indeed with regard to this point that he brings his immense metaphysico-ontological book, the *Science of Logic*, to a close.[63]

And further:

> Of course, we share with Hegel a conviction about the identity of being and thought. But for us this identity is a local occurrence and not a totalized result. We also share with Hegel the conviction regarding a universality of the true. But for us this universality is guaranteed by the singularity of truth-event, and not by the view that the Whole is the history of its immanent reflection.[64]

Trott clarifies the passage above: 'The singularity of truth-event as the flashpoint of the universal—not the totality formed in history's reflection on itself—is what makes access to the true for Badiou dialectically situated between ontology and phenomenology, between being and beings, between the philosophical and the political'.[65]

In passing, it is interesting to note that Badiou, in relation to *Science of Logic*, towards the end of *Logics of Worlds*, confesses that 'I have never ceased measuring myself up to the book, almost as unreadable as Joyce's *Finnegans Wake*'.[66] At any rate, concerning this notion of the Whole, in their commentary on Badiou and Hegel, A. J. Bartlett and Justin Clemens write that 'what disappears absolutely throughout Badiou's work is something that has always been considered to be non-negotiable from a Hegelian perspective: a consistent thinking of the Whole'.[67] And in this regard, Trott writes,

> As long as there is a whole, as long as the true infinite finds its place as the whole subsuming all things within it while remaining distinct from them, the Hegelian dialectic can achieve its absolute identity by resting in itself (with all the theological resonances of such a goal). This resting is the de-dialecticizing of dialectic, the reconciling of all difference into ultimate identity in a whole through negation, that Badiou accuses Hegel of seeking.[68]

As Trott perceptively remarks, the impossibility of the Whole makes possible another thinking of dialectic. In Hegel, dialectic is 'idealist' because the 'being unified and identical' is capable of totality, and because 'There is nothing but the Whole'. But for Badiou 'There is no Whole', as we have seen. There is a difference between the 'synthesis-driven dialectic of Hegel', and the 'subtraction-driven dialectic of Badiou'.[69] This has to do with Badiou's 'ideological struggle' or the political struggle during the 'red years' mentioned above, which has everything to do with whether 'one divides into two' or 'two fuses into one'. As Badiou clearly asserts, 'synthesis—"two fuses into one"—leads to idealism while division—"one divides into two"—leads to materialism'.[70] Badiou importantly argues that, as Trott writes, 'the contradiction between the One and the Two motivates the dialectic, both the materialist and idealist dialectics'.[71] According to Badiou, 'Under the name materialism we understand two perfectly contradictory theses: One states that there is the One, the other that the One precedes the Other, and thus that there is the Two'.[72] Trott expands on this:

yes, there is only one region of being. But by having to thus affirm the unity of being, the materialist splits the region by describing its order and thus the materialist affirms that, yes, there are two regions of being. So the contradiction that drives the materialist dialectic is that being is material and one—'there is only one world'—and that being is two since being can be described as material.[73]

According to this argument, Trott can then claim that Badiou's materialist dialectic is 'unique' and that he has gone beyond Marxist materialist dialectics, 'because with the absolute rejection of the whole, Badiou posits the possibility of a break with being and with the order of being', and that 'New political possibilities are possible because there can be a break from what is'.[74]

Much more remains to be said on the significance of Badiou's conception of dialectic in relation to the Hegelian dialectic.[75] But, at this point, I have to break and turn directly to the main concern stated at the beginning of this chapter, that is, the question of 'mass art' and Badiou's statement on dialectic and cinema. We go back, therefore, to the '*logic of scission*' or the logic of split in dialectic. In what follows I focus on the explication of this logic. As early as the *Rational Kernel of the Hegelian Dialectic*, as we have seen, Badiou distinguishes his approach from the so-called 'new-Hegel', then dominant in France, that Hegel 'must be split from within', in which, as Gabriel Riera explains, all concepts are 'internally divided between dialectical and non-dialectical side'.[76] For Badiou, as Riera puts it succinctly, 'Hegel was not dialectical enough, and the task of reading Hegel amounts to isolating dialectics and freeing it from speculative formalism'.[77]

As we know, for Badiou, art as a 'local truth' is a *condition* for philosophy along with science, politics, and love. As he puts it in *Conditions*: 'Philosophy is the place of thought where the "there is" (*il y a*) of these truths, and their compossibility, is stated. To achieve this, philosophy constructs an operational category, the Truth, which opens up an active void in thought'.[78] And insofar as 'Hegel's philosophy of art reduces art to an object of philosophy, one would expect that the protocol of scission would be at play in Badiou's assessment of Hegel in order to isolate its kernel'.[79] We should recall that in his *Handbook of Inaesthetics*, a book devoted to art as a condition of philosophy, Badiou, significantly, classes Hegel under one of the four forms of the relation between philosophy and art, namely the Romantic, and therefore problematizes Hegel's philosophy of aesthetics and his philosophy of art as if it cannot be 'put back into circulation'. So the following question can be raised, among others: 'Why is it that his golden rule for reading Hegel's dialectic, scission, does not seem to apply to his philosophy of art?'.[80] Riera reflects that in order to answer this question, along with others that he raises, one must seek the defining features of Badiou's philosophy, specifically, by way of 'two moments: Plato and Hegel':

> The former points towards the 'return of philosophy to itself' and thus towards a post-Heideggerian reformulation of the relationship between philosophy and art, more exactly the poem, a necessary move for conceiving of a new non-exhausted relationship between philosophy and art (what Badiou calls an 'inaesthetic' rapport); the latter points towards a reformulation of materialist dialectic in terms of a doctrine of the event and of its operator of inscription, the subject.[81]

In this respect, Badiou radically breaks with Romanticism and conceives art under the doctrine of *event* and the *fidelity* to the production of truths in his 're-founding of materialist dialectic'.

One of the consequences of the 'return to Plato' and the renewal of the materialist dialectic in Badiou, which dates from his masterpiece *Being and Event*, is a

> form of thinking that forces the emergence of the truth of a given situation, not through a mediation, but through an interruption, a scission, or cut in representation by means of which the real becomes a condition of possibility for a change in subjective position.[82]

For Badiou, as Riera explains, the 'real kernel' cannot be severed from the 'effect of subjectivization it induces', and further, 'Through this polemic, the fundamental concept of Badiou's philosophy emerges: scission and subject, whose idealistic and materialistic slopes must, in turn, be derived so as to form fundaments of a dialectic of the new'.[83] The argument developed by Badiou in *Being and Event*, as Riera explains, 'makes clear that Hegel's thinking should be purified from subsequent additions that, over the course of two centuries, had resulted in obscuring the fundamental message', and that

> the result of this operation would be a renewed understanding of dialectical thinking no longer based on the category of totality, but rather on the relationship between void and excess, on the split and symptomatic torsion of identity rather than on the overcoming of negation, on the exhaustion of representation rather than on the elusive self-presentation of the Concept.[84]

He further adds that 'This dialectic should be defined in terms of "splitting and torsion of the scission itself"'.[85]

Now we can come to the relationship between art and philosophy. In summary, for Badiou, artistic 'research' always takes place within the realm of the sensible: the truth of art entails a transformation of the sensible into the event of an Idea. Or, the trajectory of an artistic truth is conceived in terms of a 'relationship between the purity and impurity of forms'.[86] What is important to note is that, as Riera articulates,

> there is a difference between art and reason, or at least between art and pure thinking, that is philosophical speculation: in the real thinking, Absolute Spirit determines itself as the unity of the ideal (knowledge) and of the real (being) *in thinking*, while in art this same unity accomplishes itself in the sensible—in the three-dimensional materiality of the plastic arts, in the bi-dimensional materiality of painting, in music's evanescent sounds, or the imaginative representation of poetry. This difference is heavy in consequences, since it will ground the superiority of philosophy over art.[87]

In regard to this relationship between art and philosophy, Badiou

> places them in a non-hierarchical and asymmetric relationship. Art produces an intra-philosophical truth, external and heterogeneous to philosophy, that the latter, afterward, must elucidate but also from which it can acquire a model for its formalization. Art does not produce speculative knowledge; it presents in a consistent fashion and lasting way the vanishing passage of the event.[88]

For Badiou, the 'truth of art is always sensory, "which means transformation of the sensory into the event of the Idea"'.[89] Riera concludes his inquiry on Badiou and Hegel by pointing out that

> Badiou shares with Hegel a basic assumption: Art embodies a form of intelligibility that is essential for philosophy, which the latter cannot provide by itself. If for Hegel this form of intelligibility refers to the Absolute, for Badiou it points to the illegal and heterogeneous materiality he calls event.[90]

It is my hope that this brief investigation into dialectics has provided a context for a better understanding of what Badiou said to his audience about cinema. To recall, 'And so cinema has two qualities: it is dialectics, because it is an art of contradiction, and it is democratic. And so the cinema is a democratic dialectics. It is something exceptional'. In the continuum of 'materialist dialectic', the notion of 'democratic dialectics' has yet to be explored, which is related to Badiou's complex idea of 'democracy', in which we can enter here.

In conclusion, I want to make two points. The first is the question of architecture, which I suggest is the main locus of the 'dialectical contradiction' in capitalist society over cinema. Regarding this, one must go to Marx and his materialist dialectic over and beyond Badiou. Second, I want to provisionally interject my thesis into the statement Badiou made in his essay 'On Cinema as a Democratic Emblem'. He said: 'After the philosophy of cinema must come—is already coming—philosophy *as* cinema, which consequently has a chance of being a philosophy of the masses'. I intervene to say the following: 'After the philosophy of cinema must come—it is not *yet there*—philosophy *as architecture*, as the art of contradiction, which consequently *has had* a chance of being a philosophy *of* the masses' long before cinema. In question is the *vague* notion of 'the masses', which according to Badiou himself, as we have seen, is a *political* term. Therefore, regarding the problematic of whether it is cinema *or* architecture—as 'mass art'—grounded in dialectic that must negotiate between *philosophy* and *politics*, I contend that it must be architecture. But in order for this claim to be a credible one, the term 'masses' has yet to be analyzed and defined. Without the introduction of the 'concrete universality' of the *proletariat*, as I argue, on which Badiou remains silent in his lectures on cinema, the notion of 'masses' remains problematic. It is not enough to just say that 'mass' is a *political* notion, as I try to explicate in the next chapter.

Notes

1. Alain Badiou, 'Cinema as Philosophical Experimentation', in *Cinema*, intro. Antoine de Baecque, trans. Susan Spitzer (Cambridge: Polity, 2013).
2. Alain Badiou, 'Fifteen Theses on Contemporary Art', in *Lacanian Ink*, 23 (2004).
3. See Alain Badiou, *Handbook of Inaesthetics*, trans. Alberto Toscano (Stanford: Stanford University Press, 2005), 85.
4. Alain Badiou, *Handbook of Inaesthetics*, 83.
5. Alain Badiou, *Infinite Thought: Truth and the Return of Philosophy*, trans. and eds Oliver Feltham and Justin Clemens (London: Continuum, 2005), 84.
6. See Alex Ling, *Badiou and Cinema* (Edinburgh: Edinburgh University Press, 2011, 2013).
7. Alex Ling, *Badiou and Cinema*, 162.
8. Alex Ling, *Badiou and Cinema*, 162.
9. Quoted in Alex Ling, *Badiou and Cinema*, 162.
10. Quoted in Alex Ling, *Badiou and Cinema*, 163. Before the quoted sentence, Bazin wrote:

    > The role of cinema here is not that of a servant nor is it to betray the painting. Rather it is to provide it with a new form of existence. The film of a painting is an aesthetic symbiosis of screen and painting, as is the lichen of the algae and mushroom,

    and then 'To be annoyed by this is as ridiculous as to condemn the opera on behalf of theater and music', in André Bazin, *What Is Cinema?*, Volume I, essays selected and translated by Hugh Gray, foreword by Jean Renoir, new foreword by Dudley Andrew (Berkeley: University of California Press, 1967, 2005), 168.
11. Alex Ling, *Badiou and Cinema*, 163.
12. Alex Ling, *Badiou and Cinema*, 163.
13. Alex Ling, *Badiou and Cinema*, 164.
14. Alex Ling, *Badiou and Cinema*, 164.
15. Quoted in Alex Ling, *Badiou and Cinema*, 164.
16. Alex Ling, *Badiou and Cinema*, 165.
17. Alex Ling, *Badiou and Cinema*, 165.
18. Alex Ling, *Badiou and Cinema*, 165.
19. Alex Ling, *Badiou and Cinema*, 185.
20. Alex Ling, *Badiou and Cinema*, 192.
21. See Sarah Kofman, *Camera Obscura of Ideology*, trans. Will Straw (Ithaca and New York: Cornell University Press, 1998), 19. Kofman in her great analysis of the concept of 'ideology' writes that

even if science is no longer specular, speculative, a repetition, reflection or echo, its ideal remains that of a perfect eye, a pure retina. Nevertheless, the recognition that every eye has its camera obscura does not disqualify the eye as a model of knowledge.

19

22 Alain Badiou, 'The Common Preoccupation of Art and Philosophy', in *Badiou and His Interlocutors: Lectures, Interviews, and Responses*, ed. A. J. Bartlett and Justin Clemens (London: Bloomsbury, 2018), 37.
23 Alain Badiou, 'Cinema and Philosophy', in *Badiou and his Interlocutors: Lectures, Interviews, and Responses*, ed. A. J. Bartlett and Justin Clemens (London: Bloomsbury, 2018), 26. Badiou follows up by saying

> We cannot say that there is a 'snob access', an access which is educated and so on, or that there is a bad access, vulgar and so on. No! We cannot say that because the vulgarity is immanent to the cinema in general. It is present in a very good cinema as a form of the conflict and it is why during the last century and now, it is the only art where some evidently magnificent productions are also a massive success, seen by millions of people. It was something like that for the novel during the nineteenth century but the function of the novel during the nineteenth century today is the function of cinema.
>
> 26

24 Alain Badiou, 'Cinema and Philosophy', 26.
25 Alain Badiou, 'Cinema and Philosophy', 26.
26 Alain Badiou, 'Cinema and Philosophy', 26–27.
27 See Alain Badiou, Joël Bellassen, and Louis Mossot, *The Rational Kernel of the Hegelian Dialectics*, ed. and trans. Tzuchien Tho (Melbourne: Re.Press, 2011). Also Alain Badiou, *Theory of the Subject*, trans. Bruno Bosteels (London: Continuum, 2009). The introductory chapter by Tho, 'One Divides into Two?, Dividing the Condition', at the beginning of the former book provides an informative account of stages in the transformation of Badiou's thoughts on dialectics.
28 See Alain Badiou, *Logics of Worlds: Being and Event II*, trans. Alberto Toscano (London: Continuum, 2009).
29 See Frederick Beiser, *Hegel* (New York: Routledge, 2005), especially Chapter 7, 158.
30 Frederick Beiser, *Hegel*, 159.
31 Quoted in Frederick Beiser, *Hegel*, 159.
32 Frederick Beiser, *Hegel*, 159.
33 See Frederick Beiser, *Hegel*, especially Chapter 7.
34 Beiser informs us that

> In the *Phenomenology* Hegel did praise 'the triadic form' that had been rediscovered by Kant, describing it even as 'the concept of science'; but this is a reference to the triadic form of Kant's table of categories, not a method

of thesis–antithesis–synthesis. Although Kant's antinomies were the inspiration for Hegel's dialectic, Hegel never used Kant's method of exposition of thesis and antithesis. It has been said that this method was used by Fichte and Schelling, and then by extension wrongly attributed to Hegel; but it corresponds to nothing in Fichte or Schelling, let alone Hegel.

161

35 See Fredric Jameson, *Valences of the Dialectic* (London: Verso, 2009).
36 Quoted in Fredric Jameson, *Valences of the Dialectic*, 13. Also see Friedrich Engels, *The Dialectics of Nature* (New York: International Publishers, 1940), Chapter 2. Jameson comments that

> To be sure, these laws of Engels are not themselves wholly without content (that is to say, they bear the traces of a situation in which their formation was meant to be a political act). The Hegelian language and conceptuality are designed to include reminiscences of various moments in Marx's economic analyses; that is, they are meant to signal a kind of general applicability of Hegelianism to the economic sphere, as well as to suggest the philosophical credentials and respectability of that Marxism qua philosophy which Engels is promoting here.

37 See Fredric Jameson, *Valences of the Dialectic*, 50.
38 Fredric Jameson, *Valences of the Dialectic*, 33. He discusses the art of Piet Mondrian and remarks that

> The issue is not whether Piet Mondrian—preeminent among such dialectical artists—was or was not Hegelian (whatever the verb 'to be' might mean in this context), or whether his writings do or do not adequately articulate the philosophical dialectic as such (they do!)—but rather the objective moment in which the process of abstraction has gone far enough to reveal dialectical opposition at work, and at work in a dynamic rather than a static fashion.

33

39 Theodor W. Adorno, *An Introduction to Dialectics*, ed. Christoph Ziermann, trans. Nicholas Walker (Cambridge: Polity, 2017). The editor of this volume provides excellent complementary notes shedding light on Adorno's otherwise unexplained points and references.
40 Theodor W. Adorno, *An Introduction to Dialectics*, 3. The editor mentions that it was Johann Peter Eckermann who reported that in a conversation Goethe had asked Hegel to explain what he understood by the term 'dialectics'. The philosopher responded that 'it is basically nothing but the regulated and methodically cultivated spirit of contradiction which is innate in every human being', 257.
41 Theodor W. Adorno, *An Introduction to Dialectics*, 1.
42 Theodor W. Adorno, *An Introduction to Dialectics*, 'Lecture 2', 4.
43 Theodor W. Adorno, *An Introduction to Dialectics*, 4–5.

44 Theodor W. Adorno, *An Introduction to Dialectics*, 'Lecture 2', 7. For an extended discussion of 'Contradiction' in Hegel see Todd McGowan, *Emancipation After Hegel: Achieving Contradictory Revolution* (New York: Columbia University Press, 2019), Chapter 1.
45 Theodor W. Adorno, *An Introduction to Dialectics*, 47. Also see *Hegel's Phenomenology of Spirit*, trans. A. V. Miller (Oxford: Oxford University Press, 1977), 29.
46 Theodor W. Adorno, *An Introduction to Dialectics*, 'Lecture 3', 17. See also *Hegel's Phenomenology of Spirit*, 11.
47 In *Hegel's Phenomenology of Spirit*, 11.
48 Frederick Beiser, among others, in his *Hegel*, 169. Beiser informs us that

> Another common misconception is that the dialectic is some kind of alternative logic, having its own distinctive principles to compete with traditional logic. But for Hegel dialectic was never meant to be *formal* logic, one that determines the fundamental laws of inference governing all propositions, whatever their content. In its most general form in the *Science of Logic* the dialectic is a metaphysics whose main task is to determine the general structure of being. Such a metaphysics does not compete with logic because it has a content all its own, even if a very general one, namely, the most general categories of being.
>
> 161–162

49 See Frederick Beiser, *Hegel*, 167.
50 Frederick Beiser, *Hegel*, 160.
51 Frederick Beiser, *Hegel*, 164. As Beiser further writes,

> For Hegel, the necessity of metaphysics therefore derived from the need to explain the single source of Kant's divided faculties. Kant himself has forsworn all speculation about the single sources of understanding and sensibility, but, without such speculation, Hegel argued, there could be no resolution of the fundamental problem of the critical philosophy itself.
>
> 158–159

52 Theodor W. Adorno, *An Introduction to Dialectics*, 17.
53 Theodor W. Adorno, *An Introduction to Dialectics*, 17–18. Adorno further explains that

> The term 'mediation' in Hegel always signifies a change or alteration which must be expected of a concept as soon as we wish to be apprised of the concept itself. We might also say that mediation is the moment of 'becoming' that is necessarily involved in any form of 'being'. And, if dialectic is the philosophy of universal mediation, this implies that there is actually no being which could evade the process of becoming once you attempt to determine it as such.
>
> 18

54 Theodor W. Adorno, *An Introduction to Dialectics*, 20.
55 Theodor W. Adorno, *An Introduction to Dialectics*, 84.
56 Theodor W. Adorno, *An Introduction to Dialectics*, 85.
57 On this see the editor's note in Theodor W. Adorno, *An Introduction to Dialectics*, 281.
58 See Adriel M. Trott, 'Badiou *contra* Hegel: The Materialist Dialectic against the Myth of the Whole', in *Badiou and Hegel: Infinity, Dialectics, Subjectivity*, eds Jim Vernon and Antonio Galcagno (Lanham: Lexington Books, 2015), 59. This is an excellent collection of essays on which I am relying for much of my discussion on Badiou's relationship to Hegel.
59 In Adriel M. Trott, 'Badiou *contra* Hegel', 60. Trott helpfully highlights that,

> in *Being and Event*, Badiou affirms the multiple as ontologically basic—what is, is multiple—while arguing that ontology, being *qua* unity, presents what is as one. Furthermore, in *Being and Event*, and in *The Meaning of Sarkozy*, Badiou champions truths, especially political truths, as universal by affirming that the world is one. In *Logics of Worlds*, Badiou affirms the multiplicity of worlds seen in terms not of the being of the world but in its multiple appearing. But Badiou denies that the dialectical relation between multiplicity and differentiation, on the one hand, and unity and identity, on the other, is to be finally resolved as one non-contradictory whole, as it is for Hegel for whom the end of the dialectic really is the end of the dialectic. For Badiou, the dialectic is to be supplemented by an 'aleatory third term: Subject-truths'.
>
> 60

60 Adriel M. Trott, 'Badiou *contra* Hegel', 60.
61 Alain Badiou, *Logics of Worlds*, 141.
62 Alain Badiou, *Logics of Worlds*, 142.
63 Alain Badiou, *Logics of Worlds*, 142.
64 Alain Badiou, *Logics of Worlds*, 143–144.
65 Adriel M. Trott, 'Badiou *contra* Hegel', 68.
66 Alain Badiou, *Logics of Worlds*, 529. In relation to this, A. J. Bartlett and Justin Clemens comment that

> Something remains curious in Badiou's lifelong interest in Hegel, however. For if Hegel is regularly affirmed by Badiou as one of the 'three crucial philosophers' with Plato and Descartes, he seems the odd man out in a number of regards. Certain commentators would perhaps consider that Hegel's importance derives from Badiou's political affiliations rather than from something specific about Hegel's philosophy as such. Why? Because a received image from the history of philosophy would render Plato, Descartes, and Kant more compatible—with each other and with Badiou's own evident proclivities—in their shared divisions of worlds, their rigorous approach to Ideas, and their

commitment to Science as a thought that is not simply 'incorporable' to the philosophical concept.

> A. J. Bartlett and Justin Clemens, 'Measuring Up: Some Consequences of Badiou's Confrontation with Hegel', in *Badiou and Hegel: Infinity, Dialectics, Subjectivity*, eds Jim Vernon and Antonio Galcagno (Lanham: Lexington Books, 2015), 15–16

67 See A. J. Bartlett and Justin Clemens, 'Measuring Up', 17.
68 Adriel M. Trott, 'Badiou *contra* Hegel', 60.
69 For more see Adriel M. Trott, 'Badiou *contra* Hegel', 63.
70 Adriel M. Trott, 'Badiou *contra* Hegel', 63. Also see Badiou's interview with Tzuchien Tho, in Alain Badiou, Joël Bellassen, and Louis Mossot, *The Rational Kernel of the Hegelian Dialectics*. As Trott points out, Badiou explains to Tho that he

> had thought the dialectic in this way in the 1970s (in *Theory of the Subject*) when he did not yet have a 'path' or mechanism for thinking division in a way that held together multiplicity and unity without totalizing. Subtraction becomes that new path in *Being and Event*, a path that is articulated in the event. The event is the rupture from the situation that presents what constitutively could not be presented before and, in this sense, is subtraction.
>
> 63–64

71 Adriel M. Trott, 'Badiou *contra* Hegel', 64.
72 Quoted in Adriel M. Trott, 'Badiou *contra* Hegel', 64.
73 Adriel M. Trott, 'Badiou *contra* Hegel', 64–65.
74 Adriel M. Trott, 'Badiou *contra* Hegel', 64.
75 Readers are encouraged to consult the essays included in the aforementioned collection, *Badiou and Hegel: Infinity, Dialectics, Subjectivity*.
76 See Gabriel Riera, 'The Question of Art: Badiou and Hegel', in *Badiou and Hegel: Infinity, Dialectics, Subjectivity*, eds Jim Vernon and Antonio Galcagno (Lanham: Lexington Books, 2015), 79. For my discussion on Badiou's philosophy on art, I rely heavily on this excellent essay.
77 Gabriel Riera, 'The Question of Art', 78. As Riera further clarifies,

> This is a move that, according to Badiou, enables us to see that in the split rational kernel of Hegelian dialectic lurks a doctrine of the event (new or strong singularity). Three important protocols in Badiou are the posting of an immanent infinity; the ensuing dismantling of Hegel's conceptual opposition 'good/bad infinity' through a mathematically inflected reading; third, the interplay between the local and the global as it appears in *Logics of Worlds*. The first protocol is crucial for Badiou's doctrine of truth, while the second and the third have to do with the generic character of the Idea.
>
> 79

78 See Alain Badiou, *Conditions*, trans. Steven Corcoran (London: Continuum, 2008), 23.
79 Gabriel Riera, 'The Question of Art', 79.
80 This question is posed by Gabriel Riera, 'The Question of Art', 79.
81 Gabriel Riera, 'The Question of Art', 80. I cannot go into the details of the relation between Badiou and Plato and Hegel as Riera extensively and informatively discusses.
82 Gabriel Riera, 'The Question of Art', 83. Riera explains that

> The argument of the renewal of 'materialist dialect' is more convoluted and discontinuous. It predates the so-called mathematical turn of *Being and Event*; it disappears from the forefront in this major book only to explicitly reappear in *Logics of Worlds*.
>
> 100, n. 19

83 Gabriel Riera, 'The Question of Art', 83. Riera provides a background which is helpful: Badiou's early writings are attempts to extricate the rational (materialist) kernel from the Hegelian dialectic. Badiou makes use of Mao's famous formula

> 'the one divides into two', whereby reality is not only a process but also processing in which the process itself finds its own fundament in the ontological-dialectic principle of *scission*. The two targets of Badiou's approach are Althusser's identification of Hegel's 'real kernel' with the concept of 'process without a subject', and the Marxist reduction of the subject to an imaginary and ideological dimension.
>
> 83

84 Gabriel Riera, 'The Question of Art', 83–84.
85 Gabriel Riera, 'The Question of Art', 84.
86 Gabriel Riera, 'The Question of Art', 90.
87 Gabriel Riera, 'The Question of Art', 94. For more of this see the superb explication of the difference between art and philosophy in Hegel, which the limited space available here does not allow me to enter into.
88 Gabriel Riera, 'The Question of Art', 97.
89 Gabriel Riera, 'The Question of Art', 97.
90 Gabriel Riera, 'The Question of Art', 98.

The proletarian *mise-en-scène*

Sergei Eisenstein's *Battleship Potemkin*
Source: © Mosfilm Cinema Concern

Chapter 8

The proletarian *mise-en-scène*

> As the *mise-en-scène* is an interrelation of people in action, so the *mise-en-cadre* is the pictorial composition of mutually dependent *cadres* (shots) in a montage sequence.
> —Sergei Eisenstein, *Film Form: Essays in Film Theory*[1]

> This would be the final justification for Lenin's words, that 'the cinema is the most important of all the arts'.
> —Sergei Eisenstein, *Film Form: Essays in Film Theory*[2]

> We may truly say that with film a *new realm of consciousness* comes into being.
> —Walter Benjamin, 'Reply to Oscar A. H. Schmitz'[3]

> It should be noted ... that proletarian class consciousness, which is the most enlightened form of class consciousness, fundamentally transforms the structure of the proletarian masses.
> —Walter Benjamin, 'The Work of Art in the Age of its Technological Reproducibility'[4]

Before the 'proletariat' enters our 'consciousness' it has to be seen. But it *cannot* be seen with the naked eye. To come to visibility it must be submitted to the technological apparatus of the camera. In the age of cinema, the proletariat has to be *photographed* in order to come into being, to become visible. It must therefore become an *image* first—read *phenomenon*. It is an image, *but* it reveals that it is more than an image that is not given to sensible intuition—nowhere given to experience. I therefore name the photographed 'proletariat' by its Kantian term, the *thing-in-itself*. In its *otherness* it is *transcendental*, that is to be conceived in a *parallax* relationship to the masses. Recall that the *transcendental* seeks, in the simple term that Kojin Karatani defines, 'to cast light on the unconscious structure that precedes and shapes experience'.[5] Here I employ the resources of critical philosophy to examine the class *consciousness* of the proletarian masses. But we have to go to the cinema, to Plato's cave again, to see its *cinematic* presentation, its '*new realm of consciousness*'. The 'proletarian masses' are on the move and their *movement* cannot be seen if not through a technological operation called *cinematography*. We recall that the word *cinema* is originally derived from the French *cinématographe*, which 'comes from the Greek *kinema* meaning movement (hence the popular term *the movie*). So, the word *cinémato* plus the suffix *graphe* means variously imagining, tracing, or writing movement'.[6] In his 1932 essay 'A Course in Treatment', Sergei Eisenstein made the following remarks about the notion of 'cinematography':

> To build cinematography, starting from the 'idea of cinematography', and from abstract principles, is barbarous and stupid. Only by a critical comparison with the more basic early forms of spectacle is it possible to master critically the specific methodology of the cinema.[7]

And further: 'The art of cinematography is not selecting a fanciful framing, or in taking something from a surprising camera-angle'.[8]

Historically, in order to capture the proletarian masses in *movement* we have to go to the famous Odessa Steps. Not to the *actual* steps but to the image of them in Eisenstein's *Battleship Potemkin*—the classic revolutionary cinema, par excellence. It is in this film that the 'masses' come to their *phenomenal* visibility, or the visibility of their *image*, staged by Eisenstein's great art of *montage*. Only after seeing the specific sequences of the Odessa Steps in this film can we then submit the notion of the 'proletarian masses' to philosophical-theoretical and political scrutiny. I will come to this later. Here I would just point out that what we see in Eisenstein's *mise-en-scène* is the Sublime notion of the 'proletariat'. With Kant, as Slavoj Žižek puts it, 'the Sublime designates the relation of an inner-worldly, empirical sensuous object to

Ding an sich, to the transcendence, trans-phenomenal, unattainable Thing-in-itself'.[9] The paradox of the Sublime is as follows:

> in principle, the gap separating phenomenal, empirical objects of experience from the Thing-in-itself is insurmountable—that is, no empirical object, no representation [*Vorstellung*] of it can adequately present [*darstellen*] the Thing (the supersensible Idea); but the Sublime is an object in which we can experience this very impossibility, this permanent failure of the representation to reach after the Thing.[10]

In his 'Reply to Oscar A. H. Schmitz', published in 1927, Benjamin intervened in the debate about *Potemkin* at the time and took the occasion to raise a number of important points that he would later take up again in his Artwork essay. Discussing the political notion of 'proletariat' and 'consciousness', Benjamin foregrounded the notion of technology linked to the aesthetic and political in film and brought up the 'superiority' of the Russian revolutionary cinema, interestingly in a positive comparison with the American slapstick comedy. The 'target' of both is 'technology', he said.

> This kind of film is comic, but only in the sense that the laughter it provokes hovers over an abyss of horror. The obverse of a ludicrously liberated technology is the lethal power of naval squadrons on maneuver, as we see it openly displayed in *Potemkin*.[11]

He noted that 'The international bourgeois film, on the other hand, has not been able to discover a consistent ideological formula. This is one of the causes of its recurrent crises'.[12] In this case, 'For the complicity of film technique with the milieu that essentially constitutes a standing rebuke to it is incompatible with the glorification of the bourgeoisie'.[13] Benjamin continues by making an important point central to my concern here:

> The Proletariat is the hero of those spaces that give rise to the adventures to which the bourgeois abandons himself in the movies with beating heart, because he feels constrained to enjoy 'beauty' even where it speaks of the annihilation of his own class. The proletariat,

however, is a collective, just as these spaces are collective spaces. And only here, in the human collective, can the film complete the prismatic work that it began by acting on that milieu. The epoch-making impact of *Potemkin* can be explained by the fact that it made this clear for the first time. Here, for the first time, a mass movement acquires the wholly architectonic and by no means monumental (i.e., UFA) [Universum-Film AG] quality that justifies its inclusion in film. No other medium could reproduce this collective in motion.[14]

Benjamin called *Potemkin* 'a great film' and 'a rare achievement', and further wrote:

To protest against it calls for the courage born of desperation. There is plenty of bad tendentious art, including bad socialist tendentious art. Such works are determined by their effects; they work with tired reflexes and depend on stereotyping. This film, however, has solid concrete foundations ideologically; the details have been worked out precisely, like the span of a bridge;

lyrically concluding that 'The more violent the blows that rain down upon it, the more beautifully it resounds. Only if you touch it with kid gloves do you hear and move nothing'.[15] Here I should mention that among the notions that Benjamin employs in this essay, and that he would pick up again to discuss later in the Artwork essay, as we have seen, is the notion of 'collectivity', characteristically a feature of the 'proletariat', that he links to the 'collective urban space' that film would forever explode. He wrote:

Among the points of fracture in artistic formation, film is one of the most dramatic. We may truly say that with film, a *new realm of consciousness* comes into being. To put it in a nutshell, film is the prism in which the spaces of the immediate environment—the spaces in which people live, pursue their avocations, and enjoy their leisure—are laid open before their eyes in a comprehensible, meaningful, and passionate way. In themselves these offices, furnished rooms, saloons, big-city streets, stations, and factories are ugly, incomprehensible, and hopelessly sad. Or rather, they were and seemed to be, until the advent of film. The cinema then exploded this entire prison-world with the dynamite of its fractions of a second, so that now we can take extended journeys of adventure between their widely scattered ruins.[16]

In his 1934 essay, 'Through Theatre to Cinema', Eisenstein wrote

> No screen had ever before reflected an image of collective action. Now the conception of 'collectivity' was to be pictured. But our enthusiasm produced a one-sided representation of the masses and the collective; one-sided because collectivism means the maximum development of the individual within the collective, a conception irreconcilably opposed to bourgeois individualism. Our first mass film missed this deeper meaning.[17]

Further, he remarked: '"individuality within the collective", the deeper meaning, demanded of cinema today, would have found entrance almost impossible if the way had not been cleared by the general concept'.[18] In the same essay, Eisenstein related his influential 'theory of montage' to the notion of the 'proletariat' and wrote:

> I consider that besides mastering the elements of filmic diction, the technique of the frame, and the theory, we have another credit to list—the value of profound ties with the traditions and methodology of literature. Not in vain, during this period, was the new concept of film-language born, film-language not as the language of the film-critic, but as an expression of cinema thinking, when the cinema was called upon to embody the philosophy and ideology of the victorious proletariat.[19]

'Cinematography is, first and foremost, montage', Eisenstein declared.[20] 'Montage is conflict': 'At the basis of every art is conflict (an "imagist" transformation of the dialectical principle). The shot appears as the *cell* of montage. Therefore it also must be considered from the viewpoint of *conflict*'.[21] In his 1929 essay, 'A Dialectic Approach to Film Form', Eisenstein attempts to bring 'philosophy' to 'art', the philosophy of 'dialectical materialism' to art as conflict. He wrote:

> *Thus*: The projection of the dialectic system of things
> into the brain
> *into creating abstractly*

into the process of thinking
yields: dialectic method of thinking;
dialectic materialism—   PHILOSOPHY.
And also:
The projection of the same system of things
while creating concretely
while giving form
yields: ART.[22]

'*For art is always conflict*': (1) according to its social mission, (2) according to its nature, (3) according to its methodology.[23] In further elaboration of (1) he remarks: 'According to its social mission *because*: It is art's task to make manifest the contradictions of Being. To form equitable views by stirring up contradictions within the spectator's mind, and to forge accurate intellectual concepts from the dynamic clash of opposing passions'.[24] He further writes that 'Art is always conflict, according to its methodology', and asserting that film is the 'highest form of art', he says 'Shots and montage are the basic elements of cinema' and that '*Montage* has been established by the Soviet film as the nerve of cinema'.[25] Contesting other ideas of montage that were circulating around him, he makes it clear that for him,

> montage is an idea that arises from the collision of independent shots—shots even opposite to one another: the 'dramatic' principle. A sophism? Certainly not. For we are seeking a definition of the whole nature, the principal style and spirit of cinema from its technical (optical) basis.[26]

'For many film-makers', Eisenstein remarks,

> montage and leftist excesses of formalism—are synonymous. Yet montage is not this at all. For those who are able, montage is the most powerful compositional means of telling a story. For those who do not know about composition, montage is a syntax for the correct construction of each principle of a film fragment,

and 'lastly, montage is simply an elementary rule of film-orthography for those who mistakenly put together pieces of a film as one would mix ready-made recipes of medicine, or pickle cucumbers, or preserve plums, or ferment apples and cranberries together'.[27]

In an essay written in the same year entitled 'Methods of Montage', Eisenstein discusses 'montage principle' and distinguishes between '*Metric Montage*', '*Rhythmic Montage*', '*Tonal Montage*', and '*Overtonal Montage*'. He then adds a 'higher category' to the list and calls it '*Intellectual Montage*', which he bases on his recollection of 'Lenin's synopsis of the fundamental elements of Hegelian dialectic'.[28] Intellectual montage, he says, is 'montage not of generally physiological overtonal sounds, but of sounds and overtones of an intellectual sort: i.e., conflict-juxtaposition of accompanying intellectual affects', concluding that

> The intellectual cinema will be that which resolves the conflict-juxtaposition of the physiological and intellectual overtone. Building a completely new form of cinematography—the realization of revolution in the general history of culture; building a synthesis of science, art, and class militancy.[29]

With this brief elaboration on the principle of montage we can now go back to the Odessa Steps—also named the 'Potemkin Steps'. But first a word about the origin of the name 'Potemkin' itself. The famous battleship took its name from the Russian soldier and statesman, Prince Grigory Potemkin. He was given the responsibility to build the Black Sea Fleet under Catherine the Great (who ruled over Russia from 1762 to 1796). He was one of the favorites of Her Majesty, the Empress. It was anecdotally reported that, to impress her, Potemkin ordered the construction of a 'sham village' in order to give the false impression of rural prosperity when she was to travel to Crimea in 1787: so the famous term 'Potemkin village'. It is noteworthy to mention that this term became the title of an essay by the architect Adolf Loos in 1898, in which he sarcastically ridiculed his contemporary architects in the city of Vienna for putting historicist facades on their designed buildings, hence falsifying their actual historical time.[30]

A very brief historical account of the Odessa Steps and their description might be useful before we proceed. The stairs are a formal entrance into the city from the direction of the sea and are the best-known symbol of Odessa.

> The stairs were originally known as the Boulevard steps, the Giant Staircase, or the Richelieu steps. The top step is 12.5 meters (41 feet) wide, and the lowest step is 21.7 meters (70.8 feet) wide. The staircase extends for 142 meters, but it gives the illusion of greater length. The stairs were so precisely constructed as to create an optical illusion. A person looking down the stairs sees only the treads and the risers are invisible; whereas a person looking up sees only risers, and the treads are invisible.[31]

We are further informed that the original 200 stairs were designed in 1825 by Italian architect Francesco Boffo and St. Petersburg architects Avraam I. Melnikov and Pot'e.

> The staircase cost 800,000 rubles to build. In 1837, the decision was made to build a 'monstrous staircase', which was constructed between 1837 and 1841. An English engineer named John Upton supervised the construction. Upton had fled Britain while on bail for forgery. Upton went on to oversee the construction of the huge dry-docks constructed in Sevastopol and completed in 1853. As erosion destroyed the stairs, in 1933 the sandstone was replaced by rose-grey granite from the BOH area, and the landings were covered with asphalt. Eight steps were lost under the sand when the port was being extended, reducing the number of stairs to 192, with ten landings.[32]

The pivotal sequence of Part 4 of *Battleship Potemkin* takes place on the Odessa Steps and might be claimed to be 'the most famous single sequence of images in the history of world cinema, and especially of silent montage cinema'.[33] The sequence is also notable for its 'poetic license' as it does not follow the actual historical event of the mutiny which took place on the battleship. In this sense, as Richard Taylor notes, the Odessa Steps sequence is the 'paradigm of *pars pro toto*'.[34] Part 4 begins with the title 'That memorable day the city lived one life with the rebellious battleship'.[35] In his explanation of the 'Rhythmic Montage', in contrast to 'Metrical Montage', Eisenstein brings up the Odessa Steps as an exemplary illustration of it and writes:

> In this the rhythmic drum of the soldier's feet as they descend the steps violates all *metrical* demands. Unsynchronized with the best

of the cutting, this drumming comes in *off-beat* each time, and the shot itself is entirely different in its solution with each appearance. The final pull of tension is supplied by the transfer from the rhythm of the descending feet to another rhythm—a new kind of downward movement—the next intensity level of the same activity—the baby-carriage rolling down the steps. The carriage functions as a directly progressing accelerator of the advancing feet. The stepping descent passes into a rolling descent.[36]

As Taylor points out, the descent of the pram down the Odessa Steps 'is probably the most famous image' of *Battleship Potemkin*. Taylor writes:

> The device of using the suffering of a child to move the audience has been much imitated, although Eisenstein, unlike so many of his imitators, leaves the suffering of this particular baby to our imagination, rather than depicting it in graphic details.[37]

The next famous shot, also much imitated, is the case of 'extreme close-up' showing the face of the 'schoolmistress' or the 'nurse': 'Her pince-nez are now awry on her nose, the right lens shattered as her right eye bleeds. Her mouth gapes in horror'.[38] In his 1929 essay 'The Dramaturgy of Film Form (The Dialectical Approach to Film Form)', Eisenstein cited this scene as an instance of 'logical montage'. He wrote: 'Representation of a spontaneous action, *Potemkin*. Woman with pince-nez. Followed immediately—without a transition—by the same woman with shattered pince-nez and bleeding eye. Sensation of a shot hitting the eye'.[39] It must be noted that, as Taylor reminds us, *Potemkin*'s characteristic feature is the application of 'Eisenstein's principle of the montage of attraction', as 'objects are chosen for associations that will resonate with the audience'.[40] Taylor brings out the notion of 'seeing' and the ambiguity of 'pince-nez' in *Potemkin* and nicely observes that, in contrast to the doctor who examines the rotten meat with his pince-nez, when the 'schoolmistress' on the Odessa Steps

> wears pince-nez, these present her clarity of vision: hence, to restore the 'proper order of the society' the Cossack has to slash, not just her

face, but also her pince-nez, in order to destroy both her vision and her life.[41]

A number of things in Eisenstein's film caused reaction and debate in subsequent decades, as Taylor notes, namely the question of the historical authenticity of the mutiny on the ship, the role of montage, mass and the individual, the purpose of revolutionary art, etc. But: 'with amazing keenness Eisenstein observes nature, the human face, the machine. He listens with sensitivity to the very breathing of the ocean's depths. He loves material objects. He knows that revolution *is not an individual but the mass* and he is searching for the language to express mass emotions'.[42]

In the theoretical reception of *Potemkin*, both the psychoanalytical theory of film and the Marxian theory have noticed the importance of Eisenstein's film. Todd McGowan, from the side of psychoanalytical theory, discusses the category of the Real in Lacanian theory and perceptively writes:

> Even though cinema displays images, it has the capacity to depict the impossible real. This is one of the greatest achievements of Sergei Eisenstein's *Battleship Potemkin* (1925). The film chronicles the revolt of sailors on the *Potemkin* and their success in overthrowing the despotic rule of the officers on the ship. Eisenstein's film stresses the impossibility of the sailors' collective act, but then it shows this act occurring. The film remains compelling today because it captures the impossible real in this way. Film's commitment to visualizing the real happening is one of the reasons for the medium's appeal. One cannot imagine a cinema that did not touch on the real.[43]

In her book devoted to Marxian film theory, Anna Kornbluh, in the section 'The Capitalist Phantasmagoria', writes: 'Given the affinity between the Marxist emphasis on contradictory appearances and film theory's emphasis on the production of appearances, it makes sense that one of the very first theorists of film to conceive himself as such was a thinker deeply invested in Marx: Sergei Eisenstein'.[44] Pointing out that the name Eisenstein is associated with the first school of film ever that was founded in Russia in 1920, and that Eisenstein 'wrote one of the very first works of film theory in 1923, "The Montage of

Attraction"', she delves deeper only to remind us that the concept of 'montage' named for Eisenstein the

> dialectical character of cinema: it is an assembly of different parts, sutured together into the whole, with seams still apparent. The power of cinema to convey ideas derives from this interrelation of different shots, above and beyond the content of any individual shot, so that cinema formally resembles a dialectical idea/the dialectical method.[45]

She further remarks that Eisenstein used montage to connect 'the oppressive working conditions endured by sailors to their eventual revolt', and that *Potemkin* uses the technique of montage to illustrate the 'bond between the revolting naval sailors and the people of Odessa who have no ostensible relation to them. In turn Eisenstein hopes to trigger a similar enthusiasm for revolt among the spectators who see the montage at work'.[46] Kornbluh rightly observes that Eisenstein conceived individual parts/individual shots as themselves dialectical, since the

> pro-film event and the mise-en-scène necessarily derived from the capitalist context of contradiction, and since the pairing of sight and sound provoke sensory contrast and sensation of contradiction [...] Thus, he distinguished the dialectical energy of montage from the mere complexity of continuity editing. Montage animates the succession of images, it activates their collision—it doesn't merely line them up.[47]

She further notes that Eisenstein 'based his definition of the film medium upon this implicit promise of dialectical art: montage is at its best something like an art of contraction, formalizing the contradictions in the social world'.[48]

A contemporary critic in 1926, taking up the slogan of 'social command' which became a more important slogan decades later, commented: 'Yes, in this film Eisenstein does fulfill the social command, but not because he was working to government order. The social command does not derive from a studio director's office or a government commission. *Eisenstein derived his social command from the proletarian revolution in which he emerged as an artist*'[49] (emphasis mine). With this remark I leave the *mise-en-scène* of the 'proletarian masses' in film behind to arrive at its exposition in philosophical-theoretical and political registers. In the background of this exposition is Benjamin's point about the 'proletarian class consciousness'. In this connection we know that Benjamin in 1924 read Georg Lukács's *History and Class Consciousness*, one of the founding texts, perhaps the most important one—along with Karl Korsch's *Marxism and Philosophy*—of so-called Western Marxism, in which Lukács takes up the notion of 'reification' in its relation to the question of the 'class consciousness of the proletariat'.[50]

Before I continue, I want to pose the following questions: Who are the 'masses'? Is this word synonymous with 'crowd', or 'collectivity', or, in the case of cinema, 'audience' or 'spectator'? After all, what do we mean by the word 'proletariat'? What is the distinction between the 'masses' and the 'proletariat'?

Gustave Le Bon in his *The Crowd: A Study of the Popular Mind*, published in 1895, came up with a 'theory of the crowd' and identified modernity as the 'age of crowds'.[51] For him it was a 'period of transition and anarchy', and, as Byung-Chul Han points out, 'In taking form, the society of the future would have to reckon with a new power—the power of masses'.[52] Le Bon thus observed that 'The age we are about to enter will in truth be the ERA OF CROWDS'.[53] In his explicit reference to Le Bon and the psychologizing factor, Benjamin in the second version of the Artwork essay wrote that 'The mass as an impenetrable, compact entity, which Le Bon and others have made the subject of their "mass psychology", is that of the petty bourgeoisie'.[54] As Miriam Bratu Hansen points out, the late-nineteenth-century 'pessimistic-elitist' theories of the crowd 'essentialized, psychologized, pathologized, and demonized the crowd, or mass in the singular, as an atavistic force that required a leader'.[55] In contrast, Siegfried Kracauer, for his part, as Hansen notes, tried to complicate the 'leftist conception of masses predicated on the industrial working class and the idea of a revolutionary proletariat'.[56] In contemporary industrial-digital capitalism, the distinction between the 'mass' and the 'crowd' is blurred. As Han perceptively points out, 'The new mass is the *digital swarm*. Its features distinguish it radically from the crowd'.[57] But, as he crucially notes: 'The digital swarm does not constitute a mass because no *soul*—no *spirit*—dwells within it'.[58] And further, 'The soul gathers and unites. In contrast, the digital swarm comprises isolated individuals. The mass is structured along different lines: its features cannot be traced back to individuals'.[59]

On the other hand, Stathis Kouvelakis reminds us that 'Modernity is, irrevocably, the age of the masses, the real protagonist of history', and that this modernity irrevocably belongs to the French Revolution, which 'anticipates, in a certain sense, all subsequent' future revolutions in which the 'masses' will take center stage.[60] The masses emerge as *historical subject*. The temporality of the revolution is in fact

> pregnant with—indeed, saturated with—the future. Thus it presents itself—to paraphrase Hegel—as the temporality of the becoming-subject of the substance of politics, whatever term is used to designate this substance: *multitude*, the masses, the 'people', or, later, the 'people of the people', that is the 'proletariat'.[61]

In the chapter entitled 'Reification and the Consciousness of the Proletariat' in *History and Class Consciousness*, Lukács notes that Marx, in his *Critique of Hegel's Philosophy of Right*, gave 'a lapidary account of the special position of the proletariat in society and history, and the standpoint from which it can function as the identical subject-object of the social and historical process of revolution'.[62] He quotes Marx as saying: 'When the proletariat proclaims the dissolution of the previous world-order it does no more than reveal the secret of its own existence, for it represents the effective dissolution of the world-order'.[63] Lukács follows this up by commenting that

> The self-understanding of the proletariat is therefore simultaneously the objective understanding of the nature of society. When the proletariat furthers its own class-aims it simultaneously achieves the conscious realization of the—objective—aims of society, aims which would inevitably remain abstract possibilities and objective frontiers but for this conscious intervention.[64]

In an extensive and sympathetic discussion of Lukács's work, Slavoj Žižek takes up the analysis of *History and Class Consciousness* in its historical context and brings up Hegel along with the question of History. He grounds his analysis in the three mediated terms of Universal, Particular, and Singular, which respectively are 'History (the global historical movement), the Proletariat (the particular class with a privileged relationship to the universal), and the Communist Party (the singular agent)'.[65] Using the Hegelian terms, Žižek elaborates on these categories: 'The accent is here on the "spontaneous" revolutionary stance of the proletariat: the Party only acts in a maieutic role, rendering possible the purely formal conversion of the proletariat from Class-In-Itself to Class-For-Itself'.[66] Here Žižek is relying on the well-known Hegelian distinction between 'For Itself' and 'In Itself' to drive his point home.[67] The implication is that when the Proletariat, as a social class, becomes a class 'For Itself', not taken as an empirical entity, it begins to speak for humanity in general.

At this point I must come back to Benjamin. In relation to the concept of 'aura' (of nature), defined as 'the unique apparition of appearance of a distance, however near it may be', and in relation to its decay, Benjamin wrote that in the

> light of this definition, we can readily grasp the social basis of the aura's present decay. It rests on two circumstances, both linked to the increasing significance of the masses of contemporary life. Namely: *the desire of the present-day masses to 'get closer' to things spatially and humanly, and their equally passionate concern for overcoming each thing's uniqueness [Überwindung des Einmaligen jeder Gegebenheit] by appropriating it as a reproduction.*[68]

At the same time, in the later version, as Miriam Bratu Hansen points out, Benjamin replaces 'the masses' with the more neutral term 'audience' as 'the consumer who constitutes the market'.[69] As Hansen reminds us, 'Benjamin had no illusion regarding the contemporary masses; he knew all too well that class-conscious self-representation was not necessarily the direction in which dominant formations of collectivity were heading'.[70] 'On the contrary', Hansen continues, 'the artwork essay proceeds from the assumption that the masses are not an intrinsically progressive productive force but a problem, if not *the* problem of modern politics—which the essay links to capitalist society's failed innervation of technology and the resulting alienation of collective sense perception'.[71] Benjamin knew well that the 'capitalist film industry's "cult of the audience" (the consumerist complement to the star cult) merely enhances the "corrupt condition" of the contemporary masses, which in turn meets the objective of fascism to suppress their class consciousness'.[72] It is here that Benjamin enters sharply the political notion of the Proletariat and its 'class consciousness' in the Artwork essay.

In the second version of the Artwork essay, Benjamin begins Section XII with this remark: 'The representation of human beings by means of an apparatus has made possible a highly productive use of the human being's self-alienation'.[73] He explains that the 'nature of this use' can be grasped by the fact that the 'film actor's estrangement in the face of apparatus' is akin to the 'estrangement felt before one's appearance [*Erscheinung*] in a mirror', which now has become 'detachable from the person mirrored, and is transported'. But where? The answer: 'to the site in front of masses'.[74] He continues that 'While he stands before the apparatus, he knows that in the end he is confronting the masses. It is they who will control him'.[75] A few lines after this sentence he writes this paragraph:

> It should not be forgotten, of course, that there can be no political advantage derived from this control until film has liberated itself from the fetters of capitalist exploitation. Film capital uses the revolutionary opportunities implied by this control for counterrevolutionary purposes. Not only does the cult of the movie star which it fosters preserve that magic of the personality which has long been no more than the putrid magic of its own commodity character, but its counterpart, the cult of the audience, reinforces the corruption by which fascism is seeking to supplant the class consciousness of the masses.[76]

It is at the end of the paragraph above that Benjamin offers an extraordinary exposition of the notion of the Proletariat that he relegated to a footnote, which, by the way, won the approbation of his friend Theodor Adorno. This long footnote was subsequently omitted in the Third Version of the Artwork essay. I have before cited the footnote almost in its entirety. Here, to recall, I confine myself to highlighting only the most salient points of it. Benjamin quite perceptively wrote that '*proletarian class consciousness, which is the most enlightened form of class consciousness, fundamentally transforms the structure of the proletarian masses*'[77] (emphasis mine). He first notes that the 'class-conscious proletariat' forms a 'compact mass' in the 'minds of its oppressors'. But 'at the moment when it takes up its struggle for liberation, this apparently compact mass has actually already begun to loosen'.[78] Furthermore,

> It ceases to be governed by mere reactions; it makes the transition to action. The loosening of the proletarian masses is the work of solidarity. In the solidarity of the proletarian class struggle, the dead, undialectical opposition between individual and mass is abolished; for the comrade, it does not exist.[79]

Benjamin contrasts the class of the proletariat to the 'petty-bourgeoisie', an entity discussed as the subject of 'mass psychology' by his contemporaries, and writes that it cannot be a class. 'It is in fact only a mass', and then adds that 'the greater the pressure acting on it between the two antagonistic classes of the bourgeoisie and the proletariat, the more compact it becomes'. 'But for that very reason', he continues, 'this compact mass forms the antithesis of the proletarian cadre, which obeys a collective *ratio*'.[80]

In the critical and somewhat harsh response to the early version of the Artwork essay that Adorno wrote in his letter to Benjamin from London, dated 18 March 1936, he was otherwise full of praise for what his friend wrote in the 'footnote'. Adorno was right to tell Benjamin that, since reading Lenin's *State and Revolution*, 'I cannot conclude, however, without saying that I find your few sentences concerning the disintegration of the proletariat into "masses" through the revolution to be amongst the most profound and most powerful statements of political theory I have encountered'.[81]

To conclude: The powerful cinematic *mise-en-scène* of the *proletarian masses* by the great Eisenstein found its equally powerful philosophical-political exposition in Benjamin.

Notes

1. Sergei Eisenstein, *Film Form: Essays in Film Theory*, ed. and trans. Jay Leyda (San Diego: Harcourt, 1949, 1977), 16.
2. Sergei Eisenstein, *Film Form*, 63.
3. Walter Benjamin, 'Reply to Oscar A. H. Schmitz', in *Walter Benjamin, Selected Writing, Volume 2, 1927–1934*, trans. Rodney Livingstone and others, eds Michael W. Jennings, Howard Eiland, and Gary Smith (Cambridge: The Belknap Press of Harvard University Press, 1999), 17.

4 Walter Benjamin, 'The Work of Art in the Age of Its Technological Reproducibility', Second Version, in *Walter Benjamin, Selected Writings, Volume 3, 1935–1938*, trans. Edmund Jephcott, Howard Eiland, and others, ed. Howard Eiland and Michael W. Jennings (Cambridge: The Belknap Press of Harvard University Press, 2002), 129.

5 Kojin Karatani, *Transcritique: On Kant and Marx* (Cambridge: The MIT Press, 2003), 1.

6 See Christopher Kul-Want, 'Introduction', in his edited volume *Philosophers on Film, from Bergson to Badiou: A Critical Reader* (New York: Colombia University Press, 2019), 3.

7 Sergei Eisenstein, *Film Form*, 86.

8 Sergei Eisenstein, *Film Form*, 92.

9 See Slavoj Žižek, *The Sublime Object of Ideology* (London and New York: Verso, 1989), 203.

10 Slavoj Žižek, *The Sublime Object of Ideology*, 203. Žižek further writes that

> Thus, by means of the very failure of representation, we can have a presentiment of the true dimension of the Thing. This is also why an object evoking in us the feeling of Sublimity gives us simultaneous pleasure and dis-pleasure: it gives us displeasure because of its inadequacy to the Thing-Idea, but precisely through this inadequacy it gives us pleasure by indicating the true, incomparable greatness of the Thing, surpassing every possible phenomenal, empirical experience.
>
> 202–203

11 Walter Benjamin, 'Reply to Oscar A. H. Schmitz', 17. The editors note that Oscar Adolf Hermann Schmitz was 'a playwright and essayist', who maintained a 'close contact with the circle around Stefan Georg', and that 'Benjamin's reply to Schmitz exemplifies the tenor of the argument over *Battleship Potemkin*', 19.

12 Walter Benjamin, 'Reply to Oscar A. H. Schmitz', 17–18.

13 Walter Benjamin, 'Reply to Oscar A. H. Schmitz', 18.

14 Walter Benjamin, 'Reply to Oscar A. H. Schmitz', 18. The editors provide briefly some information about the term UFA (Universum-Film AG): UFA,

> the largest firm in the German film industry, was founded in 1917. Vertically integrated, UFA owned everything from machine shops and film laboratories to production and distribution facilities. It was acquired by the Hugenberg Group in 1927, nationalized by the German Reich in 1936–1937, and dismantled by the Allies in 1945.
>
> 19

15 Walter Benjamin, 'Reply to Oscar A. H. Schmitz', 19.

16 Walter Benjamin, 'Reply to Oscar A. H. Schmitz', 17.

17 Sergei Eisenstein, *Film Form*, 16.

18 Sergei Eisenstein, *Film Form*, 17.

19 Sergei Eisenstein, *Film Form*, 17. Eisenstein further remarks that

> Stretching out its hand to the new quality of literature—the dramatics of the subject—the cinema cannot forget the tremendous experience of its earlier periods. But the way is not back to them, but forward to the synthesis of all the best that has been done by our silent cinematography, towards a synthesis of these with the demands of today, along the lines of story and Marxist-Leninist ideological analysis. The phase of monumental synthesis in the images of the people of the epoch of socialism—the phase of socialist realism.
>
> 17

20 Sergei Eisenstein, *Film Form*, 20.
21 Sergei Eisenstein, *Film Form*, 38.
22 Sergei Eisenstein, *Film Form*, 45.
23 Sergei Eisenstein, *Film Form*, 46.
24 Sergei Eisenstein, *Film Form*, 48.
25 Sergei Eisenstein, *Film Form*, 48.
26 Sergei Eisenstein, *Film Form*, 49.
27 Sergei Eisenstein, *Film Form*, 111.
28 Sergei Eisenstein, *Film Form*, 81. He gives the categories of Lenin's synopsis of Hegelian dialectics in the following:

> These elements may be presented in a more detailed way thus: ... 10) an endless process of revealing *new* aspects, relationships, etc. 11) an endless process of deepening human perception of things, appearances, processes and so on, from appearance to essence and from the less profound to the more profound essence. 12) from co-existence to causality and from one form of connection and interdependence to another, deeper, more general. 13) recurrence, on the highest level, of known traits, attributes, etc. of the lowest, and 14) return, so to say, to the old (negation of the negation) ....
>
> 81

29 Sergei Eisenstein, *Film Form*, 82–83.
30 See Adolf Loos, *Spoken into the Void: Collected Essays 1897–1900* (Cambridge: The MIT Press, 1982).
31 I have adopted the description from Wikipedia, see https://en.wikipedia.org/wiki/Potemkin_Stairs.
32 https://en.wikipedia.org/wiki/Potemkin_Stairs.
33 See Richard Taylor, *The Battleship Potemkin* (London and New York: I. B. Tauris, 2000), 35. For my description of the film and its reception I am mainly relying on this informative text.
34 Richard Taylor, *The Battleship Potemkin*, 35.
35 Richard Taylor, *The Battleship Potemkin*, 35.
36 Sergei Eisenstein, *Film Form*, 74. Taylor cites a rather lengthy explanation of the same montage technique for the Odessa Steps by Eisenstein in his '"Eh!" On the

Purity of Film Language', published in S. M. Eisenstein, *Selected Works. Volume 1: Writings, 1922–34* (London and Bloomington: I. B. Tauris, 1988); see also Richard Taylor, *The Battleship Potemkin*.
37   Richard Taylor, *The Battleship Potemkin*, 48.
38   Richard Taylor, *The Battleship Potemkin*, 50.
39   Cited by Richard Taylor, *The Battleship Potemkin*, 50.
40   Richard Taylor, *The Battleship Potemkin*, 62.
41   Richard Taylor, *The Battleship Potemkin*, 62.
42   In Richard Taylor, *The Battleship Potemkin*, 72. Taylor devotes many pages of his book to the history of the reception of the *Potemkin*, which I do not have space here to discuss.
43   See Todd McGowan, *Psychoanalytical Film Theory and the Rules of the Game* (New York: Bloomsbury, 2015, 2018), 38.
44   See Anna Kornbluh, *Marxist Film Theory and Fight Club* (New York: Bloomsbury, 2019), 70.
45   Anna Kornbluh, *Marxist Film Theory and Fight Club*, 70.
46   Anna Kornbluh, *Marxist Film Theory and Fight Club*, 71.
47   Anna Kornbluh, *Marxist Film Theory and Fight Club*, 71.
48   Anna Kornbluh, *Marxist Film Theory and Fight Club*, 71.
49   Quoted in Richard Taylor, *The Battleship Potemkin*, 74. The critic further pointed out that 'we believe that, even if Eisenstein's next film were not made to government order and not based on the script devoted to a revolution theme, Eisenstein would nevertheless fulfill the social command of the Proletarian', 74.
50   Georg Lukács, *History and Class Consciousness: Studies in Marxist Dialectics*, trans. Rodney Livingstone (Cambridge: The MIT Press, 1971).
51   See Gustave Le Bon, *The Crowd: A Study of the Popular Mind* (New York: Macmillan, 1897).
52   See Byung-Chul Han, *In the Swarm: Digital Prospects*, trans. Erik Butler (Cambridge: The MIT Press, 2017), 9.
53   Quoted in Byung-Chul Han, *In the Swarm*, 9. Han in his further reflections aptly notes that

> Le Bon saw the received power structures were falling apart. Now the 'voices of the masses' prevailed. The masses, he observed, have founded 'syndicates before which the authorities capitulate one after the other; they are also founding labour unions, which in spite of all economic laws tend to regulate the conditions of labour and wages'.
>
> 9

Further,

> Parliamentary representatives are only their stooges. For Le Bon, the phenomenon of crowds expresses a new balance of power. The 'divine right of masses', he predicts, 'is about to replace the divine right of kings'. The ascent of the masses entails the crisis of sovereignty and heralds cultural decline.

It means the 'thoroughgoing destruction of ... Civilization', for 'civilization [requires] conditions that crowds, left to themselves, have invariably shown themselves incapable of realizing'.

9

54 Walter Benjamin, 'The Work of Art in the Age of Its Technological Reproducibility', Second Version, 129.
55 See Miriam Bratu Hansen, *Cinema and Experience: Siegfried Kracauer, Walter Benjamin, and Theodor W. Adorno* (Berkeley: University of California Press, 2012), 49.
56 Miriam Bratu Hansen, *Cinema and Experience*, 49.
57 Byung-Chul Han, *In the Swarm*, 10.
58 Byung-Chul Han, *In the Swarm*, 10.
59 Byung-Chul Han, *In the Swarm*, 10.
60 See Stathis Kouvelakis, *Philosophy and Revolution: From Kant to Marx*, preface by Fredric Jameson (London and New York: Verso, 2003), 76.
61 Stathis Kouvelakis, *Philosophy and Revolution*, 340–341.
62 Georg Lukács, *History and Class Consciousness*, 149.
63 Georg Lukács, *History and Class Consciousness*, 149.
64 Georg Lukács, *History and Class Consciousness*, 149.
65 See Slavoj Žižek 'Postface: Georg Lukács as the Philosopher of Leninism', in George Lukács, *A Defence of History and Class Consciousness: Tailism and the Dialectic*, trans. Leslie Esther, intro. John Rees and postface Slavoj Žižek (London and New York: Verso, 2000), 159.
66 Slavoj Žižek 'Postface: Georg Lukács as the Philosopher of Leninism', 159. Žižek properly contextualizes Lukács and his major work by pointing out that 'What then happened with the saturation of the "revolutionary sequence" of 1917' (using Alain Badiou's term) is that a

> direct theoretical-political engagement like that of Lukács in *History and Class Consciousness* became impossible. The socialist movement definitively split into social democratic parliamentary reforms and the new Stalinist orthodoxy, while Western Marxism, which abstained from openly endorsing any of these two poles, abandoned the stance of direct political engagement and turned into a part of the established academic machine whose tradition runs from the early Frankfurt School up to today's cultural studies—therein resides the key difference that separates it from Lukács of the 1920s.

67 Frederick Beiser in his *Hegel* (New York: Routledge, 2005) usefully explains the difference between 'For Itself' and 'In Itself' in Hegel as follows: 'something is For Itself when it is self-directing and self-conscious, fully aware of its activity and ends and striving to realize them', and 'In Itself' means two things:

> something taken by itself, apart from its relations to other things; and something potential, inchoate and undeveloped, which is not self-conscious and

completely self-directing. In this latter sense it is contrasted with something *for itself*, which is not only actual, organized and developed but also self-conscious.

318–319

68 Walter Benjamin, 'The Work of Art in the Age of Its Technological Reproducibility', Third Version, in *Walter Benjamin, Selected Writings, Volume 4, 1938–1940*, trans. Edmund Jephcott and others, eds Howard Eiland and Michael W. Jennings (The Belknap Press of Harvard University Press, 2003), 255.
69 Miriam Bratu Hansen, *Cinema and Experience*, 96.
70 Miriam Bratu Hansen, *Cinema and Experience*, 97.
71 Miriam Bratu Hansen, *Cinema and Experience*, 97.
72 Miriam Bratu Hansen, *Cinema and Experience*, 97.
73 Walter Benjamin, 'The Work of Art in the Age of Its Technological Reproducibility', Second Version, 113.
74 Walter Benjamin, 'The Work of Art in the Age of Its Technological Reproducibility', Second Version, 113.
75 Walter Benjamin, 'The Work of Art in the Age of Its Technological Reproducibility', Second Version, 113.
76 Walter Benjamin, 'The Work of Art in the Age of Its Technological Reproducibility', Second Version, 113.
77 Walter Benjamin, 'The Work of Art in the Age of Its Technological Reproducibility', Second Version, 129, n. 24.
78 Walter Benjamin, 'The Work of Art in the Age of Its Technological Reproducibility', Second Version, 129, n. 24.
79 Walter Benjamin, 'The Work of Art in the Age of Its Technological Reproducibility', Second Version, 129. n. 24.
80 Walter Benjamin, 'The Work of Art in the Age of Its Technological Reproducibility', Second Version, 129. n. 4.
81 See Walter Benjamin and Theodor Adorno, *The Complete Correspondence, 1928–1940*, ed. Henri Loniz, trans. Nicholas Walker (Cambridge: Harvard University Press), 132–133.

Epilogue

The art of the masses in the age of pornography

> The brothel, as the place of the legislation of images, the *jouissance* of simulacra.
> —Alain Badiou, *The Pornographic Age*[1]

> We must disimage, disimagine.
> —Alain Badiou, *The Pornographic Age*[2]

> The society of pornography is a society of spectacle.
> —Byung-Chul Han, *The Transparency Society*[3]

> Pornography is unmediated contact between the image and the eye.
> —Byung-Chul Han, *The Transparency Society*[4]

Contemporary capitalist society might be seen as '*The Pornographic Age*'. The term is a reference to Alain Badiou's small book, which is based on his reading of Jean Genet's play *The Balcony*.[5] From a different philosophical approach, Byung-Chul Han deploys the term 'the pornographic society', subsumed under *The Transparency Society*, which is the title of his book. He presents a set of categories, different from those of Badiou, to analyze this 'pornographic society'.[6] In a moment I will take a closer look at their different propositions.

My claim is that the contemporary 'mass arts', architecture *and* cinema, are under the 'regime of the image' in this pornographic society. They are two forms of 'mass art' that are *anaesthetized*. We can rename this *anaesthetization* in its dialectical relation with aestheticization by its Marxian–Benjaminian term *Phantasmagoria*, that verges on the Wagnerian *Gesamtkunstwerk*—the 'total work of art'.[7] I suggest another attribution, a psychoanalytical one, to qualify our contemporary pornographic society by calling it 'The *Society of Psychosis*'. I will come back to this below. Here I want to say this: If cinema after Abbas Kiarostami is 'dead', as Jean-Luc Godard declared, architecture lives on, because, as Benjamin reminded us, and I repeat it again here: 'the human need for shelter is permanent'. Thus I return to the central thesis I have pursued in the course of my investigation in this work: If architecture must be radically reconfigured, its theory and critique have to be grounded on the foundation of the philosophical teaching of revolutionary cinema as true 'mass art' at the time when cinema became the *training ground* of the individual human *apperception* in the early decades of the twentieth century, that is, the cinema of Eisenstein to Chaplin and Hitchcock, and much later, the cinema of Godard to Kiarostami. Architecture, then, must be reconfigured along the lines of *impurity* and the '*non-art* of the art' of the cinema, the philosophical foundation of which is laid down by Badiou. Still, the notion of 'mass art' must be rethought along the lines of Benjamin's thesis in 'The Work of Art in the Age of Its Technological Reproducibility'. It is my claim that in the intervening 70 years since Benjamin the choice has not changed: between the '*aestheticizing of political life*' as '*practiced by fascism*', and the response of '*Communism by politicizing art*'. This cannot be done without the agency of the proletariat. To recall, this is what Benjamin wrote in the Epilogue of his Artwork essay:

> The increasing proletarianization of modern man and the increasing formation of masses are two sides of the same process. Fascism attempts to organize the newly proletarianized masses while leaving intact the property relations which they strive to abolish. It sees its salvation in granting expression to the masses—but on no account granting them rights. The masses have a right to change property relations; fascism seeks to give them *expression* in keeping these relations unchanged.[8]

One difference between our time and Benjamin's time regarding the discourse on fascism is the noisy talk of 'democracy' in capitalist parliamentary 'representative' systems, a veritable obsession of our contemporary 'democrats' in *the pornographic society*. This is the crux of Badiou's novel argument in *The Pornographic Age* against the hackneyed and tired name of 'democracy'. Analyzing Genet's play *The Balcony*, and discussing the 'regime of images' and 'power' in our time, along with the character of 'The Police Chief' as Phallus understood in Lacanian psychoanalytical theory, Badiou writes:

> What names are put into play in the philosophical comedy of the present, of our present? What are today's pompous emblems of power? What is its untouchable value? How is it that there is an unfortunate presence of the present? To my eyes, the principal name is 'democracy'.[9]

And further:

> To avoid any misunderstanding, let us agree that the word 'democracy' does not cover any theory, or fiction, of a shared power of *demos*, of an effective sovereignty of the people. It will only be a question of the word 'democracy' in so far as it designates a form of the State and all that goes with it. It is a constitutional category, a juridical hypothesis. It is a form of public liberties, supposedly protected by the constitution and animated by the electoral process. It is a form of the 'Rule of Law' [*l'État de droit*], to which all the so-called Western powers lay claim, as those countries that live in the shelter of those powers try to do, or as their clients, pretend to agree to.[10]

Badiou goes on to say that

> To make the comedy of images exist today is thus, almost inevitably, to treat the name 'democracy' for what it is: the Phallus of our present. To win, beyond the monotonous presence of our everyday life, the life of a true present, requires the courage to go beyond the democratic fetish as we know it. Jean Genet's *The Balcony* can serve as the preliminary operator.[11]

By way of offering more explanations of Genet's play, Badiou says that the subject of the play is what is at stake in the expression 'images of the present age'. In fact, he continues, 'Genet's text asks explicitly what becomes of images when the present is disorder. For Genet, it is riots or revolution; for us, it is undoubtedly the Arab Spring, the movement of the Indignados, at the same time as that of the crisis of capitalism and its deleterious effects in Europe'.[12]

On the concept of 'democracy', before his analysis of it in *The Pornographic Age*, Badiou in two other places discussed the term extensively.[13] In his 'Democratic Emblem', Badiou points out that Plato was convinced that 'democracy would not save the Greek polis, and in fact it didn't'; he goes on to say, 'Dare one assert that democracy will not save our beloved West either? Indeed; I daresay it won't, and I would add that this brings us right back to the ancient dilemma: *either we reinvent communism or we undergo some invented form of fascist barbarity*'[14] (emphasis mine). In this statement of Badiou I find a strong affirmation of the alleged 'perplexing' dictum in Benjamin's Artwork essay almost 70 years ago: Either *politicization of art* by communism or *aestheticization of politics* by fascism. This is indeed an 'ancient dilemma', a Platonic dictum, as Badiou puts it, that Benjamin brought forth and extended to 'mass art' with foresight in a specific political-historical conjuncture facing humanity. In this regard, I recall the apt term 'democratic fascism' that Badiou has employed to characterize our contemporary capitalist 'democracy' in a lecture series he delivered on Donald Trump.[15]

Let us return to *The Pornographic Age*. Badiou writes: 'Since the idea of revolution has disappeared, our world is merely that of resumption of power, under the consensual and pornographic image of market democracy'.[16] And further:

> They propose a regulated and decent capitalism, a non-pornographic capitalism, an ecological capitalism, and always more democracy. They demand, in short, a comfortable capitalism for all: a capitalism with a human face. Nothing will emerge from these chimeras. The only dangerous and radical critique is the political critique of democracy, because the emblem of the present age, its fetish, its phallus, is democracy.[17]

Han in *The Transparency Society* takes an alternative philosophical route, different from the one taken by Badiou, to come to advance his critical scrutiny of the 'pornographic society'—one no less powerful, no less provocative. In a chapter of his book entitled 'The Society of Pornography', which is related to certain other chapters in the book, including, 'The Society of Exhibition' and 'The Society of Control', Han expands on the notion of 'pornography'. To provide a context for his argument it is appropriate to cite Benjamin from his Artwork essay, to which Han himself refers. In Section V in the third version, Benjamin wrote:

> The reception of works of art varies in character, but in general two polar types stand out: one accentuates the artwork's cult value; the other, its exhibition value. Artistic production begins with figures in the service of cults [...] Cult value as such tends today, it would seem, to keep the artwork out of sight: certain statues of gods are accessible only to the priest in the cellar; certain images of the Madonna remain covered nearly all year around; certain sculptures on mediaeval cathedrals are not visible to the viewer at ground level. With the emancipation of specific artistic practices from the service of ritual, the opportunities for exhibiting their products increase [...] The scope for exhibiting the work of art has increased so enormously with the various methods of technologically reproducing it that, as happened in prehistoric times, a quantitative shift between the two poles of the artwork has led to a qualitative transformation in its nature. Just as the work of art in prehistoric times, through the absolute emphasis placed on its cult value, became first and foremost an instrument of magic which only later came to be recognized as a work of art, so today, through the absolute emphasis placed on its exhibition value, the work of art becomes a construct [*Gebilde*] with quite new functions. Among these, the one we are conscious of—the artistic function—may subsequently be seen as incidental. This much is certain: today, photography and film are the most serviceable vehicles of this new understanding.[18]

And in Section VI, Benjamin further writes:

> *In Photography, exhibition value begins to drive back cult value on all fronts.* But cult value does not give way without resistance. It is no accident that the portrait is central to early photography. In the cult of remembrance of dead or absent loved ones, the cult value of the image finds its last refuge. In the fleeting expression of a human face, the aura beckons from early photographs for the last time. This is what gives them their melancholy and incomparable beauty. But as the

human being withdraws from the photographic image, exhibition value for the first time shows its superiority to cult value.[19]

Analyzing Benjamin's passages above, Han correctly observes that 'the compulsion for display that hands everything over to visibility makes the *aura*—the "appearance of a distance"—vanish entirely'.[20] 'Exhibition value' is in the service of capitalism but, as Han points out, it cannot fit into Marxian 'use value' and 'exchange value': 'It is not use value because it stands removed from the sphere of utility; it is not exchange value because it does not reflect any labor. It exists thanks only to the attention it produces'.[21] Han reads Roland Barthes's *Camera Lucida* and brings out the notion of '*negativity*' by taking a strong stand against 'digital photography'. He writes: 'Digital photography wipes out all negativity. It requires neither a darkroom nor developing. No negative precedes it. It is purely positive', and further, 'It is transparent photography: without birth or death, without destiny or event. Destiny is not transparent. Transparent photography lacks semantic and temporal destiny [*Verdichtung*]. That is why it *says* nothing'.[22] Observing that 'Today's photography, fulfilled entirely by exhibition value, displays a different temporality', Han perceptively remarks:

> In the society of exhibition, every subject is also its own advertising object. Everything is measured by its exhibition value. *The society of exhibition is a society of pornography.* Everything has been turned outward, stripped, exposed, undressed, and put on show. The excess of display turns everything into a commodity; possessing 'no secret', it stands 'doomed … to immediate devouring'. Capitalist economy subjects everything to compulsory exhibition. The staging of display alone generates value.[23]

(emphasis mine)

Han writes that the 'increase of image is not inherently problematic', but what proves to be problematic 'is the iconic compulsion to become a picture'.[24] Echoing what I mentioned above about the dialectic between aestheticization and anaesthetization, Han remarks that 'Today visual communication occurs through infection, abreaction, or reflex. It lacks aesthetic reflection. Its aestheticization is ultimately anesthetic', and further,

Images filled with exhibition value offer no complexity. They are unambiguous—that is, pornographic. They lack all brokenness, which would trigger physical or mental reflection. Complexity slows down communication. Anesthetic hypercommunication reduces complexity in order to accelerate itself. It is significantly faster than sensory communication. The senses are slow. They impede the accelerated circulation of information and communication. Thus transparency comes with an absence of sense. The mass of information and communication derives from a *horror vacui*.[25]

Explicating fully the various aspects of the 'transparency society', and systematically reflecting on certain constant notions that he has repeatedly explored elsewhere, including the notions of *negativity* against 'positivity', and 'the Other', Han moves to develop his thesis on 'The Pornography Society' by locating it in the center of the 'Transparency Society'.[26]

Continuing his reflection on 'exhibition value' and citing a passage by Benjamin from his text 'Goethe's Elective Affinities' at the beginning of the chapter on 'The Pornography Society', Han first moves to say that, according to Benjamin, 'beauty requires what conceals and what is concealed to be inextricably joined', and then proceeds to draw the Kantian distinction between the 'beautiful' and the 'sublime', observing that,

> Only a form or an object [*Gebilde*] can be *beautiful*. In contrast, nakedness proves *sublime*—without form or image—when secrecy, the defining trait of beauty, does not adhere to it. The sublime suppresses the beautiful. It is because it points to the work of a Creator. For Kant, too, an object is sublime when it exceeds representation, any effort to picture it. The sublime reaches beyond the imagination.[27]

Han remarks:

> To be sure, the naked body that stands exhibited pornographically is 'miserable', but it is hardly 'sublime'. The sublime, against which Benjamin sets the beautiful appearance, lacks all exhibition value. It is precisely exhibition that destroys creaturely sublimity. The sublime

generates cult value. The pornographically exhibited face that 'flirts' with the consumer proves anything but sublime.[28]

Han writes that 'the face loaded with exhibition value to the point of bursting is pornographic'.[29] And, taking issue with Giorgio Agamben's argument in his book entitled *Nudities*, Han goes on to say: 'Capitalism heightens the pornographication of society by exhibiting everything as a commodity and handing it over to hypervisibility. It seeks the maximization of exhibition value'.[30] Referring to a distinction Barthes makes between *stadium* and *punctum* in his *Camera Lucida*, Han writes: 'Transparency is obscene when it keeps nothing covered or hidden, but rather hands it all over for viewing. Today all media images are more or less pornographic. Because of their obligingness, they lack any *punctum*, all semiotic intensity',[31] and according to Barthes,

> cinematic images possess no *punctum*. The *punctum* connects with contemplative lingering: 'in front of the screen, I am not free to shut my eyes; otherwise, opening them again, I would not discover the same image'. The punctum discloses itself only to gazing that lingers in contemplation. In contrast, a sequence of images forces the observer, as Barthes puts it, to 'continuous voracity'. The punctum eludes the consuming, ravenous gaze in which no '*pensiveness*' dwells.[32]

Moving to the chapter 'The Society of Information', Han comes to reflect on Plato's allegory of the cave. He claims, in contrast to Badiou, that Plato's cave is 'constructed as a theater'. He writes: 'Plato's cave presents a kind of shadow theater, then. The objects that cast shadow are not the real things of the world: they are, one and all, theatrical figures and props. After all, shadows and reflections of real things exist only outside the cave'.[33] But, as Badiou told us, Plato's cave is rather cinematic. More accurately, we must say that it is rather Plato's 'dialogues' which is theater and not the cave. It seems that Han did not consult Badiou's 'translation' of Plato's *Republic*, which, as we have seen, is not just a 'translation' but rather a re-writing of the *Republic* for our time, which we must recognize as 'Badiou's *Republic*'. Advancing his point about Plato's cave being a theater, Han is more concerned about the idea of 'narration', by which to challenge the 'society of information' that resides in 'the society of transparency'. We must heed his point. He says, 'In the allegory of the cave, the theater as a *world of narration* stands opposed to the *world of insight*', and that 'Plato's cave is a narrative world'.[34] He writes:

> In contrast to Plato's world of truth, today's society of transparency lacks divine light inhabited by metaphysical tension. Transparency has no transcendence. The society of transparency is seen through without light. It is illuminated by light that streams from a transcendent source. Transparency does not come about through an illuminating source of light. The medium of transparency is not light, but rather lightless mediation; instead of illuminating, it suffuses everything and makes it see-through. In contrast to light, it is penetrating and intrusive.[35]

At the end, confronting 'the Society of Control', and bringing up the radical difference between Bentham's 'panopticon' space in the 'disciplinary society'—on which Michel Foucault extensively wrote—and the more dangerous and more repressive 'digital panopticon', Han offers his insights:

> Pornographic putting-on-display and panoptic control complement each other. Exhibitionism and voyeurism feed the net as a digital panopticon. The society of control achieves perfection when the subjects bare themselves not through outer restraints but through self-generated need, that is, when the fear of having to abandon one's private and intimate sphere yields to the need to put oneself on display without shame.[36]

At this point, I come to the notion of the 'society of psychosis' I suggested above. Here I wish to claim that this society is yet another dimension of the same 'transparency society' Han discussed. I claim that 'psychosis' is the general malaise of the subject in this society today, but also of the 'masses' who belong to the 'Pornographic Age', which is the general definition for contemporary capitalism as Badiou has said. In Lacanian psychoanalytical theory, the term psychosis indicates that the fundamental distinction between the Real and 'reality' is lost.[37] The pornographic society lacks the resistance of the Real—the 'Real' in the Lacanian sense of the term.

Benjamin, with his knowledge of Freud, had an inkling of this malaise in collectivity that was caused by the technological apparatus and the 'immunization' against it by the 'collective laughter' in Chaplin and slapstick films. In the second version of the Artwork essay Benjamin wrote:

If one considers the dangerous tensions which technology and its consequences have engendered in the masses at large—tendencies which at critical stages take on a psychotic character—one also has to recognize that this same technologization [Technisierung] has created the possibility of psychic immunization against such mass psychoses. It does so by means of certain films in which the forced development of sadistic fantasies or masochistic delusions can prevent their natural and dangerous maturation in the masses. Collective laughter is one preemptive and healing outbreak of mass psychosis. The countless grotesque events consumed in films are a graphic indication of the dangers threatening mankind from the repressions implicit in civilization. American slapstick comedies and Disney films trigger a therapeutic release of unconscious energies. Their forerunner was the figure of the eccentric. He was the first to inhabit the new fields of action opened up by film—the first occupant of the newly built house. This is the context in which Chaplin takes on historical significance.[38]

After the 'end' of cinema, or the so-called 'death of cinema', there is no possibility that film, as the 'world of fantasy' in Lacan's term, can fill the hole that is opened up by psychosis, as Chaplin was able to fill it. The pornographic 'digital image' has made this impossible. This hole in psychosis is exposed to the fascist manipulation. As for architecture in the contemporary transparency society, I wish to claim that it has been entirely co-opted by the pornographic image society that, in the words of Badiou, is utterly unable to 'disimage'. Architecture serves the dominant *anaesthetization* that numbs the subject, thus robbing it of its political subjectivity. We must bear in mind that the 'transparency society', as Han reminds us, directly *depoliticizes* the subject. In this situation, the subject loses its *immunization* against fascist manipulations.

In conclusion: We must, on philosophical grounds, return to the essence of *photography* in a transcendental sense supported by critical philosophy as I have discussed above. This transcendental dimension constitutes the *parallax* of photography as the locus of the *unconscious*, the absolute alterity of the Other. In this regard, we must bear in mind that, in the Lacanian theory of psychosis, there exists an unconscious in psychotic subjects but it does not function. This function must be reactivated. At the center of critical philosophy, in Hegel, resides 'dialectic' and 'contradiction'—dialectical contradiction—and above all, the *negative*, that Badiou brought out in connection to cinema.

In *Phenomenology of Spirit* Hegel talks about the 'life of Spirit' and its power that does not shrink from death. He writes:

> It is this power, not something positive, which closes its eyes to the negative, as when we say of something that it is nothing or is false, and then having done with it, turn away and pass on to something else; on the contrary, Spirit is this power only by looking the negative in the face, and tarrying with it. This tarrying with the negative is the magical power that converts it into being.[39]

Based on this Hegelian idea that 'positive' 'closes its eyes to negative', Han challenges 'the society of positivity', embedded in the Transparency Society, for taking leave of this dialectics. Thus Hegel's 'Spirit', he remarks, does not 'turn away from the negative but endures and preserves it within itself. Negativity nourishes the "life of the mind"'.[40] Significantly, Han points out that 'Theory in the strong sense of the word is a phenomenon of negativity', and further, 'Theory as negativity makes reality itself appear ever and radiantly different; it presents reality in another light'.[41] It is this 'theory of negativity' that must be brought to architecture to reconfigure it against its unconditional submission to the technological digital image in this Pornographic Society of ours.

Todd McGowan in his seminal *Emancipation After Hegel*, in which he explores Hegel's philosophy of 'contradiction', reminds us that in his analysis of the various forms of arts, Hegel 'begins with architecture and concludes with poetry'. McGowan remarks that for Hegel 'Architecture marks the beginning point of art not because it was historically primary—Hegel does not care at all about this question—but because it provides the clearest form of contradiction. It doesn't even take a philosopher to recognize it in the case of architecture'.[42] In further reflection, he states:

> Anyone can see the self-division of the architectural work of art: as with all works of art, architecture expresses the problem of subjectivity through the artwork, but in the case of architecture this expression occurs in a material form that is completely alien to subjectivity. The contours of the material building must manifest the immateriality of the subject.[43]

McGowan further notes that 'poetry doesn't eliminate the contradiction of architecture but reveals that contradiction as such is impossible to overcome'.[44] But, perhaps, it can be 'sublated', I would add. I would like to make the point here that architecture is the art of 'sensuous truth' in contrast to all other arts that are the arts of 'sensuous *Schein*'. In this respect, I wish that Badiou, in his productive conception of cinema as the 'art of contradiction', had at least acknowledged that, before the invention of cinema, in the era of capitalist modernity, architecture had been the exemplification of the 'art of contradiction'.

I would like to supplement McGowan's apt observation that, in the age of cinema—not available as such to Hegel—the analogy of architecture must be made in respect to cinema. As I have insisted all along in this work, it is under the categories of *impurity* and the '*non-art* of art' (in 'mass art')—Badiou's categories for cinema—that architecture must be understood as *the* locus of dialectic and contradiction, and *negativity*. To echo Han's point on 'theory', I say this: No theory of architecture must be thought if not with the Hegelian 'tarrying with the negative'. Building in our time must 'disimage' in order to overcome the obscenity of our Pornographic Age.

Notes

1. Alain Badiou, *The Pornographic Age*, trans. and eds with an afterword, A. J. Bartlett and Justin Clemens (London: Bloomsbury, 2020).
2. Alain Badiou, *The Pornographic Age*, 7.
3. Byung-Chul Han, *The Transparency Society*, trans. Erik Butler (Stanford: Stanford Briefs, 2015).
4. Byung-Chul Han, *The Transparency Society*, 1–2.
5. See Alain Badiou, *The Pornographic Age*. This volume includes the insightful commentary by the editors and also a commentary by William Watkin.

6 See Byung-Chul Han, *The Transparency Society*. Besides this book, Han returns repeatedly to the notion of 'pornography' in his other books for his critique of contemporary society under the 'neoliberal' system dominated by the digital image. He devotes a chapter to 'Porn' in his *The Agony of Eros*, foreword by Alain Badiou, trans. Erik Butler (Cambridge: The MIT Press, 2017). Also see his *Psychopolitics: Neoliberalism and New Technologies of Power*, trans. Erik Butler (London and New York: Verso, 2017) and *In the Swarm: Digital Prospects*, trans. Erik Butler (Cambridge: The MIT Press, 2017).

7 For more see Libero Andreotti and Nadir Lahiji, *The Architecture of Phantasmagoria: Specters of the City* (Abingdon: Routledge, 2017). Also see Theodor Adorno, *In Search of Wagner*, trans. Rodney Livingstone, with a new foreword by Slavoj Žižek (New York: Verso, 2005).

8 Walter Benjamin, 'The Work of Art in the Age of Its Technological Reproducibility', Third Version, in *Walter Benjamin: Selected Writings*, Volume 4, trans. Edmond Jephcott and others, eds Howard Eiland and Michael W. Jennings (Cambridge: The Belknap Press of Harvard University Press, 2003), 269.

9 Alain Badiou, *The Pornographic Age*, 3.

10 Alain Badiou, *The Pornographic Age*, 3–4.

11 Alain Badiou, *The Pornographic Age*, 4.

12 Alain Badiou, *The Pornographic Age*, 2.

13 See Alain Badiou, 'A Speculative Disquisition on the Concept of Democracy', in Alain Badiou, *Metapolitics*, trans. with intro. Jason Barker (London and New York: Verso, 2005), and Alain Badiou, 'The Democratic Emblem', in Giorgio Agamben *et al.*, *Democracy in What State?*, trans. William McCuaig (New York: Columbia University Press, 2011).

14 Alain Badiou, 'The Democratic Emblem', in Giorgio Agamben *et al.*, *Democracy in What State?*, 8–9.

15 See Alain Badiou, *Trump* (Cambridge: Polity, 2019).

16 Alain Badiou, *The Pornographic Age*, 16.

17 Alain Badiou, *The Pornographic Age*, 17.

18 Walter Benjamin, 'The Work of Art in the Age of Its Technological Reproducibility', Third Version, 257. Benjamin places an important large footnote to the passage quoted, which it is illuminating to cite in part:

> The polarity cannot come into its own in the aesthetics of Idealism, which conceives of beauty as something fundamentally undivided (and thus excludes anything polarized). Nonetheless, in Hegel this polarity announces itself as clearly as possible within the limits of idealism. We quote from *Vorlesungen zur Philosophie der Geschichte* [*Lectures on the Philosophy of History*]: 'Images were known of old. In those days, piety required them for worship, but it could do without *beautiful* images. Such images might even be disturbing. In every beautiful image, there is also something external—although, insofar as the image is beautiful, its spirit still speaks to the human being. But religious worship, being no more than a spiritless torpor of the soul, is directed at a *thing*. ... Fine art arose ... in the church ..., though art

Epilogue

has now gone beyond the ecclesiastical principle'. Likewise, the following passage from *Vorlesungen über die Ästhetik* [*Lecture on Aesthetics*] indicates that Hegel sensed a problem here: 'We are beyond the stage of venerating works of art as divine and as objects deserving our worship. Today, the impression they produce is of a more reflective kind, and the emotions they arouse require a more stringent test. The transition from the first kind of artistic reception to the second defines the history of artistic reception in general. Moreover, a certain oscillation between these two polar modes of reception can be demonstrated for each work of art'.

273–274

19 Walter Benjamin, 'The Work of Art in the Age of Its Technological Reproducibility', Third Version, 257–258. Benjamin further remarks, bringing up Atget's photographs of the 'deserted Paris Street' as 'crime scene' that he discussed in his 'Little History of Photography' and I discussed in Chapter 1:

> It has justly been said that he [Atget] photographed them like scenes of crimes. A crime scene, too, is deserted; it is photographed for the purpose of establishing evidence. With Atget, photographic records begin to be evidence in historical time [*Prozeß*]. This constitutes their hidden political significance. They demand a specific kind of reception. Free floating contemplation is no longer appropriate to them. They unsettle the viewer; he feels challenged to find a particular way to approach them.
>
> 258

20 Byung-Chul Han, *The Transparency Society*, 9.
21 Byung-Chul Han, *The Transparency Society*, 9.
22 Byung-Chul Han, *The Transparency Society*, 10–11. See also Roland Barthes, *Camera Lucida: Reflections on Photography*, trans. Richard Howard (New York: Hill & Wang, 1981).
23 Byung-Chul Han, *The Transparency Society*, 11.
24 Byung-Chul Han, *The Transparency Society*, 13.
25 Byung-Chul Han, *The Transparency Society*, 13.
26 See especially Byung-Chul Han, *The Burnout Society*, trans. Erik Butler (Stanford: Sandford Briefs, 2015), and Byung-Chul Han, *In the Swarm*.
27 Byung-Chul Han, *The Transparency Society*, 21–2. The following is the passage in Walter Benjamin's 'Goethe's Elective Affinities' that Han quotes:

> The beautiful is neither the veil nor veiled object but rather the object in its veil. Unveiled, however, it would prove to be infinitely inconspicuous [*unscheinbar*] … For that object, to which in the last instance the veil is essential, is not to be characterized otherwise. Since only the beautiful and outside it nothing—veiling or being veiled—can be essential, the divine ground of the being of beauty lies in the secret.
>
> 21

See also Walter Benjamin, 'Goethe's Elective Affinities', in *Selected Writings, 1913–1926*, Volume 1, eds Marcus Bullock and Michael W. Jennings (Cambridge: The Belknap Press of Harvard University Press, 1996).
28 Byung-Chul Han, *The Transparency Society*, 22.
29 Byung-Chul Han, *The Transparency Society*, 24.
30 Byung-Chul Han, *The Transparency Society*, 24. See also Giorgio Agamben, *Nudities*, trans. David Kishik and Stefan Pedatella (Stanford: Stanford University Press, 2010).
31 Byung-Chul Han, *The Transparency Society*, 26–27.
32 Byung-Chul Han, *The Transparency Society*, 27.
33 Byung-Chul Han, *The Transparency Society*, 37.
34 Byung-Chul Han, *The Transparency Society*, 38.
35 Byung-Chul Han, *The Transparency Society*, 39.
36 Byung-Chul Han, *The Transparency Society*, 46.
37 For more see *The Seminars of Jacques Lacan: Book III, The Psychosis, 1955–1956*, ed. Jacques-Alain Miller, trans. Russell Grigg (New York and London: W. W. Norton, 1993).
38 Walter Benjamin, 'The Work of Art in the Age of Its Technological Reproducibility', Second Version, in *Walter Benjamin: Selected Writings, Volume 3, 1935–1938*, trans. Edmund Jephcott, Howard Eiland, and others, eds Howard Eiland and Michael W. Jennings (Cambridge: The Belknap Press of Harvard University Press, 2002), 118.
39 See *Hegel's Phenomenology of Spirit*, trans. A. V. Miller (Oxford: Oxford University Press, 1977), 19. Also see Slavoj Žižek, *Tarrying with the Negative: Kant, Hegel, and the Critique of Ideology* (Durham: Duke University Press, 1993). Further we read,

> This power is identical with what we earlier called the Subject, which by giving determinateness as existence in its own element supersedes abstract immediacy, i.e., the immediacy which barely is, and thus is authentic substance: that being or immediacy whose mediation is not outside of it but which is this mediation itself.
>
> 19

40 Byung-Chul Han, *The Transparency Society*, 4.
41 Byung-Chul Han, *The Transparency Society*, 6.
42 See Todd McGowan, *Emancipation After Hegel: Achieving Contradictory Revolution* (New York: Columbia University Press, 2019), 20.
43 Todd McGowan, *Emancipation After Hegel*, 20.
44 Todd McGowan, *Emancipation After Hegel*, 21.

References

Adorno, Theodor, *In Search of Wagner*, trans. Rodney Livingstone, with a new foreword by Slavoj Žižek (New York: Verso, 2005).

Adorno, Theodor W., *An Introduction to Dialectics*, ed. Christoph Ziermann, trans. Nicholas Walker (Cambridge: Polity, 2017).

Agamben, Giorgio, *Nudities*, trans. David Kishik and Stefan Pedatella (Stanford: Stanford University Press, 2010).

Agamben, Giorgio et al., *Democracy in What State?*, trans. William McCuaig (New York: Columbia University Press, 2011).

Andreotti, Libero, and Nadir Lahiji, *The Architecture of Phantasmagoria: Specters of the City* (Abingdon: Routledge, 2017).

Badiou, Alain, *The Century* (Cambridge: Polity, 2007).

Badiou, Alain, *Cinema* (Cambridge: Polity, 2013).

Badiou, Alain, *Conditions*, trans. Steven Corcoran (London: Continuum, 2008).

Badiou, Alain, 'Fifteen Theses on Contemporary Art', in *Lacanian Ink*, 23 (2004).

Badiou, Alain, *Handbook of Inaesthetics*, trans. Alberto Toscano (Stanford: Stanford University Press, 2005).

Badiou, Alain, *Infinite Thought: Truth and the Return of Philosophy*, trans. and eds Oliver Feltham and Justin Clemens (Continuum: London: 2005).

Badiou, Alain, *Logics of Worlds: Being and Event II*, trans. Alberto Toscano (London: Continuum, 2009).

Badiou, Alain, *The Meaning of Sarkozy*, trans. David Fernbach (London and New York: Verso, 2008).

Badiou, Alain, *Metapolitics*, trans. with intro. Jason Barker (London and New York: Verso, 2005).

Badiou, Alain, *Plato's Republic: A Dialogue in 16 Chapters*, trans. Susan Spitzer, intro. Kenneth Reinhard (New York: Columbia University Press, 2012).

Badiou, Alain, *Polemics*, trans. and intro. Steve Corcoran (London and New York: Verso, 2006).

Badiou, Alain, *The Pornographic Age*, trans. and ed. and with an afterword A. J. Bartlett and Justin Clemens (London: Bloomsbury, 2020).

Badiou, Alain, *Rhapsody for the Theatre*, ed. and intro. Bruno Bosteels (London and New York: Verso, 2013).

Badiou, Alain, Joël Bellassen, and Louis Mossot, *The Rational Kernel of the Hegelian Dialectic*, ed. and trans. Tzuchien Tho (Melbourne: Re.Press, 2011).

Badiou, Alain, with Fabian Tardy, *Philosophy and the Event* (Cambridge: Polity, 2013).

Barthes, Roland, *Camera Lucida: Reflections on Photography*, trans. Richard Howard (New York: Hill & Wang, 1981).

Bartlett, A. J., *Badiou and Plato: An Education by Truths* (Edinburgh: Edinburgh University Press, 2011, 2015).

Bartlett, A. J., and Justin Clemens, eds, *Badiou and His Interlocuters: Lectures, Interviews and Responses* (London: Bloomsbury, 2018).

Bartlett, A, J., and Justin Clemens, 'Measuring Up: Some Consequences of Badiou's Confrontation with Hegel', in *Badiou and Hegel: Infinity, Dialectics, Subjectivity*, eds Jim Vernon and Antonio Galcagno (Lanham: Lexington Books, 2015).

Baudry, Jean-Louis, 'The Apparatus: Metaphysical Approaches to Impression of Reality in Cinema', in *Narrative, Apparatus, Ideology: A Film Reader*, ed. Philip Rosen, trans. Jean Andrews and Bernard Augst (New York: Columbia University Press, 1968).

Bazin, André, *What Is Cinema?*, Volume I, trans. Hugh Gray, foreword Jean Renoir and new foreword Dudley Andrew (Berkeley: University of California Press, 2005 [1967]).

Bazin, André, *What Is Cinema?*, Volume II, essays selected and trans. Hugh Gray, foreword François Truffaut (Berkeley: University of California Press, 1971).

Beiser, Frederick, *Hegel* (New York: Routledge, 2005).

Benjamin, Walter, *The Arcades Project* (Cambridge: The Belknap Press of Harvard University Press, 1999).

Benjamin, Walter, *Selected Writings, Volume 1, 1913–1926*, ed. Marcus Bullock and Michael W. Jennings (Cambridge: The Belknap Press of Harvard University Press, 1996).

Benjamin, Walter, *Selected Writings, Volume 2, 1927–1934*, eds Michael W. Jennings, Howard Eiland, and Gary Smith, trans. Rodney Livingston and others (Cambridge: The Belknap Press of Harvard University Press, 1999).

Benjamin, Walter, *Selected Writings, Volume 3, 1935–1938*, eds Howard Eiland and Michael Jennings, trans. Edmund Jephcott, Howard Eiland, and others (Cambridge: The Belknap Press of Harvard University Press, 2002).

Benjamin, Walter, *Selected Writings, Volume 4, 1938–1940*, ed. Michael W. Jennings (Cambridge: The Belknap Press of Harvard University Press, 2003).

References

Benjamin, Walter, and Theodor Adorno, *The Complete Correspondence, 1928–1940* (Cambridge: Harvard University Press, 1999).

Buck-Morss, Susan, 'Aesthetics and Anaesthetics: Walter Benjamin's Artwork Essay Reconsidered', in *October*, 62 (Autumn 1992).

Buck-Morss, Susan, *The Dialectic of Seeing: Walter Benjamin and the Arcades Project* (Cambridge: The MIT Press, 1989).

Buden, Boris, 'It Is Getting Darker around the Central Sun of Freedom: *Capital* Translation and the Re-feudalization of Capitalism', in *Capitalism: Concept, Idea, Image, Aspects of Marx's Capital Today*, eds Peter Osborne, Éric Alliez, and Eric-John Russell (London: CRMEP Books, 2019).

Cavell, Stanley, *The World Viewed: Reflections on Ontology of Film, Enlarged Edition* (Cambridge: Harvard University Press, 1971).

Caygill, Howard, *Walter Benjamin: The Color of Experience* (London and New York: Routledge, 1998).

Deleuze, Gilles, *Cinema 1: The Movement-Image*, trans. Hugh Tomlinson and Barbara Habberjam (Minneapolis: University of Minnesota Press, 2003).

Deleuze, Gilles, *Cinema 2: The Time-Image*, trans. Hugh Tomlinson and Robert Galeta (Minneapolis: University of Minnesota Press, 1994).

Deleuze, Gilles, *Francis Bacon: The Logic of Sensation*, trans. and intro. Daniel W. Smith, afterword Tom Conley (Minneapolis: University of Minnesota Press, 2003).

Eisenstein, Sergei, *Film Form: Essays in Film Theory*, ed. and trans. Jay Leyda (San Diego: Harcourt, 1949).

Elena, Alberto, *The Cinema of Kiarostami* (London: Saqi, 2005).

Engels, Friedrich, *The Dialectics of Nature* (New York: International Publishers, 1940).

Ferris, David, ed., *The Cambridge Companion to Walter Benjamin* (Cambridge: Cambridge University Press, 2004).

Finchelstein, Federico, *A Brief History of Fascist Lies* (Oakland: University of California Press, 2020).

Genet, Jean, *The Balcony*, trans. Bernard Frechtman (New York: Grove Press, 1966).

Giedion, Sigfried, *Building in France: Building in Iron, Building in Ferroconcrete*, trans. J. Duncan Berry (Los Angeles: The Getty Center for the History of Art, 1995).

Gilloch, Graeme, *Myth and Metropolis: Walter Benjamin and the City* (Cambridge: Polity, 1996).

Gilloch, Graeme, *Siegfried Kracauer* (Cambridge: Polity, 2015).

Gumbrecht, Hans Ulrich, and Michael Marrinan, *Mapping Benjamin: The Work of Art in the Digital Age* (Stanford: Stanford University Press, 2003).

Han, Byung-Chul, *The Agony of Eros*, foreword Alain Badiou, trans. Erik Butler (Cambridge: The MIT Press, 2017).

Han, Byung-Chul, *The Burnout Society*, trans. Erik Butler (Stanford: Sandford Briefs, 2015).

Han, Byung-Chul, *Psychopolitics: Neoliberalism and New Technologies of Power*, trans. Erik Butler (London and New York: Verso, 2017).

Han, Byung-Chul, *In the Swarm: Digital Prospects*, trans. Erik Butler (Cambridge: The MIT Press, 2017).

Han, Byung-Chul, *The Transparency Society*, trans. Erik Butler (Stanford: Stanford Briefs, 2015).

Hansen, Miriam Bratu, *Cinema and Experience: Siegfried Kracauer, Walter Benjamin, and Theodor W. Adorno* (Berkeley: University of California Press, 2011).

Hegel's Phenomenology of Spirit, trans. A. V. Miller (Oxford: Oxford University Press, 1977).

Herzogenrath, Bernd, ed., *Film as Philosophy* (Minneapolis and London: Minnesota University Press, 2017).

Horkheimer, Max, and Theodor W. Adorno, *Dialectic of Enlightenment*, ed. Gunzelin Schmid Noerr, trans. Edmund Jephcott (Stanford: Stanford University Press, 2002).

Jameson, Fredric, *Valences of the Dialectic* (London: Verso, 2009).

Kaes, Anton, 'The Debate about Cinema: Charting a Controversy (1900–1929)', in *New German Critique*, Special Issue on Weimar Film Theory, 40 (Winter 1987).

Karatani, Kojin, *Isonomia and the Origins of Philosophy* (Durham and London: Duke University Press, 2017).

Karatani, Kojin, *Transcritique: On Kant and Marx* (Cambridge: The MIT Press, 2003, 2005).

Kettle, Petra, and Robert Pfaller, 'The End of Cinema as We Know It: Or How a Medium Turned from a Promising Graduate into an Old Folk', in *Crisis and Critique* 2, vol. 7 (June 2020).

Kiarostami, Abbas, BFI Interviews in the *Guardian* (28 April 2005).

Kienzl, Hermann, 'Theater und Kinematograph', in *Der Strom*, 1 (1911/1912).

Kofman, Sarah, *Camera Obscura of Ideology*, trans. Will Straw (Ithaca: Cornell University Press, 1998).

Kornbluh, Anna, *Marxist Film Theory and Fight Club* (New York: Bloomsbury, 2019).

Kouvelakis, Stathis, *Philosophy and Revolution: From Kant to Marx*, preface Fredric Jameson (London and New York: Verso, 2003).

Kracauer, Siegfried, *The Mass Ornament, Weimar Essays*, trans., ed., and intro. Thomas Y. Levin (Cambridge: Harvard University Press, 1995).

Kracauer, Siegfried, *Theory of Film: The Redemption of Physical Reality*, intro. Miriam Bratu Hansen (Princeton: Princeton University Press, 1997 [1960]).

Kul-Want, Christopher, ed., *Philosophers on Film from Bergson to Badiou: A Critical Reader* (New York: Columbia University Press, 2019).

Lacan, Jacques, 'The Mirror Stage as Formative of the *I* Function as Revealed in Psychoanalytical Experience', in *Écrits: The First Complete Edition in English*, trans. Bruce Fink (New York and London: W. W. Norton, 2002, 2006).

Lahiji, Nadir, *An Architecture Manifesto: Critical Reason and Theories of a Failed Practice* (Abingdon: Routledge, 2019).

Lahiji, Nadir, *Architecture or Revolution: Emancipatory Critique After Marx* (Abingdon: Routledge, 2020).

Le Bon, Gustave, *The Crowd: A Study of the Popular Mind* (New York: Macmillan, 1897).

Lenin, V. I., 'Notes of a Publicist: On Ascending a High Mountain ...', in *Collected Works*, Volume 33 (Moscow: Progress Publishers, 1965), 204–211.

Lenin, V. I., 'State and Revolution', in *Essential Works of Lenin*, ed. Henry M. Christman (New York: Dover, 1987).

Ling, Alex, *Badiou and Cinema* (Edinburgh: Edinburgh University Press, 2011, 2013).

Loos, Adolf, *Spoken into the Void: Collected Essays 1897–1900* (Cambridge: The MIT Press, 1982).

Lukács, Georg, *A Defence of History and Class Consciousness: Tailism and Dialectic*, trans. Leslie Esther, intro. John Rees, postface Slavoj Žižek (London and New York: Verso, 2000).

Lukács, Georg, *History and Class Consciousness: Studies in Marxist Dialectics*, trans. Rodney Livingstone (Cambridge: The MIT Press, 1971).

Macy, David, *Lacan in Context* (New York: Verso, 1988).

Marcus, Laura, and Lynda Nead, eds, *The Actuality of Walter Benjamin* (London: Lawrence and Wishart, 1998).

Marx, Karl, 'A Contribution to the Critique of Hegel's *Philosophy of Right*: Introduction', in *Critique of Hegel's 'Philosophy of Right'*, trans. Annette Jolin and Joseph O'Malley, ed., intro., and notes Joseph O'Malley (Cambridge: Cambridge University Press, 1970).

Marx, Karl, and Frederick Engels, *The Communist Manifesto* (Lexington: SoHo Books, 2010).

McCole, John, *Walter Benjamin and the Antinomies of Tradition* (Ithaca and London: Cornell University Press, 1993).

McGowan, Todd, *Emancipation After Hegel: Achieving Contradictory Revolution* (New York: Columbia University Press, 2019).

McGowan, Todd, *Psychoanalytical Film Theory and the Rules of the Game* (New York: Bloomsbury, 2015).

References

Metz, Christian, *Language and Cinema*, trans. Donna Jean Umiker-Sebeok (The Hague and Paris: Mouton, 1974).

Miller, Jacques-Alain, ed., *The Seminars of Jacques Lacan: Book III, The Psychosis, 1955–1956*, trans. Russell Grigg (New York and London: W. W. Norton, 1993).

Mottahedeh, Negar, *Displaced Allegories: Post-Revolutionary Iranian Cinema* (Durham and London: Duke University Press, 2008).

Osborne, Peter, Éric Alliez, and Eric-John Russell, *Capitalism: Concept, Idea, Image: Aspects of Marx's Capital Today* (CRMEP Books, London: 2019).

Pippin, Robert B., *The Philosophical Hitchcock: Vertigo and the Anxieties of Unknowingness* (Chicago and London: The University of Chicago Press, 2017).

Plato, *Complete Works*, ed. John M. Cooper (Indianapolis and Cambridge: Hackett, 1997).

Rancière, Jacques, *Film Fables* (Oxford and New York: Berg, 2006).

Rancière, Jacques, *The Intervals of Cinema* (London and New York: Verso, 2014).

Riera, Gabriel, 'The Question of Art: Badiou and Hegel', in *Badiou and Hegel: Infinity, Dialectics, Subjectivity*, eds Jim Vernon and Antonio Galcagno (Lanham: Lexington Books, 2015).

Ruda, Frank, *For Badiou: Idealism without Idealism*, with a preface by Slavoj Žižek (Evanston: Northwestern University Press, 2015).

Ruda, Frank, 'Marx in the Cave', in Slavoj Žižek, Frank Ruda, and Agon Hamza, *Reading Marx* (Cambridge: Polity, 2018).

Saeed-Vafa, Mehrnaz, and Jonathan Rosenbaum, *Abbas Kiarostami*, Expanded Second Edition (Urbana: University of Illinois Press, 2003, 2018).

Simmel, Georg, 'The Metropolis and Mental Life', in *On Individuality and Social Forms: Selected Writings*, ed. Donald Lewis (Chicago: The University of Chicago Press, 1971).

Stedman Jones, Gareth, *Karl Marx: Greatness and Illusion* (Cambridge: The Belknap Press of Harvard University Press, 2016).

Taylor, Richard, '"Eh!" On the Purity of Film Language', in *S. M. Eisenstein, Selected Works. Volume 1: Writings, 1922–34* (London and Bloomington: I. B. Tauris, 1988).

Taylor, Richard, *The Battleship Potemkin* (London and New York: I. B. Tauris, 2000).

Trott, Adriel M., 'Badiou *contra* Hegel: The Materialist Dialectic against the Myth of the Whole', in *Badiou and Hegel: Infinity, Dialectics, Subjectivity*, eds Jim Vernon and Antonio Galcagno (Lanham: Lexington Books, 2015).

Vernon, Jim, and Antonio Calcagno, *Badiou and Hegel: Infinity, Dialectics, Subjectivity* (Lanham: Lexington Books, 2015).

Virilio, Paul, *The Logics of Perception*, trans. Patrick Camiller (London and New York: Verso, 2009).

Weigel Sigrid, *Body- and Image-Space: Re-reading Walter Benjamin* (London and New York: Routledge, 1996).

Wolfarth, Irving, 'The Measure of the Possible, the Weight of the Real and the Heat of the Moment: Benjamin's Actuality Today', in *The Actuality of Walter Benjamin*, eds Laura Marcus and Lynda Nead (London: Lawrence and Wishart, 1998).

Žižek, Slavoj, 'How to Begin from the Beginning', in *The Idea of Communism*, eds Costas Douzinas and Slavoj Žižek (London and New York: Verso, 2010).

Žižek, Slavoj, *A Left That Dares to Speak Its Name* (Cambridge: Polity, 2020).

Žižek, Slavoj, *Living in the End Times* (London and New York: Verso, 2010).

Žižek, Slavoj, *The Sublime Object of Ideology* (London and New York: Verso, 1989).

Žižek, Slavoj, *Tarrying with the Negative: Kant, Hegel, and the Critique of Ideology* (Durham: Duke University Press, 1993).

Index

actuality [*Aktualität*] xviii, 21, 39, 50
Adorno, Theodor 8, 20, 22–4, 36, 49–50, 82, 92–3, 101–5, 114–15, 134–5, 138–9, 153; dialectics 101, 104–5, 115n52
aestheticization 5–6, 15, 21, 42, 78–80, 144, 145; of politics 5–6, 21, 79, 144
Agamben, Giorgio 148, 153
anaesthetics 15, 23–4, 78, 80, 82
apparatus xiv, xvi–xviii, 1–2, 4, 11–12, 16, 25, 30, 40, 43, 45, 53, 67, 75, 76, 89, 120, 134; collective 53; technical xvi, xvi
apperception xvi–xvii, 2, 4, 12, 16, 30, 32, 75–6, 142
architecture ix, xi–xiv, xvi–xviii, xx, 1–2, 4, 6–7, 10–12, 14–18, 33, 35, 38, 41, 53, 71–2, 74–9, 81, 87–9, 93, 97, 99, 101, 111, 141–2, 150–3
architecture after cinema xiii–xiv
architecture *as* philosophy xviii
Arp, Hans 88
art ix–xxi, 1–39, 43–50, 52, 54–64, 67, 72, 74, 81, 94, 96, 100, 102, 104, 109–112, 116, 123, 125–36, 141, 145, 151, 153, 155
Atget, Eugène 34, 35, 154
aura 5, 34–5, 38, 41, 78, 83–4, 87–9, 133, 145–6
avant-garde 5, 44, 87, 90, 93n29

Badiou, Alain ix, xi, xiii, xv–xvi, xix–xx, 2, 6, 8–11, 14, 22–3, 39, 50–1, 53–5, 67–9, 94, 112, 115–17, 139–40, 151–2; cinema xiii, xvi–xviii, 2–4, 6, 12, 16–18, 39, 44, 46–63, 95–6, 151; dialectics 97–9, 105–9, 111; mass art 14, 43, 45, 94, 141; Plato's cave xiii, xvii–xviii, 55, 57, 59–65, 67
barbarism xvii, 14–15, 78, 83–4n44, 85–8
Bartlett, A. J. xix, 8, 23, 51–2, 53, 67–70, 107, 113, 115–16, 152
Battleship Potemkin x, 119, 121, 127–9, 136–8
Baudelaire, Charles 77, 83, 104
Baudry, Jean-Louis 55, 67–8
Bazin, André 4, 6, 41, 52, 95, 112
Behn, Adolf 87–8
Beiser, Frederick 22, 99–100, 103, 113–15, 139
Benjamin, Walter v, xi, xiii–xiv, 1, 7, 8, 10, 22–5, 27, 35–9, 50–4, 71, 81–5, 91–3, 97, 104, 120, 135–6, 138–9, 153–5; artwork essay xiv–xv, xvii, 1–4, 6, 10, 15, 18, 20–4, 30, 31–3, 40–4, 50n4, 71–5, 77–8, 82n14, 83n42, 122–3, 131, 133–5, 142, 144–5, 150; building xvi, 1, 2, 12, 17, 34, 74, 87, 89; human sensorium xiv, xvi, xvii, xviii, 1, 4, 11, 12, 40, 76; perceptual apparatus xiv, 1, 4, 11, 12; reception in distraction xvii, 2, 74, 75, 78; thinker of the Proletariat xv
Bergson, Henri 41
Berlin 71, 73, 77, 87, 50n4, 93n24

165

Index

Berman, Marshall xv, xxn5
bourgeoisie 19, 90, 135
Breuer, Joseph 13
Buck-Morss, Susan 15, 23–4, 80, 82
Buden, Boris xv, xix–xx
building xi, xvi–xvii, 1–2, 12, 17–18, 34, 67, 74, 87, 89, 92, 97, 126, 152; age of cinema 12
capitalism xiv–xv, xviii–xx, 4–5, 10–11, 14, 21, 40–3, 64–6, 70, 91, 131, 144, 146, 148–9
cave xiii–xiv, xviii, xx, 56–70, 121, 148, 149; allegory of xiii, xviii, 55, 59–61, 63, 148–9
Cavell, Stanley 41, 52
Caygill, Howard 32, 37, 72, 75–7, 81–2, 92
Chaplin, Charlie 43, 71, 142, 150
cinema ix–xiv, xvi–xx, 1–4, 6–19, 21–5, 32, 35–41, 43–55, 57, 59–64, 67–71, 75, 77–8, 82–4, 92–101, 105, 108, 111–13, 119–29, 130–1, 135–6, 138–42, 148, 150–2
cinema *as* philosophy xviii
Citizen Kane x
Clemens, Justin xix, 8, 23, 51, 53, 67–8, 107, 112–13, 115–16, 152
collective xvi–xvii, 2, 9, 19, 34, 42, 53n36, 71–5, 80, 87, 89, 123–4, 129, 133, 135, 150
communism xiv–xv, 5–7, 10, 15–16, 21, 40, 42, 65, 72, 80, 87, 92, 142, 144; Eastern Bloc, xv
contradiction x, xi, xiii–xiv, xvi, xviii, 39, 50, 59–61, 63, 94, 97–9, 101–5, 107–8, 111, 114, 125 ; art of xiii, xiv, 94, 150; dialectical 111, 151
Copjec, Joan 7
critical theory xvi
critique xviii, 10, 12–13, 21, 25–6, 28–9, 59, 64–6, 98, 99, 132, 142, 144

Daguerre, Jacques-Mandé 25
David, Jacques-Louis 33
Debord, Guy 1
Deleuze, Gilles 3–4, 6, 8, 41, 52–3, 66, 69

democratic: dialectic xiii, xviii, 98, 111; emblem 9n22, 29n23, 39, 41, 45, 50n3, 53, 144, 153n14; fascism xiv, 11, 14–15, 144
dialectics xiii, 61–4, 67, 80, 94–117, 137, 138, 151
disimage xi, 141, 150, 152
distraction [*Zerstreuung*] xvii, 2, 12, 71–84; theory of 71–2, 81n1
Duchamp, Marcel 95

Eisenstein, Sergei x, 3, 119–21, 124–30, 135–8, 142; *Battleship Potemkin* 121, 127–9
El Lissitzky 88
emancipation xvi, xix, xxi, 34–44, 64, 66, 94, 114, 145, 151, 155n42
experience xiv, 4, 8–9, 12, 14–16, 22–4, 27, 30, 32, 36–40, 50–2, 54, 66, 72–3, 75–80, 82–93, 98, 121–2, 136, 139

fascism xiv, 3, 4, 5, 10–11, 14–15, 19–21, 24, 40–2, 72–3, 79–81, 84, 133–4, 142, 144
film x–xi, xvi–xvii, xx, 1–9, 11–13, 16–18, 22, 32–3, 35, 41–3, 45–55, 67, 71–2, 75–6, 81–3, 88–9, 95–6, 112, 119–25, 128–31, 133–6, 138, 145, 150
Forrest Gump x
Freud, Sigmund 13, 30–2, 36, 73, 150

Gabo, Naum 88
Genet, Jean 141, 143
Gide, André 72
Giedion, Sigfried 87–9, 92–3
Gilloch, Graeme 71, 77, 81, 83
Godard, Jean-Luc ix, xvii, xx, 1, 2, 18, 97, 142
Griffith, D. W. 1–2

Han, Byung-Chul 131, 138, 141, 152, 154–5
Hansen, Miriam Bratu 4–6, 8–9, 15–16, 19, 21–4, 32, 33, 36–43, 49–52, 54, 73, 77–8, 80, 82, 84, 88–9, 91–3, 131, 133, 138–9
Hausmann, Raoul 88

166

Index

Hegel, G. W. F. xiv, xvi, xix–xxi, 12, 22, 31, 36, 48, 63, 94, 98–109, 111, 113–15, 117, 126, 132–3, 137, 139, 151–4, 155
Hilberseimer, Ludwig 88
Hitchcock, Alfred 4, 52, 142
human sensorium xiv, xvi–xvii, 1, 4, 11–12, 40, 76, 80

image x–xi, xiii, xix–xx, 3–4, 8, 13, 25–7, 29–30, 32, 36, 45–9, 51–3, 56–7, 59–63, 65, 79, 84, 95, 116, 120–1, 124, 127–30, 136, 141, 143–8, 150–1, 153
impure art xviii, 18, 43, 45–6, 61, 94–5
impurity 39–54, 60, 95–7, 110, 142, 152
industrial capitalism 10, 11, 14, 41, 43, 91, 131
inessential art 43, 67, 95, 97

Jameson, Fredric 100–1, 113–14, 138
Jones, Ernest 73
Jünger, Ernst 80

Kaes, Anton 13, 22
Kant, Immanuel xiv–xvi, xx, 12, 22, 25–6, 28–32, 35, 36, 51, 99, 102–13, 115–16, 121, 136, 138, 147, 155
Karatani, Kojin xx, 22, 25–31, 35–6, 121, 136
Kiarostami, Abbas xvii, xx, 2, 7–8, 18, 68, 96, 142
Kornbluh, Anna 129, 137–8
Korsch, Karl 131
Kouvelakis, Stathis 132, 138
Kracauer, Siegfried 8, 22, 36, 40, 50, 71, 81–2, 88–9, 92–3, 131, 138
Krauss, Rosalind 32, 37n27
Kul-Want, Christopher 136

Lacan, Jacques 73, 82, 155; mirror stage 73
Le Bon, Gustave 131, 138
Left xv, 5–6, 14, 16, 27, 91; architecture on the 14; intellectual on the 5, 6; thinker of xv
Ling, Alex 8, 43, 52–4, 67, 95, 112
Loos, Adolf 17–19, 87–8, 93, 126, 135, 137

Lucas, George x
Lukács, Georg 83, 131–2, 138–9
Lumière, Louis and Auguste 12, 13

McCole, John 22–3, 37, 85, 89–93
McGowan, Todd 7, 13, 22, 114, 129, 137, 151–2, 155
Marx, Karl xv–xvi, xx–xxi, 55, 67, 131; *Capital* xv, xixn4, 16, 66
Marxism xiv, 6, 64, 90, 108, 117n83, 129, 136n19–138n45
mass art x–xi, xvi, 1–4, 14, 17–18, 39–40, 45–8, 94, 96–9, 101, 108, 142, 144, 152
masses xx, 1–8, 10, 11–14, 16–24, 34, 38–44, 52, 71–5, 77–9, 83, 96–7, 111–12, 120–1, 124, 130–5, 138, 141–2, 149–50; art of 3, 4, 97; Badiou, Alain 44, 141; Benjamin, Walter 1, 43, 72, 74, 77–9, 120, 133–5, 142, 150; cinema 5; pedagogy of xiii, xiv–xvi; political theory of 1; proletarian 19, 42, 120–1, 130, 135
metropolis 13–14, 22n13, 77, 83n36
Mickey Mouse xi
Mies van der Rohe, Ludwig 38, 87, 88
mise-en-scène 8, 120–2, 124–39
modernity xvii–xviii, 4, 12, 32, 35, 39, 50, 71, 80–1, 85, 86, 88, 95, 101, 131–2, 152
montage 94, 120–1, 124–30, 137

Naples 77
negativity 63, 67, 97–8, 146–7, 151–2
Neue Sachlichkeit [New Objectivity] 88, 93
Niépce, Joseph Nicéphore 25
non-art xviii, 12, 45–9, 54n39, 61, 94, 95, 142, 152
non-cinema xvii

Odessa Steps 121, 126–7, 137
ontology 4, 57, 107
optical unconscious 25, 31, 32, 37, 71
Oud, J.-J. P. 87

parallax xvi, xx, 26–32, 36, 121, 151
Parsifal 15

167

Index

pedagogy ix, xi, xiii–xvii, 1, 10; of cinema ix, xi; of the masses ix, xiii, xvi–xvii
perception 1, 5–6, 8n12, 9n17, 13, 15, 27, 34, 41–3, 58, 74–7, 79, 83n42, 87, 133, 137n28
perceptual apparatus xiv, 1, 4, 12
phantasmagoria 40, 66, 80–1, 129, 141, 153
philosophy ix–xi, xiii–xvi, xviii–xxi, 7–8, 10–13, 15–41, 44–5, 47, 51, 53, 55, 59–65, 67–70, 73, 86, 95–102, 105, 108–14, 116, 121, 124–5, 131–2, 138, 151, 153; and cinema xi, xiii–xiv, xviii, 7, 12, 14, 16, 18, 39, 40–1, 44–5, 47, 55, 59, 60–2, 64, 95–9, 111, 121, 124; *as* architecture xviii; *as* cinema xviii; of masses 111
photography 5, 25–7, 29–35, 37, 38, 41, 72, 88, 145–6, 150–1, 153
Picasso 71
Pippin, Robert 41, 52
Plato xiii, xvii–xviii, 18, 48, 54–67, 69–70, 96, 101, 109, 116–17, 121, 144, 148–9; *Republic* xiii, 55–7, 59, 64–7, 68n6, 148
political: category 7, 10, 17; crisis 5, 6, 12, 14, 40, 43, 77; subjectivity xiv, 150
politics x, 2, 4–6, 11, 15, 21, 41–2, 72–3, 79, 100, 108, 111, 132–3, 144
pornographic age xi, 141–4, 147, 152–3
pornography xi, 141–4, 147–53
poverty 14–15, 22n15, 23n17, 78, 85–8, 90–1; of experience 15, 23n17, 78, 85–6, 88, 90
proletarian aristocratism 44, 96
proletariat xv–xix, xxi, 6, 9, 11, 14, 18–20, 42, 73, 79, 90, 120–4, 131–5, 142
pronounced parallax 26–9, 31
psychoanalysis xvi, 7, 30, 82n14, 129, 137n43, 142–3, 149–55; experience 73, 82n14; object 30; theory xvi, 129, 143, 149
public use of reason xv

Rancière, Jacques 41, 52, 95
representation 36n18, 45, 51, 59–60, 65, 67–8n4, 78, 109–10, 122, 124, 128, 133–4, 136n10, 147
Richter, Hans 38n34, 88
Riera, Gabriel 109–11, 116–17
Ruda, Frank 64–7, 70

Scheerbart, Paul 87
Schein [semblance] 4, 12, 22n8, 152
Simmel, Georg 13, 22, 80
Socrates 18, 51, 55, 57, 62
Sohn-Rethel, Alfred 64
Star Wars x
Stone, Sascha 33, 38n34; subjectivity xiv, 27, 32, 62, 63, 67, 115n58, 116n66, 150, 152; political xiv, 150
Stedman Jones, Gareth xix, xxi
sublime 121–2, 136, 147–8

tactile 71, 74–6
Taylor, Richard 127–9, 137–8
technological reproduction 2, 5, 39, 41
thing-in-itself xvi, 12, 27, 29–30, 36–7n18, 121–2
Trott, Adriel 106–8, 115–16
Tzara, Tristan 88

utopian collective 9, 42

van Doesburg, Theo 88
Vernunft [reason] 103
Verstand [understanding] 100, 103

weak messianism xiv
Welles, Orson x

Zemeckis, Robert x
Žižek, Slavoj xv, 7, 66, 69–70, 86, 92, 101, 121, 132–3, 136, 138–9, 153, 155